CW01468088

The Pebble in My Shoe

An Anthology of Women's Cricket

Roy Case

authorHOUSE®

AuthorHouse™ UK
1663 Liberty Drive
Bloomington, IN 47403 USA
www.authorhouse.co.uk
Phone: 0800.197.4150

Published by AuthorHouse 10/30/2018

ISBN: 978-1-5462-9981-3 (sc)
ISBN: 978-1-5462-9982-0 (hc)
ISBN: 978-1-5462-9980-6 (e)

Print information available on the last page.

Contents

Chapter 1

Knocking up

One of the most consummate sporting personalities of all time was undoubtedly the charismatic former world heavyweight boxing champion Muhammad Ali [1942-2016]. Who encapsulated the sentiments of all truly great sporting champions when summoned to overcome the difficulties they are called upon to face in their quest to fulfil their sporting aspirations, when he proclaimed, *'It isn't climbing the mountain ahead that wears you out, it's the pebble in your shoe.'* For the most part the world of sport has for centuries been dominated by the male gender. So it is hardly surprising those participating in most forms of women's sport have time after time been called upon to overcome the irritation of the countless obstacles encountered in pursuit of their sporting dream.

Records exist which suggest in medieval England young men left work early to compete for their village in games similar to that of football. With the ball booted around an indefinable pitch, carried, or driven, through village streets, over fields, hedges and streams. With the rules of the game such as they were, inconsistent from county to county. Such rough *'kick-abouts'* were usually held at holiday times or times of celebration such as Shrove

Tuesday. However, in Tudor times, laws were passed forbidding such a '*devilish pastime*', since excessive injuries and fatalities were seriously depleting the towns and villages available workforce. England became the first country to develop a '*kicking game*', seemingly similar to that of modern day football. With compelling evidence in existence to suggest that in the county of Nottinghamshire team games were being played in schools as early as 1581. And although there is diversity of opinion regarding the accuracy of dates, there is also information suggesting an ancient form of a similar game was being played in China. But it is England which is internationally recognised as the source of the oldest football clubs in the world, with the earliest rules of the game established in London in 1863. The global game as we know it today was first organised around 1857, even though it is claimed an annual match was held in Scotland as early as the 1790s, although the first match recorded by the Scottish Football Association was held in Glasgow in 1892.

Women's football in England has a relatively long and chequered history, and women may well have also been playing a form of the game for as long as it has been in existence. The first recorded game between women took place in 1895, in a decade when it is claimed a number of English women's clubs were reported as being active. One such ladies club, situated in north London, is believed to have attracted around 10,000 spectators in support of a match held at Crouch End.

In its formative years Lancashire was a stronghold of women's football, where in 1894 the charitable Dick Kerr's Ladies Club came into being. It is claimed a club match, held on Boxing Day in 1920, against the St. Helen's Ladies club, attracted 53,000 spectators which were crammed into the ground at Goodison Park, Everton, with thousands more believed to be locked outside. At the time, it was the confirmed view of the Football Association [FA] that football was *'quite unsuitable for females',* and the following year it initiated a ban prohibiting women's football from being played on the grounds of its member clubs. And although this ruling was rescinded in July 1971, at the time it symbolised a sizeable *'pebble'* in the boots of the women.

The Women's Football Association [WFA] was formed two years earlier in 1969, and within three years the inaugural women's FA Cup Final and the first England women's international match had taken place. And in August 2017, England's heroic *'Lionesses'* almost managed to dislodge that infuriating *'pebble'* in the semi-finals of the Women's European Football Championship, suffering defeat by 3-0 in Enschede, by the eventual winners the Netherlands. Soccer is now the world's leading women's team sport, with upwards of 180 national teams competing internationally at professional level.

Meanwhile, the nation's reign as the women's rugby world champions was brought to an end on a summer evening in Belfast, in the final of the rugby World Cup, with a magnificently ruthless performance by the New Zealand *'Black Ferns'*.

The origins of a game roughly comparable with that of rugby can be traced back over 2000 years, when the Romans played a ball game called *'harpastum'*. Sourced from the Greek *'to seize'*, implying that the player carried or handled the ball. The roots of the modern game are well documented and can be traced to a school for *'young gentlemen'*, which outgrew its cramped surroundings in 1749 and was moved to a new site on the edge of the town of Rugby in Warwickshire. The new Rugby school came with an eight-acre plot known as the Close, upon which the game of football was subsequently played. At the time the game had few rules, and the ball could be caught and handled, although running with ball in hand was not permitted. *'Touchlines'*, marking the boundaries of the playing area were introduced, and in the autumn of 1823, during a football match which was taking place on the Close, the features of the game were radically changed, which would ultimately lead to the origin of the sport now known throughout the world as rugby. A local historian recorded the momentous incident, as follows, *'with a fine disregard for the rules of the game as played in his time, William Webb Ellis first took the ball in his arms and ran with it, thus originating the distinctive feature of the Rugby game'.* According to the rules of the day, Ellis [1806-1872] should have moved backwards to give himself sufficient room to either punt the ball up field, or to place it for a kick at goal. He would have been protected from the opposing team, as it was only permitted to advance to the spot where the ball had been caught. Disregarding the rules Ellis ran forward with the ball in hand towards the opposite goal, a move which in 1841, found its way into the fast developing rule book.

More often than not the concept of women playing contact sports habitually resulted in rude and disrespectful criticism, usually generating an adverse reaction from the general public. Reports relating to the early years of women's sport, especially rugby union, are rather vague, and it is difficult to accurately determine when and where the women's game actually began.

In 1881, two teams engaged in a number of exhibition *'football games'* in Scotland and northern England, several of which had to be abandoned due to riotous and violent behaviour. While most such games appear to have been played in accordance with the new FA rules, a report in an edition of the *Liverpool Mercury* dated the 27 June, suggested that a match held at the Cattle Market Inn Athletic Grounds in Stanley, Liverpool, involved scoring goals following *'touchdowns'*. Implying the match may have been played using a modified version of the rules of rugby. Other than this, for most of the nineteenth century, official records are unclear.

However there is evidence in existence to suggest that some girls played rugby unofficially, as members of school teams. Indeed, the earliest corroboration of a female playing rugby anywhere in the world relates to a school game. At the Portora Royal School, Enniskillen, County Fermanagh, Ireland, it is implied Miss Emily Valentine [1878-1967] practised with the school's first rugby team as a young girl. Remarkable since there are no other records of any other female rugby players in the nineteenth century.

While there are a few vague suggestions women's rugby teams may have been playing in France, and possibly New Zealand, as early as the 1890s, the first documented evidence of attempts to form a purely English women's team was in 1891, when a tour of New Zealand by a team of female rugby players was cancelled due to public protestation. Women's rugby union is reported as having been played in France as early as 1903, and in England a decade later, however it was usual at the time for the games to be held behind closed doors.

From 1983 until May 1994 women's rugby was organised throughout the United Kingdom by the Women's Rugby Football Union [WRFU]. However, in 1992 Ireland broke away, with Scotland following suit a year later.Consequently, in 1994, England and Wales established their own Unions. England's Union became the Rugby Football Union for Women [RFUW], which now has over 500 member clubs, including more than 200 senior clubs, the majority of which operate as women's sections within larger men's clubs. In September 2010 the RFUW was integrated into the Rugby Football Union [RFU], whilst retaining significant levels of independence, in the main it adopted the structures operated by the RFU. Subsequently in 2017, ten women's rugby union clubs were awarded a place in the newly formed domestic rugby union competition Women's Super Rugby.

It was in July of the same year an England women's team of professional cricketers fleetingly enjoying indisputable global sporting success. Led by twenty-six year-old Heather Knight OBE [born 1990], England defeated India by 9 runs in a thrilling final before a full house at Lord's, to win the International Cricket Council [ICC] Women's World Cup for the third time in eleven appearances.

The game of cricket is by far one of the oldest of the country's most popular team sports, with a wealth of information chronicled for those with an interest in the history of village and county cricket to explore. Its is perhaps understandable that a great deal more attention has been attributed to examining the men's game than has been devoted to that of the women's game. Even though the women's game can itself be traced back at least 250 years and reveals a rich and varied history.

Throughout the nineteenth century the schooling of upper and middle-class girls contrasted unequivocally with that of the education of boys. Boys were taught discipline, the benefits to be accrued from academic proficiency, and the qualities of leadership. While the education of girls centred upon the teaching of social graces and femininity, with tuition delivered on such subjects as needlework seemingly quite normal. The primary motive for this delineation was said to be based upon the roles boys and girls were each expected to assume upon reaching maturity, and in particular to ensure female students made a more attractive matrimonial prospect.

From the mid-nineteenth century, recreational pursuits, such as gentle walking, dancing, and moderate keep-fit exercise, were each regarded as welcome pastimes for their respective scholars by the school teachers at influential girls' schools. Such activities were considered beneficial in facilitating the feminine qualities of posture and grace. On the other hand, boys' public schools placed more emphasis on character building, through a variety of in-house sporting competitions. Predictably, with the passing of time, a growing number of elite girls' schools began to emulate boys' schools, with team games and physical education introduced as a fundamental element of the syllabus, and simple keep-fit exercise replaced by sport and gymnastics.

Founded in 1885 the influential public school for girls Roedean, situated on the outskirts of Brighton and formerly known as Wimbledon House, began to actively encourage numerous forms of sporting activity for its pupils. Its spacious grounds housed eight tennis courts a swimming pool and a cricket pitch with a pavilion. In summer, three hours each day, were reserved exclusively for sport, and two in winter, which included hockey, tennis, running, fencing, swimming, lacrosse and cricket, considered most important as a team game.

In 1929 the *'Times'* published numerous letters submitted by its female readers recalling memories of cricket played at schools which they attended. One such account, from a Mrs. E. Lombe of Torquay, described playing cricket at a Brighton school in 1857-1858. And in 1868, the *'Shepton Mallet Journal'* reported, *'in a ladies' school near Frome the pupils are allowed to play cricket, and the best cricketers are said to be the best scholars'*.

For the most part the women's game evolved separately from the men's game, and as such quite logically developed its own characteristics. From the late nineteenth and early twentieth centuries, perhaps one of the most distinguishing features was the *'class'* of women who engaged with the sport. The governing bodies of women's cricket which were gradually evolving around that time were for the most part influenced by women from an upper socio-economic position, women who were able to spare the time and had the resources to be able to administer and affiliate to such associations. In the early twentieth century a measured change in the lifestyle of middle and upper class women was begun. Women began to acquire a new found independence, which eventually led to an increase in their involvement in leisure activities, which in turn began to encourage the growth of women's cricket amongst the middle classes.

When compared with the comprehensive range of literature associated with the men's game, with very little is recorded on the subject of the women's game. Consequently, for this reason the flourishing sport of women's cricket is deserving of much closer inspection.

The true origin of the game of cricket remains a mystery. From the collection of folklore and fact expertly assembled over time, it is likely a simplified version of the game was played by children living in the south-east of England, in the counties of Kent, Sussex and Surrey, a region of the country then known as the Weald. It is thought the pastime survived as a children's game for many generations before the game was taken up by adults around the beginning of the seventeenth century.

There have been a number of speculative anecdotes regarding the origin of the game, including some which suggest it was created in France or Flanders. The earliest of these unconfirmed suppositions date back as far as 1300, when it is claimed the future King Edward II [1284–1327] played *'creag'* and other games at Westminster and Newenden in Kent. It is suggested *'creag'* was an old English word for cricket, although conflicting opinion suggests it was an early spelling of *'craic'*, which roughly translated meant *'fun and games'*.

It has also been suggested a form of cricket stemmed from the game of bowls. With a *'batsman'* introduced to intervene and try to hit the *'bowl'* in order to prevent it from reaching its target the *'jack'*. Since cricket can be reliably traced back to the thirteenth century, it may be assumed bowls is the older of the two sports. The game of bowls can also be traced back to the thirteenth century, and hypothetically to the twelfth century. For in a biography of Thomas Becket [c1120-1170], the Archbishop of Canterbury, in a graphic sketch portraying the city of London, the summer amusements of young men are recorded as including the sport of *'casting of stones'* which is believed to mean the game of bowls.

Undoubtedly the first definitive reference to the game of cricket is dated as Monday, 17 January, 1597, when a disagreement over a piece of common land was heard in court in Guildford, Surrey. John Derrick, a fifty-nine year-old former pupil at the Free School in Guildford, testified under oath that, some fifty years earlier, he and some of his school friends played the game of *'creckett'* on the disputed site. It is universally accepted this is the earliest reference to the game. Proving beyond doubt that cricket was being played in Surrey circa 1550, around the time of the death of the Tudor monarch, Henry VIII [1491–1547], described as *'one of the most charismatic rulers to sit on the English throne'*.

A number of words are thought to be the potential foundation of the term cricket, with the source most likelyto have been based upon words in use in the south-east of England at the time. This region of the Country had incorporated a number of Middle Dutch words into its southern English dialect, since at the time the area enjoyed trade connections with the historic and affluent County of Flanders. In the earliest definite reference it was spelled *'creckett'*, and the name may well have been derived from the Middle Dutch *'krick'*, meaning a stick. Alternatively, it is quite possible the old English word *'cricc'* or *'cryce'*, meaning a crutch or staff, may have been the origin. Perhaps the French word for a wooden post, *'criquet',* or even the Middle Dutch word *'krickstoel',* a long, low stool used for kneeling in church, which resembled an early form of low wicket with two stumps.

However, according to the European language expert, Dr. Heiner Gillmeister, of the University of Bonn, a specialist in medieval sports, especially ball games, who claims the word cricket derives from the Middle Dutch phrase for hockey *'met de krik ket sen'*, which translates as *'with the stick chase'*. You take your pick !

By and large the game continued to be played by children for generations, and cricket can be found defined in a dictionary of the day as a boys' game. The game was played in clearings, or on pieces of land grazed by sheep, when amongst the earliest items of equipment used may well have included a matted lump of sheep's wool, a small lump of wood, or even a stone, to serve as the ball. A stick was used as the bat, and a tree stump or a *'wicket-gate'* functioning as the wicket.

The game was later embraced by adults during the early part of the seventeenth century, when the first reference to the game being played as an adult sport occurred in 1611, when two Sussex men were prosecuted for playing cricket on Sunday instead of going to church.

It is generally considered village cricket had developed by the middle of the seventeenth century, and there are a number references in existence to suggest the game was contested between parish teams consisting of adult players right up to the English Civil War [1642–1651] fought between the *'Roundheads'* [Parliamentarians] and the *'Cavaliers'* [Royalists]. After the war ended the puritanical government clamped down on *'unlawful assemblies'*, in particular more boisterous games such as football, demanding stricter observance of the Sabbath as a day of worship and rest from work. Since Sunday was usually the only day of the week in which a limited amount of free-time was available to the lower classes, the popularity of cricket, along with other sports such as football, might well have gone into decline, however this was seemingly not the case in fee-paying elite public schools such as Winchester and St. Paul's.

There is no evidence to suggest the English political leader, Oliver Cromwell [1599-1648], banned cricket specifically. Indeed there are references which suggest the game continued to take place during the Interregnum [1649- 1660], the period of parliamentary and military rule after the end of the English Civil War. Maintaining it was acceptable to the authorities providing it did not cause any *'breach of the Sabbath'*. It is also thought that at the time the considerable enthusiasm shown by the nobility to engage in village games may well have encouraged the landed gentry to actively adopt and participate in the sport of cricket.

Charles II [1630-1685] became the first monarch to reign over the kingdoms of England, Ireland and Scotland following the Restoration in 1660. At which point cricket began to thrive, primarily since it began to attract a significant amount of gambling. In 1664 Parliament introduced the Gaming Act, limiting stakes to a maximum sum of £100, an absolute fortune at the time. By the end of the seventeeth century gambling on the results of cricket matches had certainly become enormously significant.

'Freedom of the press' was granted in 1696, and newspapers could for the first time publish detailed accounts of cricket matches. In 1697 a

newspaper reported a *'great match'* played in Sussex for the high stake of 50 guineas a side. Widespread gamblingcontinued to typify the game during the eighteenth century, with newspaper reports apt to lay greater emphasis on the wagers than on the play.

Chapter 2

The 'Cradle of Cricket' The Hambledon Club

The eighteenth century was a critical period in the development of the game of cricket.

The first recorded game of cricket in which teams were distinguished by the use of county names was reported as being held in 1709. Although there can be little doubt these types of event were being arranged long before then. Especially since the local nobility, along with others of considerable influence, were inspired by the notion that as ardent gamblers it would be highly likely they would improve the probability of winning their respective wagers by forming their own teams. As a consequence competent village cricketers were employed from neighbouring communities to serve as early professionals.

The oldest cricket bat in existence belonged to John Chitty of Surrey, and dates from, 1729. It can be found in the Sandham Room in the members pavilion at the Oval, and resembles a hockey stick in shape, rather than that of the modern bat of today. In the early eighteenth century the ball was never pitched, but rolled *'underarm'* along the ground, in a similar manner to bowls, and the curved shape of the bat enabled the batsman to play the ball.

The transition to the *'pitched'* delivery came about some thirty year later. Bowlers still continued to deliver the ball *'underarm'*, but pitched the ball towards the wicket through the air. This method of bowling led to the invention of the straight bat, and was the first of the resulting evolutionary *'roundarm'* and *'overarm'* style of bowling.

As the game continued to spread nationwide, Hambledon in Hampshire was by far the most famous of the early cricket clubs, and it is claimed the *'curved'* bat was the type used in the early Hambledon matches. Initially it was purely a local parish team which had been in existence since before 1750. Often referred to as the *'Squire Land's Club'*, after Squire Thomas Land [1714-1791] who was the principal organiser of the cricket teams in the village prior to the formation of the club. Hambledon came to prominence in 1756, when it is reported to have played a series of three matches against Dartford, itself a major club for at least thirty years. Formally established in 1727, Dartford Cricket Club is one of the oldest cricket clubs in England, its earliest known match, against a team from London, said to have taken place in 1722.

In spite of its rural location, Hambledon developed as a private club incorporating amongst its membership noblemen and country gentry, for whom one of the main attractions was the potential the game presented for gambling. Although occasionally some of these gentlemen played in matches, the players employed were mainly professionals.

The Reverend Charles Powlett [1728-1809] was the curate of Itchen Abbass, and illegitimate son of the Duke of Bolton and the actress Lavinia Fenton, best remembered for her role as Polly Peachum in John Gay's *Beggar's Opera*. Charles Powlett was a patron of English cricket, and often described as the founder and mainstay of the Hambledon Club, serving as its steward for many years. Described as *being 'the life and soul of the club'*, when the end came, he *was 'the last to abandon the sinking ship'*.

Despite being ordained and a Steward of the club and a member of the Laws of Cricket Committee which revised the Laws of Cricket in 1774, Powlett was not above gambling on the outcome of matches, or of betting against his own team. In 1775 Hambledon hosted Surrey on Broadhalfpenny Down, and when at one point in the second innings Surrey victory seemed certain, Powlett and his associate Philip Dehany, another Hambledon member, decided to bet heavily on Surrey to win. However, John Small and his team captain Richard Nyren delivered the earliest known century partnership in first-class cricket history to turn the game around. When Nyren's wicket eventually fell he was confronted by the irate Powlett and Dehaney who complained he had cost them money. At which the outraged Nyren replied, *'Another time, don't bet your money against such men as we are'.*

Another notable Hambledon cricketer was the left-handed batsman James Aylward [1741-1827]. Born in Warnford, Hampshire the first recorded reference of Aylward's cricketing feats remained undiscovered until 1773, when he was 32 years of age. He is known to have played 107 first-class matches from 1773 until 1797. Arthur Haygarth [1825-1903] an amateur cricketer, who later became one of the sports most eminent historians, wrote, *'he must have played several years previously, the records being unfortunately lost'*.

Aylward is perhaps best remembered for an extraordinary achievement in the summer of 1777, when he set the record for the highest individual score in first-class cricket, scoring 167 runs in a single innings, pitted against the best bowlers and fielders of the day, smashing the record of 136 set two years earlier by John Small [1737-1826]. A cobbler, and extremely influential player in his day, Small was the first person to be described a *'superstar'*, and was involved in the permanent addition of two significant *'Laws of Cricket'*, the maximum width of the bat and the introduction of the middle stump in the wicket. In 1775, during an innings which endured for two and three-quarter hours, while making the 14 runs Hambledon required to defeat a visiting England side, it was observed that three balls had passed between his two stumps. Acclaimed as one of the greatest players to grace the pitch at the famous Hambledon Club, Small was named by the *Times* as one of the *'100 Greatest Cricketers of All Time'*.

Aylward played for the Hambledon club until 1779, following which he continued to play in minor matches. He was offered employment as a water bailiff for the politician Sir Horation Mann [1744-1814], and moved to Mann's house at Bourne Paddock in Kent, where he continued to play for his patrons' teams, but failed to satisfy his preceding promise as a batsman or water bailiff. He is buried in St John's Wood Churchyard alongside Lord's Cricket Ground.

Another prominent player to routinely turn out for the Hambledon club was the gypsy inn-keeper Noah Mann [1756- 1789]. A left-handed powerful all-rounder Noah made his first-class debut in 1777, and made 55 appearances for Hambledon in his 12 year spell with the club. It is claimed he was a medium fast seam bowler and the creator of the *'swerve'* bowling technique. The eminent cricket historian Arthur Haygarth [1825-1903], recounts how Mann was *'extremely athletic and could cover an immense deal of ground, darting about like lightning'*. He would entertain the early arrivals at matches by performing daring bareback riding performances of agility, picking up handkerchiefs from the ground at full speed. Noah Mann's death at the age of 33 was caused as a result of a bizarre accident. He had been out shooting, and on returned to the Half Moon Inn, at Northchapel, wet and tired, where he spent a drunken evening with his companions. Refusing to go to bed, Noah slept all night in his chair in front of the fire. According to the Hambledon cricketer John Nyren, during the night *'he fell upon the embers, and was so severely burned that he died the next day'*. At the subsequent inquest a verdict of accidental death was returned. A friend of the musician Ivor Novello, John Nyren [1764-1837] was a large bald headed man who played the fiddle, and it was said particularly fond of black Kent cherries, however he found fame as an author, when in 1833 he published *The Young Cricketer's Tutor*, a classic and colourful recollection of the legendary figures who dominated the final years of the eighteenth century, widely regarded as cricket's first great work of literature, and *Cricketers of My Time*. Nyren's father Richard *'Dick'* Nyren [1734-1797] was the landlord of the *Bat and Ball Inn* overlooking Halfpenny Down. A professional cricketer who played first-class cricket for the Hambledon club in its heyday.A genuine all-rounder and the earliest known left-hander of note, Nyren was the captain of Hambledon and was known as the team's *'general'* on the field of play. He also acted club secretary and for many years took care of matchday catering.

Educated at Westminster, John Frederick Sackville [1745-1799], the 3rd Duke of Dorset, was an eminent devotee of cricket, before joining Hambledon Cricket Club, the leading cricket club of the day. Sackville was returned unopposed as the Member of Parliament for the county of Kent in 1768, sitting until he succeeded to the dukedom in 1769 following the death of his uncle Charles. Best remembered for his love of cricket, which was undoubtedly stimulated by his interest in gambling, he was a nonetheless a good player and an important patron.

In 1773 Sackville presented the Vine Cricket Ground to the town of Knole in Sevenoaks, Kent at a peppercorn rent. Described as being one of the oldest cricket grounds in England, it is said the first nationally reported cricket match took place there in the season of 1734, when *'The Gentlemen of Kent'* beat *'The Gentlemen of Sussex'*. Lord Middlesex, the 2nd Duke of Dorset, Charles Sackville [1710-1769] played for the Kent team, alongside his brother Lord John Philip Sackville [1713–1765] the father of John Frederick Sackville.

In 1782 the *'Morning Chronicle'*, reporting on John Frederick Sackville noted, *'His Grace is one of the few noblemen who endeavour to combine the elegance of modern luxury with the more manly sports of the old English times'*. However the Duke of Dorset's patronage of cricket did not come cheap, and a year later, in 1783, the *'Whitehall Evening Post'* recorded the annual cost of maintaining his team, before wagers, as being £1,000. Although considerable, it was considerably less than the sum some of his contemporaries were spending on horse racing. The report continued, saying that the Duke of Dorset was unrivalled among noblemen *'at cricket, tennis and billiards'*. Presumably his reputation as a serial womaniser was benevolently overlooked. In spite of his well documented fondness for the fair sex, it was subsequently suggested Sackville would *'turn in his grave'* if a woman ever played cricket for England. *'Mind not, my dear ladies, the impertinent interrogatories of silly coxcombs, or the dreadful apprehensions of semi-men. Go on, and attach yourselves to the athletic.'*

Thomas 'Daddy' White [1740-1831] was a genuine all-rounder, successful as both batsman and bowler, who appeared frequently for Surrey and All-England in the 1760s and 1770s. Although there was some confusion in various cricketing circles between him and the similarly named *'Shock'* White of Middlesex, it has been conclusively proved the wide bat was used by his namesake Thomas White of Reigate. The main cause was in relation to the *'wide bat controversy'* when, *'White of Reigate' tried to use a bat that was fully as wide as the wicket'*. The incident occurred when White was playing for Chertsey against Hambledon, whether White had been seeking an unfair advantage, or merely playing a prank, the Hambledon players objected and it is rumoured the Hambledon players held down White while his bat was planed down to an acceptable width. In any event a formal protest was later made by Hambledon's opening bowler Thomas Brett, the captain Richard Nyren, and the master batsman John Small. White's real motive remains a mystery, but the Hambledon objection was preserved by the MCC, and the Laws were formally changed in 1774 when the maximum width of the bat was set at four and one quarter inches.

Straight bats had replaced the old hockey stick shape several years earlier, and the issue of the width of the bat may have been rankling.

The English cricket season was coming to an end when the first ever women's cricket match was played on Gosden Common, near Guildford in Surrey, on the 26 July, 1745, during the reign of the George II [1683-1760], the last British monarch to have been born outside Great Britain. Almost 150 years since the earliest known reference to the game in 1597. The first significant battle of the Jacobite Rebellion took place in September at Prestonpans in the East Lothian, Scotland.

Two years later, In April 1747, *'Bonnie Prince Charlie'*, Charles Edward Stuart [1720-1788], *'The Young Pretender'*, suffered a crushing defeat on the windswept Drummossie Moor in the final conflict of the rebellion at Culloden, one of the most harrowing battles in British history. Loyalist troops conquered the supporters of *'The Old Pretender'*, the Catholic challenger who sought to restore the Stuart monarchy to the British throne. The Scottish Jacobite, Simon Fraser [1667-1747], known as *'the Fox'*, and Chief of Clan Fraser of Lovat, was amongst the highlanders defeated at the battle of Culloden, he was later tried and convicted for high treason against the Crown, and sentenced to death. He was subsequently beheaded on Tower Hill, London, the last man in Britain to be executed by beheading, although this method of execution was not formally abolished in United Kingdom law until 1973. Nevertheless, the brutal Jacobite conflict had little impact, if any, on women's cricket taking place in the south-east of England.

Regrettably the identities of the rival players competing in the historic ladies match held at Gosden Common remain unknown. Even so this momentous event in the chronicles of women's cricket was somewhat diffidently reported in the '*Reading Mercury*', as '*the greatest cricket match that was played in this part of England ... between eleven maids of Bramley and eleven maids of Hambledon, all dressed in white. The Bramley maids had blue ribbons and the Hambledon maids red ribbons on their heads. The Bramley girls got 119 notches and the Hambledon girls 127. There was of both sexes the greatest number that ever was seen on such an occasion, the girls bowled, batted, ran, and catched, as well as any men could do in that game.*'

The next women's cricket match for which written records exist was held three months later in July, between the teams of Charlton, and those of Westdean and Chilgrove, in Sussex. A charge was made for admission to the famous Artillery Ground, clearly highlighting the importance attached to the contest. Unfortunately, the match turned out to be a somewhat unruly affair, and was disrupted by crowd trouble, and as a consequence ran on into the following day. In the eighteenth century the Artillery Ground was home to the original London Cricket Club, and at the time served as the featured venue for all London cricket. Due to uncontrolled gambling, the club unfortunately fell into disrepute, and subsequently brought to an end first-class cricket there. The last known match taking place in 1778, some years after the London Club had disbanded.

Early women's cricket matches were especially popular in the counties of Sussex, Hampshire and Surrey, where local fixtures were played between the neighbouring communities. Women's matches were however not necessarily refined occasions, and it was quite usual for crowds in excess of 2,000 to be in attendance. Partly due to competitive rivalry and partly due to the large wagers placed on the results of matches, crowd trouble was commonplace. One variety of contest matched single women against their married counterparts, with an assortment of prizes on offer for the victors, ranging from *'ladylike'* lace gloves to barrels of ale !

In 1777, the ardent cricket enthusiast and supporter of the Hambledon club, John Sackville, the 3rd Duke of Dorset in what must have resulted from an earlier change of heart, wrote a letter to *'a circle of ladies, his intimate friends'*, in which he enquired, *'What is human life but a game of cricket ? And if so, why should not the ladies play it as well as we ?'* Fickle as the Duke usually was in most of his dealings with the fair sex, he remained abidingly charitable towards the cause of women's cricket. He liked his women sporty, and his eventual support for the women's game was just one of his many endeavours in assisting women to participate, irrespective of the hostility they were frequently called upon to endure.

Best remembered for his love of cricket, John Sackville was a competent player and an important benefactor for the game. Throughout the entire eighteenth century since cricket had become an extremely appealing pastime for gamblers, and the Duke's passion was without doubt stimulated by his love of gaming. The Duke's other leisure pursuits, whilst probably secondary to his reputation as a womaniser, included billiards and tennis.

Women's cricket continued to broaden its horizons and gained a further level of respectability in 1777 when the English peeress, Elizabeth Smith-Stanley, [née Hamilton] the Countess of Derby [1753-1797], organised a cricket match which was played between two teams drawn entirely from upper-class society women, and ladies of quality and fashion, in private at the Oaks in Surrey, one of the favourite havens of the Countess. An English peeress, the Countess of Derby was the eldest daughter of the 6th Duke of Hamilton, popular amongst society and considered a leader of fashion. It is said Miss Elizabeth Anne Burrell [1757-1837], the sister of the 1st Baron Gwydyr, Peter Burrell, a fine batsman in his day, *'got more notches in the first and second innings than any Lady in the game'*. Such was the impression she made upon the Scottish peer, nobleman, and politician, Douglas Hamilton, the 8th Duke of Hamilton, who fell instantly head over heels in love with her, and they were married before the start of the next cricket season.

Amongst the invited guests was another infamous member of eighteenth century society, the most notorious rake of the day, John Frederick Sackville. Early in 1778, just five years after her marriage to the 12th Earl of Derby, rumour spread alleging Lady Derby was engaged in a very public and torrid affair with Sackville, causing a scandal which led to her eventual separation from her husband, and her exile from society.

Chapter 3

Victorian cricket

The nineteenth century heralded a period of enormous development and growth, during which Victorian Britain became a powerful manufacturing force and the British Empire reached its zenith. Having originated in south-east England, cricket became the country's national sport in the course of the eighteenth century and developed globally in the nineteeth and twentieth centuries. The first international matches were played, and Test cricket was retrospectively recognised in 1877.

The growth of cricket in the mid and late nineteeth century was aided by the development of the rail travel. For the first time teams were able to play against each other without enduring long, time-consuming journies, and spectators were able to travel further to support matches, which led to an increase in the size of crowds. Most of the army units spread throughout the British Empire had time on their hands, and encouraged the locals to embrace cricket, which most did with the exception of Canada.

The first recorded men's international game of cricket was held in 1844 between North America and Canada at the St. Georges Crciket Club in New York, and in 1859 a team of leading English professionals, led by George Parr [1826-1891] of Nottinghamshire, embarked on the first ever overseas tour to Canada and North America, and in 1862 the first English men's team toured Australia. Six years later a team of Aborigines toured England and became the first Australian cricket team to travel overseas. It was not until 1877 that an England team would tour Australia, where it played two matches that are now regarded as the inaugural Test matches. The following year an Australian team toured England, and such was its success it popular demand warranted similar future events, which eventually led to the tense Australian victory at the Oval in 1882 which gave rise to The Ashes.

Fundamental change also occurred with the formation of Sussex as the first of the county clubs in 1839. However, no sooner had the first county clubs become established, they faced *'player action'* when in 1846 a 'one-eyed' bricklayer by the name of William Clarke [1798-1856] created a travelling All-England XI. as a commercial venture with the aim of popularising the sport in regions of the Country which had never been visited by first-class cricketers. A number of similar teams were formed, and the trend lasted for about thirty years before the counties and the MCC eventually won through. Born in Nottingham, William Clarke is recognised as the founder of Nottinghamshire cricket and has since been described as *'one of certain figures who, in the history of cricket, stand like milestones along the way'*.

It was not until eight short years after its formation in 1926, that the Women's Cricket Association received an invitation to send a touring team to Australia and New Zealand, which it eagerly accepted. Meanwhile, women's matches continued to thrive and attract large crowds, providing a rare source of entertainment which captivated the public. The first ever women's county match was held in October 1811, in a field at the back of Newington Green, near Ball's Pond in the ancient parish of Newington, Middlesex, between the counties of Surrey and Hampshire. The teams, ranged in age from 14 to 60 years, and were defined by blue and orange coloured ribbons pinned to their respective bonnets. Underwritten by two noblemen in the total sum of 1,000 guineas, with 500 guineas allocated to each side, the match was, lasted for three days and was won by Hampshire by 15 runs. The *Times* reported there had been *'some very excellent play and much skill'* and *'a great concourse of people attended to witness this singular contention'.* Consequently, a return match was immediately arranged.

From time to time the provincial press reported similar village diversions, one such match held at Southborough, which lies to the north of Tunbridge Wells, Kent. In this specific match the older lady players pitted their skills against the young. The old ladies won by 55 runs and promptly set about enjoying the spoils of their victory, *'three bottles of gin, and three bottles of best gunpowder tea'*, a form of Chinese tea in which each leaf is rolled into small round pellets resembling grains of gunpowder.

There was at least one occasion when the ladies fell some way short of demonstrating the recognised and approved standards of decorum. The *Nottingham Review* of 4 October 1833 reported, *'Last week, at Sileby feast, [a village which lies between Loughborough and Leicester], the women so far forgot themselves, and by their deportment, as well as frequent applications to the tankard, they rendered themselves objects such as no husband, brother, parent or lover could contemplate with any degree of satisfaction'.*

Such games pale into insignificance when compared with the contest at Newington Green. It has to be said, most women did not show the slightest interest in the game being played, or exhibited any motivation to take part. The majority occupied themselves in the local hostelry preparing suitable refreshment for their respective men-folk who were engaged on the field of play. And from time to time they even turned their hands to washing clothes or making tea, a practice which persists to this day in some village cricket.

Long before writing reports and articles on the subject of cricket became as popular as it is today, a cricket-loving woman who showed no desire to help out by acting as tea-lady, or washer-woman, might on rare occasions offer her assistance to men's cricket as a teacher.

By way of example, one such handsome matriarch, who in her day was an inspiration among cricket enthusiasts, was the strong-willed harp-playng mother of nine, Martha Grace [née Pocock] [1812-1884]. Martha studied, taught, and commented on the performance and development of each of her five cricketing sons. Whether on the field of play, or in the orchard where their father Henry had felled a few trees to create a cricket pitch, Martha taught them everything they knew, and attended every game she could to see them play.

Even as women's cricket continued its development, and far less resistance was displayed towards the concept of women participating in the sport. Despite the help and guidance Dr. William Gilbert Grace received from his devoted mother as a young man, some time later the *'folk-hero'* was said to have given support to the common belief that cricket was ostensibly, *'not a game for women,and although the fair sex occasionally join in a picnic game, they're not constitutionally adapted for the sport !'*

During cricket's formative years the ball was initially delivered under-arm to the batsman, but there are those who claim it was actually a woman that later introduced the favoured *'round-arm'* bowling style. The early nineteenth century woman cricketer, Christiana Willes [1786-1873] of Headcorn, Kent, frequently known by her married name Christiana Hodges, found the under-arm style of bowling difficult to deliver when wearing a hooped skirt. Consequently, it is claimed she eventually developed the higher *'round-arm'* style of bowling to avoid her hand becoming ensnared in the folds of her voluminous skirt. It is said Christiana found this far more successful than the *'under-arm'* style of bowling when helping her brother John, who played for Kent, when bowling to him in practice. However, the ardent cricket devotee, and former Tory Prime Minister, Sir John Major, in his best-selling *book 'More than a Game, a History of Cricket'*, rejects the *'hooped skirt'* anecdote, claiming that the hooped skirt was *'no longer in vogue by 1807.'* The same story was also rejected in 1970 by Rowland Bowen, in his book '*Cricket: A History of its Growth and Development* '. Nevertheless, it remains guardedly accepted by some writers as part of cricketing folklore. It is equally well documented the *'round-arm'* action was first developed by the useful bowler, Tom Walker [1762-1831] of the Hambledon Club, who is credited with introducing *'round-arm'* bowling, the predecessor of modern *'over-arm'* bowling. It is claimed Walker, together with some of his fellow Hambledon players, used to practise in a barn during the winter. It was during these practice sessions that he discovered he could generate more bounce and variation of pace if he bowled with his arm away from his body, and soon realised such deliveries caused serious problems for the batsman. However, having sown the seeds of a bowling revolution, he failed to see the new style of bowling accepted during his career, which did not come about until a later generation. Known as *'old everlasting'*, Walker was renowned for his skilful defensive batting, and was notoriously difficult to dismiss. On one occasion he faced the terrifying right-arm under-arm bowling of David Harris [1755-1803], the most fearful bowler of the age, for a total of 170 balls scoring just a single run. In old-age the redoubtable Harris supported himself on a crutch to help brush away the effects of gout, and would rest in an armchiar behind the wickets between overs. On another occasion Walker faced the frustrated right-arm slow under-arm bowler, the clergyman Lord Frederick Beauclerk [1773–1850] the fourth son of the 5th Duke of St Albans, is reported to have thrown down his hat in disgust and shouted, *'You confounded old beast ! '* Walker's laconic response to his team-mates being, *'I don't care what he says'*. On his retirement in 1826, Lord Beauclerk went on to serve as President of the Marylebone Cricket Club [MCC].

Widespread outbreaks of cholera and typhoid were quite commonplace in Victorian England, and improving the general health of the nation was an important concern. Smallpox, diphtheria, scarlet fever and measles all contributed to the nation's death rate on a scale which these days would be considered wholly unacceptable. Water supplies for the majority of towns and villages usually came from wells and streams, with unpolluted water and effective sewage disposal essential for improved well being. Cholera was discovered in Soho, in the West End of London in 1932. It was thought to have spread through a *'miasma'* or *'haze'*, or *'bad smell'* in the atmosphere. The epidemic swept throughout England, and subsequent burial register and inquest reports on victims identified poor sanitary conditions and overcrowding as the possible source. Some housing was reported as being very unhealthy, a significant number of which incorporated pigsties and privies. The *'great stink'* would last for over 20 years before the Government was forced to act upon the hideous state of the River Thames and deal with London's polluted source of water by developing an effective sewage system. Nevertheless, the late nineteenth century was the pinnacle of the contribution made by women in assisting the development of men's cricket, but even more importantly it was the starting-point at which women's cricket was played seriously as a sport rather than an amusing form of entertainment.

Women cricket writers have always been in the minority, since Mary Russell Mitford [1787-1855] published her article *'The Cricket Match'* in *The Lady's Magazine* in 1823, and again in the following year, with great success her first publication of *'Our Village'*. Born at Alresford in Hampshire, Mary Russell Mitford was an author and dramatist, best remembered for her *'Our Village'*, series of drawings of village scenes and characters based upon life in the hamlet Three Mile Cross, near Reading in Berkshire, where she lived.

Just over a century later, the career of the sports writer Marjorie Pollard OBE [1899-1982] was drawing to a close in an age when the enthusiasm for all forms of women's sport was steadily gaining momentum. Born in

Rugby, Warwickshire, she wrote a regular cricket column for the *Morning Post* and *London Evening News*, and in 1926 helped found the Women's Cricket Association [WCA].

Three years after the death of Martha Grace, and almost 150 years from the time of the historic mid-summer match between the villages of Hambledon and Bramley held on Gosden Common, the first women's cricket club was founded in 1887. The White Heather Club was formed by eight noblewomen at Nun Appleton in North Yorkshire, and within the next four years the membership of the Club had risen from 8 to 50, mostly made up of well-to-do Yorkshire ladies with sufficient money to meet their own expenses.

Included amongst its number was founder member and writer, Lucy Baldwin, Countess Baldwin of Bewdley [née Ridsdale] [1869-1945], the wife of the Prime Minister, Stanley Baldwin. During the General Strike of 1926, Countess Baldwin convened a General Meeting of the White Heather Club at 10 Downing Street. And in 1930, penned a letter to the editor of '*Women's Cricket*' affirming, *'The crack of bat against ball amid the humming and buzzing of summer sounds is still to me a note of pure joy that raises haunting memories of friends and happy days. The one game in the world for me.'*

The White Heather Club survived until 1951, and its scorebook still exists and can be viewed in the library of the MCC at Lord's. The copper plate inscription written inside the front cover of the book describes the reason behind the decision to form the club as being *'the large amount of cricket being played at Normanhurst and Eridge, the country seats of the Brassey and Neville families.'*

However, this genteel form of *'country house'* cricket was soon to have a professional rival, for three years later two teams of women were formed by a Mr. Matthews, confusingly named the Original English Lady Cricketers. His objective being to demonstrate how appropriate the game of cricket was in which the fair sex might engage, in preference to lawn tennis and other games. Young women and girls were carefully selected by Matthews and underwent a rigorous programme of training and practice in the sport which subsequently became recognised as England's national game.

During 1890, two teams of eleven women set about touring the principal towns of the United Kingdom, competing in a series of *'select and refined'* exhibition matches. The players competing in such events were usually mature women of good social standing. They were always accompanied by a suitably respectable and virtuous manager, and at all *times 'elegantly and appropriately attired'*. Players were not permitted to play under their real names, and were each allocated the sum of sixpence a day [2½ pence] to cover their respective expenses. They were each provided with a suitable uniform, red for one team, and blue for the other.

The Original English Lady Cricketers opening match was held in Liverpool, and attracted a crowd of around 15,000 spectators. The *Liverpool Daily Post,* first published in 1855 at a cost of one penny per copy, proclaimed in its report on the game, *'They came to scoff but stayed to praise'*. Advertisements publishing the tour depicted the lady cricketers as a *'genuine novelty'*, but stressed the entertainment provided was *'sport not clowning',* portraying the women cricketers as *'refined lady athletes, not burlesque masqueraders'.*

A good many newspaper reporters of the time acknowledged the formation of the Original English Lady Cricketers with more than a little sarcasm. One extremely patronising, and widely published report, relating to the schedule of forthcoming matches, insisted, *'when scrambling across the pitch to steal a short run, we fear that dignity and elegance can with difficulty be preserved. The appearance of pads beneath a short skirt is very clumsy. It will be curious, again, to see how many of the team can throw properly, without causing the ribald populace to snigger. Of one thing there can be no doubt, that these lady cricketers are brave, very brave women, and also highly original'.*

In a short article on women's cricket, published in Lillywhite's Cricketers Annual for 1890, James Lillywhite observed, *'As an exercise, cricket is probably not so severe as lawn tennis, and it is certainly not so dangerous as hunting or skating, and if, therefore, the outcome of the present movement is to induce ladies more generally to play cricket, we shall consider that a good result has been attained'.*

The Attraction for 1890.
A Genuine Novelty.
Complete in itself. Matchless.
The "Original English
LADY CRICKETERS."
Idea Protected.
Title a Registered Trade Mark.
Two Complete Teams,
Splendidly Equipped,
Excellently Trained
Sport, Daily for Months past
not by George Hearne,
Clowning. Maurice Read,
and other Players.
THE "ORIGINAL ENGLISH LADY CRICKETERS"
have arranged to visit
Scarborough,
Skegness,
Blackpool (Raike's Hall),
Eastbourne (Devonshire-park),
See Brighton (Preston Park),
The Star, Northampton (Franklin's),
March 7th. Hastings,
Plymouth,
Wales, and
nearly every large City in the Kingdom.
Elaborate Pictorials, Blocks, and Lithos,
by Hill-Siffken, David Allen, Hal Berte, Phillips, &c.
Magnificent and extensive Wardrobe, Photos., and Properties.
Complete Day Show.
Assault-at-Arms at Night.
Cricket, Crocketta, Bicycling, Fencing, Boxing, and Drill.
Refined Lady Athletes, not Burlesque Masqueraders.
For full particulars and few remaining dates
(Easter open),
Address, the MANAGER (E. C. and A. An., Limited),
13, Chesterfield-grove, London, S.E.
THE "ORIGINAL ENGLISH LADY CRICKETERS."
Agent for the North,
F. W. Walden, 13, Parker-street, Liverpool.

British Newspaper Archive - The Era - 15 March 1890
(www.britishnewspaperarchive.co.uk)

With matches frequently played on county grounds all over the country, the Original English Lady Cricketers proved highly successful, until after two years, in somewhat mysterious circumstances, it was disbanded, when it was alleged the male organisers made off with the accumulation of hard-earned profits.

The concept of the Original English Lady Cricketers was not unlike that fashioned in 1846 by the Nottinghamshire born cricketer William Clarke, who signed up the best English cricketers of the age and created an All England XI touring team to play matches in the prosperous big cities of the north. With no rival organised team games to challenge his bold initiative, thousands of eager spectators flocked to watch his top-class team of cricketing stars. Clarke was inundated with requests for fixtures, receiving a substantial fee from the opponents of his All England XI, who in turn hoped for a large attendance and a financial return on their investment. Within a few short years Clarke's venture became very profitable and the pounds, shillings and pennies just kept on rolling in. Especially for Clarke, who was astute enough to keep his players enthusiastic by ensuring he paid them more than the MCC could afford. The surplus he kept for himself and as a consequence he became a very wealthy man. Leslie Thomas John Arlott OBE [1914–1991] an English journalist, author and iconic cricket commentator for the BBC's *Test Match Special*, wrote, *'William Clarke was the first man to make a fortune out of cricket. He was also the first to see that a fortune was to be made out of it'.*

The format for the first County Championship was also launched as an official competition 1890. In a private meeting held at Lord's in December of the previous year, representatives of the eight leading county clubs met to discuss a procedure by which future County Championships might be decided. A new format for the competition was formally approved, initially including the counties of Gloucestershire, Kent, Lancashire, Middlesex, Nottinghamshire, Surrey, Sussex and Yorkshire. And the first official County Championship match was held in Bristol where Yorkshire defeated Gloucestershire by 8 wickets. In the same year, Surrey after winning nine out of its fourteen games, were crowned as the first official county champions.

Just as the British Empire continued its expansion throughout the world, the tentacles of cricket were also beginning to spread, and the first international match was played during the second half of the nineteenth century. Meanwhile, in 1894 a women's cricket league was formed in Australia, and in Port Elizabeth, South Africa, the Pioneers Women's Cricket Club had already been founded, while in Canada a women's team was playing cricket at Beacon Hill Park in Victoria.

THE ORIGINAL ENGLISH LADY CRICKETERS.

Marjorie Pollard - *Cricket for Women and Girls* [London, 1934]

Chapter 4

Heroines' of 19 Century Cricket

Martha Grace [1812-1884] [née Pocock]:

Martha Grace, the first woman to be mentioned in *Wisden*. in 1915.
Photo courtesy: *Reminiscences* [W.G. Grace].

The Grace family was an extremely famous and influential English cricketing family during the latter part of the nineteenth century. Fourteen of its members played first-class cricket at some time during their lives, the most celebrated and controversial of which was Dr. W.G. Grace [1848-1915] *'the big-un'*. Together with his elder brother, Edward Mills Grace [1841-1911], and younger brother, Fred Grace [1850-1911], the trio were frequently referred to as the *'three Graces'*. In 1880, the siblings created cricketing history when they played in the same England Test team, the first time three brothers had played together in Test cricket.

Martha Pocock married Henry Mills Grace, a local doctor, in Bristol in November 1831. The family lived out their lives in the village of Downend, *'a distinct village surrounded by countryside'*, situated about four miles outside Bristol. In every respect the Grace's were a typical Victorian family, raising a family of nine children, including five sons and four daughters.

Both Henry and Martha were *'full of enthusiasm for the game of cricket'* and the subject was *'a common theme of conversation at home'*. But it was the large-featured, matriarch Martha who first taught her children the fundamentals and techniques of the game, around the vegetable patch in the family back garden. It is claimed the legendary W.G. Grace first handled a cricket bat at the age of two, and when asked was he *'born a cricketer'* he replied, *'cricketers are made by coaching and practice'*, adding that in his opinion, if he was not *'born a cricketer'*, he was *born 'in an atmosphere of cricket'*.

In 1850, Henry and Martha relocated to a nearby house called *'The Chestnuts'*, which boasted a good sized orchard, which Henry soon set about clearing to fashion a rudimentary practice pitch. All the children, including their four daughters, were encouraged to play cricket in the re-designed orchard, although the girls, along with the family dogs, were generally only required to perform fielding duties.

It was in the Downend orchard, and as members of the local cricket club, that the Grace family fashioned their considerable cricketing skills. To a great extent with the support and guidance of their uncle, Alfred Pocock [1814-1897], who was considered by many an exceptional coach, who spent countless long hours tutoring the Grace boys on the practice pitch at the family home.

Whenever she could Martha would go to watch the games in which her children were competing, and according to historical record proved to be a severe critic, repeatedly scolding the young W.G following the execution of a bad shot. She would be heard to forcefully cry out, *'Willie, Willie, haven't I told you over and over again how to play that ball?'* or, by way of a change, *'Gilbert, how many times have I told you how to play that ball?'*

The majority of elite sportsmen and women do not reach their optimal level of achievement without enormous commitment and support from their immediate family, and undoubtedly Martha must number amongst the earliest of elite sport's *'pushy parents'*. Although it is claimed Martha was the primary cricket coach of her children, according to the MCC's official memorial biography, it is argued she played almost no role in the cricketing education of the great W.G.

It is suggested the Grace family name became exaggerated in cricketing history when in 1859 Martha is said to have written a technically knowledgeable letter to Nottinghamshire's George Parr. The successor of the famed *'father of Nottinghamshire cricket'* William Clarke. The letter, is supposed to relate to her young son Edward Mills Grace, and is considered one of cricket's most precious pieces of prose, although Parr declared he had either lost, or destroyed the prized item of correspondence, casting some doubt as to whether the letter really existed ! By all accounts Martha wrote, *'I am writing to ask you to consider the inclusion of my son, E.M. Grace – a splendid hitter and most excellent catch – in your England XI. I am sure he would play very well and do the team much credit. It may interest you to learn that I have another son, now twelve years of age, who will in time be a much better player than his brother because his back stroke is sounder, and he always plays with a straight* bat. *His name is W.G. Grace.'*

Martha's enthusiasm for the game yielded a total of ten first-class cricketers under the Grace family tree. But what is most revealing is the reference in the letter to W.G's back foot technique and straight bat. Martha's concern for the improvement of his technique makes her one of the game's most influential coaches of all time, especially since W.G. was soon to be acknowledged as the first batsman to play off both the front and back foot.

Martha died on the 25 July 1884. Her death led to the abandonment of what initially appeared to be just another Championship match between the counties of Gloucestershire and Lancashire. On the second day of the match a telegram arrived at the Old Trafford ground bearing the news that Martha Grace, who had been ill for some time, had passed away a week after her 72nd birthday. In a magnanimous gesture the Lancashire captain, who undoubtedly knew of Martha's significance in the development of modern cricket, immediately abandoned the match as a mark of respect, allowing the bereaving Grace siblings to leave for home.

The Indian cricket historian, and senior cricket writer at *Cricket Country*, Arunabha Sengupta [born 1973] wrote, *'The matriarchal role in the development of the Grace supremacy cannot be exaggerated. Martha was a tall, strong, imperious woman who arguably knew more about cricket than the most addicted gentleman following the game'.*

The former Nottinghamshire captain, and one of the era's finest batsmen, Richard Daft [1835-1900], declared that Martha Grace *'knew ten times as much about cricket as any lady ever knew'.*

Lucy Baldwin [née Ridsdale] [1869–1945]

Countess Baldwin of Bewdley, GBE, DGStJ.

Lucy Ridsdale. Wife of the former Prime Minister, Stanley Baldwin 1st Earl Baldwin of Bewdley, KG,PC,JP,FRS [1867–1947].

Three years after the death of Martha Grace, the first women's cricket club, the White Heather Club, was founded at Nun Appleton in Yorkshire. Its members were ladies of independent means and within three years, its numbers had swelled to 50. The club, which only folded in 1951, counted among its number Lucy Ridsdale.

Born in Bayswater, London, Lucy Ridsdale was known as 'Cissie', and grew up with her sister and three brothers in the historic Sussex village of Rottingdean, within the City of Brighton and Hove on the Sussex coast. Her elder brother was Sir Edward Aurelian Ridsdale GBE [1864–1923], a British Liberal politician for Brighton and leading member of the British Red Cross Society.

From 1892 until her death Lucy was the wife of Stanley Baldwin, a Conservative politician who held office as Prime Minister of the United Kingdom on three occasions, serving under three monarchs.

As an eighteen year-old girl, Lucy was a founder member of the first women's cricket club, the White Heather Club, which was established in 1887 at Nun Appleton Hall near Appleton Roebuck in Yorkshire. During the General Strike of 1926 she convened a meeting of the White Heather Club which was held at 10 Downing Street.

It was on the cricket field that Lucy met her husband, Stanley Baldwin, and in the cricket season of 1892, the year they became engaged to be married, she notched up a seasonal average score of 62. The couple were married in September later that year, in Rottingdean, amongst the wedding guests were her husband's aunt Alice, and her son Rudyard Kipling

[1865-1936], one of the United Kingdom's most popular and prolific writers of both prose and verse in the late nineteenth and twentieth centuries.

The couple had seven children, the first of which was stillborn, but in addition to raising her children, she was a remarkable person in her own right. Unlike her husband, she was extremely sociable and much preferred the city life of London to the country. Their daughter Lady Margaret Huntington-Whiteley [1897-1976] suggested, *'two people could not have been more unlike, but should they ever differ, it was always done quietly and politely.'*

Lucy Ridsdale loved her cricket and rarely missed the fiercely contested annual varsity match between the rival universities of Oxford and Cambridge, habitually held at Lord's. In a note written to the editor of the magazine '*Women's Cricket*' in 1930, she wrote. *'The crack of bat against ball amid the humming and buzzing of summer sounds is still to me a note of pure joy that raises haunting memories of friends and happy days. The one game in the world for me.'*

Lucy and her husband Stanley shared a deep Christian faith, and she became involved in several charitable bodies for women, including the Young Women's Christian Association [YWCA], although largely associated with youth hostels and fitness centres, the YWCA is a human rights-based organisation with activities advocating gender equality and the empowerment of women. Lucy Baldwin was a writer and activist for maternity health. She was particularly concerned with improving maternity care, undoubtedly due to the fact that she had herself suffered difficult pregnancies and the loss of her first child. In his capacity as President of the National Birthday Trust Fund, a charity promoting the provision of maternity services, the successful British businessman, philanthropist and cricket enthusiast Sir Julien Cahn, 1st Baronet [1882-1944] became friendly with the Trust's vice president, Countess Baldwin of Bewdley. And in honour of her work for maternity care, Cahn donated funds to build the Lucy Baldwin Maternity Hospital in Stourport-on-Severn, Worcestershire, which was commemorated by the Labour Prime Minister, Ramsey MacDonald in April 1929. The hospital would later become known as the Lucy Baldwin Hospital until its closure in 2006, where the bronze dedication plaque over the main entrance read, *'What she wanted most in the world. Presented to her by Julien Cahn Esq.'*

Cahn grew up in a strict Orthodox Judaism household in Nottingham where, following his success in business, he established himself as a philanthropist. One of his most eminent gifts was the rescue of the 12th-century Augustinian priory Newstead Abbey, the ancestral home of Lord Byron [1788-1824]. Cahn purchased the Abbey and donated it to the Nottingham City Council to help preserve Byron's legacy. His main love, however, was cricket, which he began playing as a teenager, during a time when it was quite common for business owners to organise teams. He would later serve as President of both the Nottinghamshire and Leicestershire County Cricket Clubs.

Lucy Baldwin was invested as a Dame of Grace, Order of Saint John of Jerusalem and a Dame Grand Cross, Order of the British Empire, and styled as Countess Baldwin of Bewdley in June 1937.

She died suddenly of a heart attack in 1945 at the couples country home Astley Hall, a three storey country house set in 20 acres of parkland, two miles outside Stourport-on-Severn, in Worcestershire. She was cremated and her ashes interred in the nave of Worcester Cathedral with those of her husband, following his death two years later.

Harriott 'Lily' Poulett-Harris [1873-1897]:

Lily Poullet-Harris

Harriet 'Lily' Poulett-Harris, and her twin sister Violet, were born on the 2 September, 1873, and grew up in the former penal colony of Hobart, the capital of the Australian island state of Tasmania.

Her father Richard Deodatus Poullet-Harris [1817-1899] travelled from England Tasmania in 1856, where he became head of the Hobart

Boys' High School, and renowned as a founding father of the University of Tasmania. He was also a part-time rector at the Holy Trinity Anglican Church in Hobart, and as a consequence Lily and her sister were raised in a devout, resolutely low church environment.

Richard Deodatus Poulett-Harris

When her father retired in 1885, he purchased the Woodbridge Hotel at Peppermint Bay, on the south side of Hobart. He later converted it into a house and re-named it *'The Cliffs'*, where the young Lily spent most of the remainder of her brief and difficult life.

Said to be *'melancholy in outlook and prone to depression',* Richard Poulett-Harrish grieved over the separation from his three daughters by his first marriage, and the early death of his son Richard from severe burns.

His second daughter Charlotte Maria became of *'unsound mind'*, and was committed to an institution in 1872.

He was also charged with assaulting boys with a cane in 1860, and again in 1868. Even though the first case was dismissed and the second was settled out of court, somehow he managed to maintain the school's pre-eminent position in the colony until 1878. The school was closed down in August 1885, after Richard's health went into serious decline as he began to suffer acute physical pain and mental depression. Following which he was offered and accepted an annuity of £ 300.

The early indications of young Lily's strength of character emerged when she was only twelve years old. One warm November day in 1885, May Harris, together with her younger twin sisters Violet and Lily, decided to pay a visit to the beach to enjoy a swim.The sisters were joined by a Miss Gaynor, a guest who was staying at the hotel, and after a short while by Lily's mother, Mrs. Elizabeth Eleanor [née Milward] Harris, who went along to ensure the group were alright. On her way down to the beach, Lily's mother's attention was drawn to an area of brushwood and dry grass, which she thought might harbour snakes, and with the initial intention of safely removing it she rather foolishly set it on fire. The blaze spread quickly and suddenly the sleeves of her dress caught alight and burst into flame. Screaming in terror she began to roll on the ground, in a futile attempt to put the fire out. The only person near enough to assist her mother was young Lily, who had the presence of mind to tear off her wet bathing dress and wrap it around her mother's burning body, saving her from serious injury. Only to discover on her arrival home she too was suffering from severe burns on her arms and back.

Following the death of her father in December 1899, a plaque was installed in the Holy Trinity Anglican Church, North Hobart, which was dedicated to him. There is also a memorial fountain in the grounds of the old campus of the University of Tasmania raised in honour of Richard Deodatus Poulett-Harris..

Lily was a *'bright, inquisitive, adventurous and active child'*, who was educated by her father. And it came as no surprise when, in common with several of her siblings, she eventually followed him into a career in education. Lily's older sister Eleanor, who was known as Nellie, first taught at the Hobart Ladies' College before teaching at her father's home, prior to founding the Ladies' Grammar School and Kindergarten in 1894, where the twins Lily and Violet would eventually also teach.

In due course Lily and Violet left Peppermint Bay to teach at the Ladies' Grammar School and Kindergarten in Hobart, when it was reported they were presented with a dinner and tea service by local inhabitants, including members of the Oyster Cove Ladies Cricket Club. The report stated, *'There is a general feeling of regret throughout the district at the Misses Poulett-Harris leaving, as they have always taken a deep interest in the Bay and its institutions and inhabitants, and they carry with them the sincerest wishes of all that they will prosper in the new school life on which they are entering in Hobart'.*

The Ladies' Grammar School and Kindergarten moved to Battery Point in 1898, where it was run by Nellie Poulett-Harris until her retirement in December 1919. Lily's twin sister Violet became a relatively well-known actress on the Australian theatre circuit, under the stage-name of Mary

Milward. Following which she spent her remaining days teaching music and elocution, by 1931 she was working as a governess for four young children. Violet died in 1941, and her sister Nellie died in the New Norfolk asylum in 1935 from arteriosclerosis, the thickening, and hardening of the arteries.

Having permanently relocated to the city of Hobart from Peppermint Bay, Lily lived at the Ladies' Grammar School, and was a regular member of the congregation at the All Saints church in South Hobart, a short walk from the school. Lily also taught music classes at the school, which in the beginning had only ten pupils, but it was always well regarded throughout its entire existence, and within a few years, the number had grown to reach a total of seventy.

Whenever possible she loved to visit her home at '*The Cliffs*', where she remained keenly involved in social and church activities, and importantly continued to play for the Oyster Cove Ladies Cricket Club.

A notable sportswoman, Lily's love of cricket was undoubtedly influenced by her father, who throughout his career as a teacher encouraged the boys at the High School to actively participate all forms of sport. In 1882 he was elected a trustee of the Southern Tasmanian Cricket Association, which was founded in the 1850s and from the outset was situated on Hobart's urban park known as Queens Domain.

Lily Poulett-*Harris 'was a great admirer of athletic exercises, firmly believing that it was very necessary to develop the physical as well as the mental part of our nature. Cricket had her warm sympathy and support.*

She was a good horsewoman and cyclist. Fear, it is said, was a thing unknown to her.'

Lily is unquestionably accepted as being the founding mother of women's cricket in Australia. In 1894, at the age of 20, her enthusiasm for the game led her to establish the Oyster Cove Ladies' Cricket Club, which according to news reports was almost certainly the first female cricket club to be formed in the Australian colonies. Unanimously elected to serve as the team's captain, Lily *'was remarkably successful in piloting her team to many a victory'.* She continued to play for the Oyster Cove ladies team until she was forced to retire due to ill health. Generally opening the batting or appearing as the third-order batswoman. Her brief sporting career was well-documented in the newspapers of the time, with the sports journalists of the day consistently praised her performances, with comments such as a *'prettily played innings'*, and *'the feature of the match was undoubtedly the fine not out innings of Miss L. Poulett-Harris, captain of the winning team, who, going in first, carried her bat right through the innings for 64 runs.'*

Lily was instrumental in establishing the first women's cricket league in 1894, which in the opening year included three other teams, Atalanta [Hobart Quakers], Heather [Hobart] and North Bruny. In the following year Green Ponds, Ranelagh and Huonville also joined the annual contest. By the end of the following year the league had become well-established, and a Hobart sports journalist noted that interest in *'cricket seems to be growing, and extending to the weaker sex, who often have a quiet match upon a romantic little plateau on the Domain immediately beyond the upper cricket ground'.*

As well as playing matches against each other, the ladies' teams frequently supported their male counterparts by providing lunches for them, and from time to time organising concerts and playing music.

A Tasmanian correspondent writing for a Melbourne newspaper reported that, '*The ladies cricketing season was concluded at Oyster Cove on May 6, with a match between the Oyster Cove and North Bruny clubs, resulting in a win for the local team by an innings and 41 runs. The past season has been very successful, consequently the outcome has been good cricket and high scoring. The captain of the Oyster Cove CC., Miss L. Poulett-Harris, heads the batting list with the remarkably good average of 32.6, her batting throughout the season has been very good. She has also the honour of having put up the record for Tasmania, making 64 [not out] in an innings, which included five fours, and 78 in a match. Miss K. Denne, North Bruny CC, comes next with an average of 18 runs.*' In the 1895 season, Lily was described in one match as having '*batted in good style, her contribution being well earned for the winners.*' On one occasion her bowling was described by a sports journalist of the *Hobart Mercury* as '*very good indeed*' when she got two opponents out for a total of one run between them. The teams did not adopt the '*rational dress*' that had become popular in some women's sports overseas by that time. Rather, '*they all appeared in prim summer dresses, and presented a pretty picture.*'

Although the Oyster Cove Ladies' Cricket Club no longer exists, Australia now has a thriving women's cricket culture, inspired by the success of the Oyster Cove club. Other ladies clubs quickly formed throughout Tasmania, and by the end of the 1890s, cricket and rowing were two of the most popular competitive sports for women in Australia.

The Victoria Women's Cricket Association was founded shortly afterwards in 1905, and the Australian Women's Cricket Association [AWCA] followed in 1931. The Australian Women's Cricket Association Championships were replaced in 1996 by a national competition for women's cricket organised by the Women's National Cricket League [WNCL], involving six member teams which play each other annually in two 50 limited-over matches.

Lily's older brother, Henry Vere Poulett-Harris [1865–1933] was a gifted footballer, runner and cricketer, who represented both Tasmania and Western Australia in a first-class cricket career. In an early news report he was described as being a *'sterling cricketer and footballer'* and a *'sterling batsman and good field'.*

He played cricket for the Wellington Club and was regarded as one of the most graceful batsmen in the State. As a youth Henry was a member of the State team, and toured New Zealand with the Tasmanian team. He would later progress to earn success as a batsman on the mainland.

Henry later owned a Western Australian gold mine, although he remained best known as being *'one of the outstanding athletes in the State, winning great success as a cricketer and footballer'*, and as a runner who defeated many of the recognised champions of his day. It is said it was Henry's consuming interest in sport which appears to have been a powerful incentive which helped to stimulate Lily.

In the October of 1896, shortly before her death, a fire destroyed most of the Poulett-Harris homestead at Peppermint Bay. As a result, most of her father's papers were lost, including all references and personal records of his youngest daughter's life.

As a young girl Lily had learned to play both the violin and piano extremely well, and enjoyed giving public performances in Peppermint Bay and Hobart, up until a few months before tuberculosis claimed her life at the tender age of 23.

On the evening of the 15 August 1897, Lily Poulett-Harris died of tubercular peritonitis, at the school's 26 Davey Street address, two weeks prior to her birthday, after what was described as a painful illness. She is buried alongside her father and sister Nellie in the Cornelian Bay Cemetery, Hobart. A memorial plaque dedicated to Lily is to be found on the rear wall of All Saints' Anglican Church in South Hobart. Donated by the teachers and students of the Ladies' Grammar School and Kindergarten, it describes her as *'bright and lovable'*. There is also a plaque dedicated to her memory at the Saint Simon and Saint Jude Anglican Church in Woodbridge.

In her obituary Lily was described as having *a 'mirthful and happy disposition, ever endeavouring to make those with whom she came in contact, and those not a few, cheerful and happy also'*. The obituary also incorporated an anecdote related by one old man who *told 'how she stopped and obliged by cutting up some tobacco for him, and by many of such little acts and kindnesses, Miss Lily endeared herself to the whole community.'*

In March 2016, an article appeared in the Sydney *Daily Telegraph* newspaper. The headline read, *'The Southern Stars owe a huge debt to the Tasmanian schoolteacher who became Australia's first female cricket star'*. The accompanying article recalls the life of Lily Poulett-Harris, her enduring legacy and her impact on women's cricket in Australia, noting that she had been *'responsible for inspiring many other women to take up the sport.'*

Chapter 5

Social Change The Fight for Equality

Nationalism became a major political issue in the twentieth century world, during which the first global-scale wars took place, with technological advancements changing the way wars were fought.

Strong discrimination based on race and sex remained significant in society, and although the transatlantic slave trade had come to an end, the fight for equality for non-white people in the white-dominated societies of North America, Europe, and South Africa persisted. However, by the end of the twentieth century women were granted the same legal rights as men in many parts of the world, racism had come to be seen as abhorrent, as were opinions regarding homosexuality.

Europe appeared to be at a sustainable peace for the first time in recorded history, although parts of the world remained blighted by small-scale wars, and terrorism emerged as a grave concern demanding serious attention.

Research conducted by climate scientists indicated environmental problems which put at risk the inhabitability of the planet. Disease and newly discovered viruses threaten to destabilise specific regions of the world. Medical advances, and improved methods of communication and information technology, have radically altered our daily lives, with mass media and information providing an opportunity to access an immediate understanding of what is going on in the world today.

Meanwhile, the sport of cricket was structured and played independently by both men and women for a number of years after World War I came to an end. Everyday life for women was slowly but surely becoming less restricted. Convention gradually eased allowing them the opportunity to benefit from the rights and privileges previously enjoyed by a relatively small group of people, usually as a result of their wealth or social status. A number of girl's public schools had begun playing cricket, and over the next couple of decades became a regular part of life at the larger girls' public schools, and a growing number of women's cricket clubs began to emerge.

As a consequence of this increase in interest, the first national organisation for women's cricket, the Women's Cricket Association [WCA], was founded in 1926, following a cricketing holiday arranged by a group of hockey, lacrosse and netball playing women held in the Worcestershire spa town of Malvern, at the foot of the Malvern Hills. A series of matches were arranged and played at the Cheltenham Ladies College and the Malvern Boys College, and so successful was the festive week of cricket, the ladies who took part decided to found an association with the aim of enabling an organised form of women's cricket to continue to take place.

The WCA adopted the laws of the game as practiced by the MCC, and within a year of its inauguration had enlisted 10 clubs and affiliated a total of 28 schools. Organised women's cricket began to develop very quickly, and the WCA was soon organising matches throughout the country, with the first organised public match held in 1929, three years after its launch.

The following year the first *'unofficial'* county match was held between the neighbouring counties of Leicestershire and Nottinghamshire, heralding the beginning of a flourishing decade for women's cricket. By 1931 the first county associations had evolved, and a match was played between Durham and a combined XI made up of women cricketers from the counties of Cheshire and Lancashire. Inside seven years, the number of clubs affiliated to the WCA had increased to 80, and by 1938 a total of 123 clubs had been formed. At its peak, the WCA numbered 208 affiliated clubs, including 94 schools and a number of junior teams.

Although the game remained expensive for those taking part, it was no longer considered so bizarre as to attract large, inquisitive crowds. And yet, neither was it well enough established as a major sport to attract financial sponsorship. Consequently, it remained a minor sport, with few women understanding the purpose of the game, and even less knowing how to play it. A questionable recipe if the WCA aimed to ensure long-standing success.

However, under the guidance of the WCA, the game achieved international recognition when in 1933 an England women's team played a match against The Rest at Leicester. And the first women's international cricketing tour was held in Australia and New Zealand in 1934-1935. The team selected were chosen sufficiently early enough to allow each of the team members to start saving in order to meet the estimated cost of the tour, which ran out at around £80 for each of the players. A series of three Test matches were played in Australia where England won two games and drew the third. From there they travelled to New Zealand for a further Test series. In Christchurch, in February 1935, in the first ever Women's Test match between the two countries, the redoubtable Betty Snowball [1908-1988] scored 189 runs in 222 minutes, setting a world record for the highest individual innings in women's Test cricket which stood for half-a-century.

That same year the WCA was sub-divided into five regional associations, the East, Midlands, North, South and West, each organised by its own local administrative working group.

Chapter 6

Heroines of 20 Century Cricket

Marjorie Pollard [1899-1982]:

Born in Rugby, Warwickshire, in August, 1899 Marjorie Pollard was the youngest of three children. She was educated at the Peterborough County Grammar School for Girls, Cambridgeshire, and the Bedford College, before later becoming a journalist and attending the St. Peter's College in Saltley, Birmingham.

Marjorie played hockey for the Northamptonshire County Hockey Association, representing England from 1921 to 1937. She served as the President of the Midland Counties Women's Hockey Association [MCWHA] from 1936 to 1963. At the time Marjorie Pollard was undoubtedly one of the most famous names in women's hockey, as a player, coach, journalist, publisher and film maker. As far back as the 1930s, Marjorie was producing films many of which addressed the subject of coaching. In turn these were loaned to clubs and schools by the All England Women's Hockey Association [AEWHA], the governing body of women's hockey. Marjorie also recorded international hockey matches on film. One of which was the famous match held in 1938 between England and Wales at the Oval.

Filming alongside the BBC television cameras, which was broadcasting an international team sports match live for the first time ever. The BBC covered the match in black and white, while the ever creative Marjorie filmed it in colour !

Shortly before her death in the spring of 1982 at the age of 82, Marjorie bequeathed her hockey collection to The Hockey Museum. Including dozens of reels of fragile film, subsequently all digitalised after the Hockey Museum received a Heritage Lottery Fund award. Amongst the reels were two marked *'Coronation 1953'*, which revealed the preparation and ensuing celebrations of the Coronation of Queen Elizabeth II, held in the village of Bampton in Oxfordshire, where Marjorie lived. Bampton village is well-known today given that scenes from the historical period television drama Downton Abbey were filmed there, and where a small museum is housed.

It is difficult to know which sport was Marjorie's greatest passion, hockey or cricket. Since she edited and wrote mostly for the weekly magazine *Hockey Field.* Notwithstanding, she was an extremely accomplished cricketer and played regularly for the Midlands County Association, and in 1926 was actively involved in founding the WCA.

Through her media work for the AEWHA and the WCA, Marjorie Pollard was arguably the most prominent female sports journalist in Britain at the time. In 1932 she created and edited the magazine *Women's Hockey*, as an alternative to the AEWHA magazine *Hockey Field.* Edith Thompson, the editor of *Hockey Field*, praised Pollard's writing abilities proclaiming, *'Pollard has the real journalistic touch, and is very readable. She writes easily with humour'.* Three years later Pollard established her own publishing house, Pollard Publications, located in the village of Knebworth, Hertfordshire.

Her growing reputation within the sports of hockey and cricket led to her appointment as the National Women's Organiser for the government driven Keep Fit Campaign. Her responsibility extended to cover the sports of hockey, lacrosse and netball for the Women's Team Games Board at an annual salary of £ 400. During the first six months of her appointment, it is claimed she visited twenty different counties, held interviews with thirty-three local newspapers, attended three conferences and made twenty-one public speeches. It is further reported a crowd of young people exceeding 1,200 in number, listened to her speech at a conference held in Manchester. Furthermore, she contributed a series of articles to twelve different newspapers and periodicals, and produced instructional films on hockey, cricket and netball. And even found time to produce and market her own brand of women's hockey shoes!

Pollard worked tirelessly campaigning to publicise and promote women's cricket and the values of the WCA, constantly challenging the depressing and damaging article published at the time by some newspapers on the subject of women's cricket. Compelled to contact the journalist, or editor, of the publications concerned, Pollard frequently offered to discuss the published articles in an effort to change their point of view. By way of example, following an article printed in *Women's Cricket*, she wrote, *'I have in mind a criticism I saw in a paper not long ago. The editor had seen a picture of girls presumably playing cricket, and on the leg side, quite close to the batsmen were three fielders. The whole thing looked silly and was silly. I ferreted the matter out and found that the photographer had asked square leg to move in and two players from the slips to go over and so make a better picture. This was done with the ultimate result that women's cricket was held up to ridicule in that paper. I have since cleared up the matter with the paper concerned and a good and proper picture has been published, and I believe there is goodwill between us'.*

Pollard was referred to by the *Wisden Book of Obituaries* as *'the first official reporter of women's cricket in the national press and the first woman radio commentator on the game'.*

She was awarded an OBE in 1965 for *'services to local government and sport'.*

Elizabeth 'Betty' Alexandra Snowball [1908-1988]:

Betty Snowball

Born in Burnley, Lancashire, 'Betty' Snowball played international cricket for England, and international squash and lacrosse for Scotland.

Snowball was educated at St Leonards School in St Andrews, Scotland and then Bedford Physical Training College, before becoming a teacher of physical education at St Swithun's School in Winchester, where she turned out for the Hampshire ladies cricket team.

Her father, Thomas Snowball, was an eminent Scottish eye doctor, an active local club cricketer, and bearer of a discomforting cricketing misnomer, who encouraged his daughter to play the game when she was still at school. She later became a gifted right-handed opening bat and perhaps the most outstanding wicketkeeper of her generation. After leaving school Betty was coached for a while by the West Indian cricketer Sir Learie Constantine [1901–1971], developing what she described as her *'aggressive inspiration'*. Born in Trinidad, Constantine established an early reputation as a promising cricketer, and as a member of the West Indies teams that toured England in 1923 and 1928. Later to pursue a professional career in England, with the Lancashire League club Nelson. He was knighted in 1962, and became the United Kingdom's first black life peer in 1969.

Snowball played in 10 Test matches for England from 1934 to 1949, including the first women's Test against Australia in Brisbane in 1934 until her seventh appearance at the Oval in 1937, when was dismissed for 99, a single run short of doubling her record for the number of centuries she scored in Test cricket. During her Test career she scored a total of 613 runs at a batting average of 40.86. And behind the wicket took 13 catches and made eight stumpings.

Batting and fielding averages:

Tests:	Innings:	Not out:	Runs:	Highest score:	Average:	100:	50:	Caught:	St:
10	18	3	613	189	40.86	1	4	13	8

Standing at a little over 5ft tall, Betty Snowball was an effective foil to one of the best known women cricketers of the day, the powerful all rounder, Myrtle Maclagen MBE [1911-1993]. Both as a fellow-opening bat, or when crouched behind the stumps taking Maclagan's fearsome spin bowling. The pair regularly opening the batting for England, and were considered the female equivalent of *'The Master'*, Sir John 'Jack' Berry Hobbs [1882-1963] and his resourceful opening partner Herbert 'Bert' Sutcliffe [1894-1978], still regarded by many as the greatest opening pair of male batsmen in Test history. The eldest of 12 children, Hobbs was a man of great dignity who bridged the classic and modern periods of the game. An elegant Surrey batsman he made 61, 237 runs throughout his career.

Snowball had something of the Australian wicket-keeper William Albert Stanley 'Bert' Oldfield [1894-1976] in her style. Always immaculately turned out, and neat and tidy in technique, her passion and commitment adding an additional flourish to her undoubted efficiency.

In February 1935, in the women's Test match played, against New Zealand in Christchurch, Betty put her wristy square cut to good use in an outstanding innings of 189 runs in 222 minutes, setting a world record for the highest individual innings made in women's Test cricket, which stood for over half-a-century, before it was surpassed at Worcester in 1986 by the former Indian women's cricket team captain, Sandhya Agarwal [born 1963], who notched up her highest score of 190 against England. In the following year Agarwal's record score was overtaken by the Australian Denise Annetts [born 1964] who recorded her top score of 193 runs against England at Wetherby in Yorkshire, before being run out in a record partnership of 309 playing alongside Lindsay Anne Reeler [born 1961].

Betty Snowball was described in Wisden Cricketers' Almanack as *'one of the major figures of women's cricket for two decades from 1930'*. When her cricketing career came to an end, Betty retired to the Worcestershire village of Colwall, where she taught cricket and mathematics at The Elms Prep School. The Colwall Cricket Club is often referred to as *'the cradle of women's cricket'*, and remains home to the annual Colwall Cricket Festival. The former English international cricketer, and ECB Director of Women's Cricket, New Zealander Gill McConway [born 1950], describing the Colwall Cricket Festival, said *'Cricket Week has a special place in the women's cricket calendar. It provides everyone with a chance to play the game, take some time out in a beautiful part of England in summer, make new friends and enjoy themselves'*.

Betty Snowball, what an exquisite name for a cricketer, and perhaps an even more appropriate one for an umpire ! Which would without a shadow of a doubt have caused a ripple of amusement amongst the spectators when Betty donned the white coat and took to the field as the umpire in her first, and only appearance, for the 1951 summer womwn's Ashes Test match at the County Ground, Worcester against Australia.

Snowball died in Colwall at the age of 80.

Myrtle Ethel Maclagan MBE [1911-1993]:

Myrtle Maclagan

Myrtle Maclagan was born in April, 1911 in the city of Ambala, bordered by the northern state of Punjab, in the former United Provinces of British India.

The daughter of an officer in the Royal Engineers, who became bursar of Haileybury College on his retirement, where Myrtle was raised with her two cricketing brothers and a sister. Founded in 1806 the school was known as the East India College, and was originally a boys' public school, which later served as a training establishment for administrators of the Honourable East India Company. It is now a co-educational independent school situated near Hertford in England.

Myrtle's primary education was at the Royal School in Bath, where her outstanding aptitude for the game of cricket was soon revealed. From the age of 12, young Myrtle made regular appearances for the school first XI throughout a period which spanned six years. During which the youngster notably bagged a total of five wickets in five balls with her off-breaks in a school match against Cheltenham Ladies College.

She was coached by the five-foot-two-inches tall prolific England international wicket taker Alfred Percy *'Tich'* Freeman [1888-1965], a right-arm bowler of leg-breaks, googlies and top-spinners for the Kent County Cricket Club. Tich took 3,776 wickets throughout his career, once collecting a total of 300 wickets in a season.

Myrtle was soon to develop into a complete all-rounder in every sense of the word. Her introduction to the sport coincided with the formation of the WCA in 1926. And her name was soon to become synonymous with the development of women's cricket in England, celebrated for her propensity of recording high scores especially when playing against the Australians.

It was following her performance in the pioneering tour of Australia and New Zealand in 1934-35, that Maclagan matured as a national cricketing personality, renowned as one of the most accomplished women cricketers of her era. On her debut for England in the first women's Test match held in December 1934 in Brisbane She opened the bowling against Australia in its first innings, claiming 7 wickets for just 10 runs with her awesome off-break, as England skittled out the home side for the meagre total of 47 runs in 49 overs.

In England's reply Maclagan opened the batting alongside Betty Snowball, scoring 72 in the visitor's total of 154. Australia fared a little better in its second visit to the crease, putting on 138 more runs, but England knocked off the deficit in 12.5 overs to wicket to win by 9 wickets. Maclagan fell for 9 runs to the tantalising leg-spin bowling of Peggy Antonio [1917-2002], who following her marriage later became known as Peggy Howard.

First Innings:	Overs:	Maidens:	Runs:	Wickets:	Economy:
	17	11	10	7	0.59
Second Innings:	Overs;	Maidens:	Runs:	Wickets:	Economy:
	28	12	31	0	1.11

A few days later, in January of the following year, she scored the first Test century recorded in women's cricket, contributing 119 for England on the opening day of the Test against Australia at the Sydney Cricket Ground, before being trapped leg before wicket once again to the bowling of Peggy Antonio. Myrtle set another distinguished record in the same historic Test match, which England won by 8 wickets, when she became the first woman cricketer to open the batting, as well as the bowling with her fearsome right-arm off-spin.

First Innings:	Overs;	Maidens:	Runs:	Wickets:	Economy:
	33.2	22	33	4	0.99
Second Innings:	Overs;	Maidens:	Runs:	Wickets:	Economy:
	29	15	35	2	1.24

A few months earlier the England men's team had lost the Ashes and the *Morning Post* praised Maclagan's batting prowess with the verse:

What matter that we lost, mere nervy men
Since England's women now play England's game,

Wherefore Immortal Wisden, take your pen

And write Maclagan on the scroll of fame.

Maclagan would also play in the second series of the Women's Ashes against Australia at the County Ground, Northampton in June 1937. In the opening Test Australia won the toss and elected to bat, scoring 300 all out from 119.5 overs in its first innings, with Maclagan taking one wicket for 65 runs. England mustered 204 all out in reply, with Myrtle carrying her bat with a score of 89. In its second innings Australia put on a further 102 runs, with Maclagan bowling 7 overs, claiming one wicket for 7 runs. In its response England could only muster 167, with Maclagan caught behind the wicket for 28 runs by Winifred Una Margaretta George [1914-1988], off the right-arm medium fast bowling of Ellen 'Nell' Mary McLarty BEM [1912-1988]. Australia won the first of the series of three matches by 31 runs.

Myrtle added to her growing tally of records when later that same month she went on to score the first Test hundred for her country in England, when facing the Australians at the Stanley Park cricket ground in the Lancashire seaside resort of Blackpool, reversing the previous result and squaring the series. The England captain Mary 'Molly' Edith Hide [1913-1995] won the toss and chose to bat first. The customary partnership of Maclagan and Snowball opened the batting, with Myrtle contributing 115 runs towards the England total of 222, before being stumped by Alice Wegemund [1907-1976] off a right-arm off break delivered by Alicia Walsh [1911-1984]. She then collected three wickets in the Australian reply of 302 all out, for the sum of 78 runs in a bowling spell of 28 overs. In England's second innings total of 231, Maclagan fell one run short of her half-century to the right-armed fast bowler Molly Flaherty [1914-1989]. As a result Australia were left needing 151 runs to win the match and clinch the series, but fell short by 25 runs after being bowled out for 126, in which Maclagan collected a further 2 wickets for 29 runs.

The final Test was played in mid-July at the Kennington Oval. Australia opening the batting and put on 207 for the loss of 9 wickets before declaring the innings closed. England replied with a score of 308 for 9 declared, with Maclagan falling to Nell McLarty caught and bowled for 34 runs. Australia's second innings yielded a further 224 runs, in which Maclagan claimed 3 wickets for 58 runs, leaving England needing 124 runs to win the match and the Ashes. But time was against the home side, which made just 9 runs for the loss of 3 wickets from three overs, and the series was tied on one win apiece and one drawn game.

Myrtle returned to cricket after World War II came to an end in 1945, and again toured Australia and New Zealand in 1948–49. She was then selected as a member of the England team to face Australia in July, 1951. England won the match by 137 runs. In what was to be her final Test, Maclagan contributed 59 runs in 152 minutes in her first visit to the crease, before being caught by Mavis Jones [1922-1990] off the right-arm fast bowling of Betty Norma Whiteman [1927]. In her second innings she was out lbw to an off-break bowled by Una Lillian Paisley [1922-1977] for 16 runs. In her final Test appearance with the ball in hand she took a total of 3 wickets for 34 runs in a spell of 29 overs, which included 14 maidens.

She played her last official game of cricket for the Combined Services at the age of 52 against her favourite adversary, 29 years after her Test debut against Australia in Brisbane in 1934. She had lost none of her class and with HRH Mary, the Princess Royal, watching on, scored an effortless unbeaten 81.

Myrtle Ethel Maclagan MBE died at Farnham Surrey on March 11, 1993, aged 81. Baroness Rachel Heyoe Flint OBE, DL, wrote in her obituary for *The Independant, 'Myrtle Maclagan qualified for the Combined Services when she joined the Army in 1951, having served in the Second World War as a senior ATS officer in the anti-aircraft regiment in Dover in 1944 during the flying bomb raids. She was an Inspector PT, WRAC, but rose to the rank of Major and was appointed MBE for Army services in 1966, which would have greatly pleased her military antecedents'.*

Batting and fielding averages:

Tests:	Innings:	Not out:	Runs:	Highest score:	Average:	100:	50:	Ct:
14	25	1	1007	119	41.95	2	6	12

Bowling averages:

Tests:	Inns:	Balls b'led:	Runs:	Wkts:	Best b'ling:	Avr:	Econ:	SR:
14	27	3432	935	60	7/10	15.58	1.63	57.2

Mary 'Molly' Edith Hide [1913-1995]:

Molly Hide

Born in Shanghai, China in October 1913, Molly Hide was one of England's greatest pioneeof early women's cricket. Once described as *'the personification of women's cricket'*, she dominated the women's game for 20 years, from her Test debut in Brisbane in 1934, to her eventual retirement from first-class cricket in 1954, following the Test against New Zealand at the Oval.

Molly Hide brought credibility and panache to the women's game, such as had never been seen before. Tall and lithe of stature, her 17 year reign as England captain was deemed by many to have been faultless.

The development of women's cricket was significantly advanced through Molly's conduct, performance and achievements, both on and off the field of play. She was held in such high regard by her cricketing peers, that almost 60 years after her maiden Test appearance in Brisbane, she was invited as guest of honour at Lord's in 1993 when England's triumphant women won the cricket World Cup.

Molly came to live in England at the age of six, shortly after the end of the World War I, where she was educated at the Wycombe Abbey Girls School, situated in Hertfordshire, some 35 miles west of London. Founded in 1896, the school promoted equal opportunities for girls during the Victorian age, and to this day remains numbered amongst the list leading girls' boarding schools in the UK. It was at Wycombe Abbey that Molly first learned to play cricket, before graduating to study agriculture at Reading University. This would eventually prove to be a great benefit to her father, who she helped throughout World War II, working tirelessly on the family farm in Haslemere, Surrey.

Molly never married, choosing to devote her entire life to cricket. From her schooldays at Wycombe Abbey, through the cricketing summers she spent with Surrey and England, and in her later years, as a selector, broadcaster and administrator.

In the opinion of Gerald Durani Martineau [1897-1976], a captain in the Royal Sussex Regiment, and prolific writer on English cricket, *'The chief characteristic of Molly Hide on the cricket field was a very positive attitude that asserted what a game of cricket should be like. She put her ideas into practice, making great declarations, trusting her keen eyes, ready to hit the first ball for four, and always on the attack. There have been less chancy batsmen but her aim was ever to get on top of the bowling, so that the rate of scoring almost always quickened on her arrival. With a particularly strong on drive 'off her toes', she put character into her strokes, and there has been no better batsman'.*

Hide represented Worcestershire in first-class County representative matches in 1932 and 1933, and toured with Elizabeth 'Betty' Archdale [1907-2000], the captain of the first English women's touring team of Australia and New Zealand in 1934-1935.

Born in London, Betty Archdale was the daughter of Helen Alexander Archdale [née Russel] [1876-1949], a suffragette who was jailed for smashing windows in Whitehall. Her godmother was Emmeline Pankhurst [1858-1928], a political activist and leader of the British suffragette movement. Betty's early education was delivered at one of the most expensive public schools in the United Kingdom, the Bedales School in the village of Steep, near the market town of Petersfield in Hampshire. It was at Bedales that she first learned to play cricket. She completed her studies at the St. Leonards School in St. Andrews, Fife, founded in 1877 by the St Andrews School for Girls Company, firmly committed to the belief that *'a girl should receive an education that is as good as her brother's, if not better'*.

In February 1935, in the famously noteworthy, one-sided three-day Test match, when England crushed New Zealand, at the AMI Lancaster Park Stadium, Christchurch, Molly notched up 110 runs, before being caught by a substitute fielder off the bowling of Merle Hollis. In the second wicket partnership alongside Betty Snowball the pair put on 235 runs, in a spell at the crease lasting less than two-and-a-half hours. The home side won the toss and chose to open the batting against a fearsome England bowling attack led by the incomparable Myrtle Maclagan. Lack lustre New Zealand could only muster a miserable 44 runs from 28.2 overs in its opening innings, of which Merle Hollis contributed 24, with Maclagan claiming 5 wickets for 22 runs, in a bowling spell of 14.2 overs. England put on 503 before declaring for the loss of just 5 wickets, including an outstanding innings from Betty Snowball, who personally contributed 189 runs. The dejected *'White Ferns'* fared little better when they returned for their second visit to the crease, adding a further paltry total of 122 runs to the first innings score.

The tour of Australia and New Zealand in 1934-1935 did a great deal to improve the significance of women's cricket, as well as helping repair some of the damage caused to the Anglo-Australian cricket relationship, detonated by the controversial bodyline discord which surfaced during the 1932–33 men's Ashes tour of Australia. Devised by the English team to specifically combat the matchless Australian batting skills, bodyline bowling was a strategic approach perceived by many as being extreme and unfairly aggressive. Such was the anger generated through the use of the bodyline technique, diplomatic relations between the two countries was threatened for some time, before the situation eventually calmed.

Hide played in the first ever women's Test in Brisbane in December 1934, and was made captain of the South of England team two years later. In the following year Molly captained England against the Australian women's touring team, taking charge of the position until her ultimate retirement in 1954. The 1937 series ended 1-1, with the visitors taking the first Test at the County Ground in Northampton by 31 runs. Batting at number 7, Molly was caught by Nell McLarty, off the off-spin bowling of Alicia Walsh without making a contribution. In her second innings she made just four runs before falling to the left-arm medium pace bowling of Kathleen Mary 'Kath' Smith [1915-1993].

England squared the series at Stanley Park, Blackpool, winning the Test by 25 runs. Molly won the toss and elected to bat, losing her wicket again to McLarty for 34 runs, however with the ball in hand she took three wickets for 38 runs from 114 balls. In her second innings she made 31 before being bowled by Peggy Antonio, and took a further 5 wickets for 20 runs from 74 balls bowled.

Having been persuaded by her parents not to go gallivanting around the world, but to stay at home and work on the farm, Molly would have missed the 1939-40 tour of Australia. However, in any event, the tour was cancelled, when Test cricket was temporarily suspended for 11 years due to World War II.

When cricket was eventually resumed, Molly joined the England team in 1948-1949 on its Test tour of Australia, in which the visitors came up short, losing 1-0. However, Molly swiftly returned to form scoring five centuries during the tour, including 124 not out in a drawn game at the Sydney Cricket Ground, where a portrait of her was subsequently hung in the pavilion.

A comprehensive and charming account of the events of the tour is recorded in Sylvia Nancy Joy's [1915-1997] captivating book *'Maiden Over'* first published in 1950 and dedicated to Molly Hide. On the outward voyage to play the official Test tour, the Women's Cricket Association [WCA] decided to break the journey, and play an additional unusual *'whistle stop'* match, hastily arranged against a women's team at the Colombo Cricket Club Ground in Colombo, where at the time, cricket was practically non-existent. En route the England team manager, Netta Rheinberg had received a telegram from the Ceylon cricketing authorities, saying it had decided to put forward a men's team to play against the WCA. Rheinberg hastily responded announcing that, *'our WCA rules forbid our playing officially against men'*, a condition which had been in place since the WCA's inauguration in 1926.

Consequently, in the intervening weeks a female Ceylon team had to be quickly gathered together, which it seems was made of up five European and six Sinhalese women. Some of which were schoolgirls, with most having never handled a cricket bat until six weeks previously. Prior to the match, *'members of the Ceylon cricketing fraternity'* took the English ladies sight-seeing. *'Lovely women in bright saris, men wearing sarongs, rickshaw boys, bullock carts, roadside bazaars selling huge bunches of bananas, mixed with marvellous American cars, Europeans in white suits, buses straight from London,and English road signs, with the newly-independent island of Ceylon of 1948, brimful full of colonial leftovers, leaving an ever-lasting impression on the England party'.*

The match was not a long one, but it attracted a great deal of local interest, and was watched by a crowd of 8,000 enthusiastic spectators. According to Netta Rheinberg the crowd was '*one of the most appreciative ones I've ever come across. Absolutely everything one did was watched and applauded or the reverse !*' Numbered amongst the throng were members of the British armed forces who were stationed in Ceylon at the time. After clearly enjoying the game they were heard to comment that the English women had, '*started to put English cricket back on the map*'.

England made 168 for 7 and declared after 38.3 overs, with the England captain Molly Hide, probably the best batsman of her generation, making a century. Ceylon was dismissed for 51 in just 92 minutes. Their top scorer, E. Fernando, one of the Sinhalese players who little is known about, made 22 runs, out-performing the rest of her team and the majority of the England players as well.

After the match, the President of the Board of Control for Cricket in Ceylon, arranged a party for the teams at the Ceylon Cricket Club, and presented the England players with '*a silver chip bearing an elephant and the crest of the Ceylon Cricket Board*'.

The England team manager, Netta Rheinberg MBE [1911-2006], played just one Test match for the English women's cricket team, but was a notable figure in the women's game as an administrator and journalist. Rachael Heyhoe-Flint [1939-2017], the former England captain, said, *'Netta was an action girl. We had very few people then, and she galvanised activity, partly just by having a great personality and a sense of humour.'*

Rheinberg's one and only Test appearance was during England's tour of Australia in 1948-1949. Although she was acting in the capacity of team manager, she was called upon to turn out in her one and only appearance match since other members of the squad had sustained injuries. Sadly, she scored no runs on both her visits to the crease in the two-innings match, consequently making a *'pair'*, or a *'pair of spectacles'* or a *'pair of ducks'* [0–0], to famously become the first woman cricketer to register a *'pair'* on her Test debut.

It was not simply the classical batting which elevated Molly Hide above the rest, for she could drive the ball beautifully, astonishing many a cynical male spectator. Her tenacious slow off-cutters, which she bowled so reluctantly, coupled with her competent fielding, made her the complete all-rounder. During her entire term of captaincy she was strict but fair. Molly also captained England at home against Australia in 1951 and New Zealand in 1954, before continuing her association with the game, as a selector, and as President of the Women's Cricket Association in 1973. According to Netta Rheinberg, Molly Edith Hide was the personification of women's cricket, who contributed an immense amount to give the game credibility.

Having also represented England at lacrosse in the early stages of her sporting career, Molly Hide died in hospital in Guildford, Surrey on September 10, 1995, aged 81.

Roy Case

Batting and fielding averages:

Tests:	Innings:	Not out:	Runs:	Highest score:	Average:	100:	50:	Caught:
15	27	3	872	124 not out	36.33	2	5	10

Bowling averages:

Tests:	Innings:	Balls:	Runs:	Wickets:	Best Innings:	Average:	Economy:	SR:
15	26	2064	549	36	5/20	15.25	1.59	57.3

Elizabeth Rebecca 'Betty' Wilson [1921-2010]:

Betty Wilson

Organised women's cricket has been played in Australia since the turn of the 20th century. The Victoria Women's Cricket Association [VWCA] was first established in 1905, followed by the Australian Women's Cricket Association [AWCA] in 1931.

In 1937, just prior to the start of World War II, a team of Australian women visited England to compete in a series of three Test matches, and with one win each and one drawn game the honours were shared. Held during the early summer months of May to July, the tour was the second series of the Women's Ashes, and included 16 additional tour matches played by the Australian women. In the first ever series of women's Test matches held in England, Molly Hide captained the home team, while the right-handed bat Margaret Elizabeth Maynard Peden [1905-1981], led the visitors as the Australian captain.

The opening Test was played in June at the County Ground, Northampton, which Australia won by 31 runs. The second was played two weeks later at Stanley Park in Blackpool. England reversed the earlier result, winning a tight match at the popular seaside resort on the Lancashire coast, by the slender margin of 25 runs to level the series. The first female cricket commentator, Marjorie Pollard, broadcast on the deciding contest held at the Kennington Oval, where Betty Snowball fell one short of a century in the England opening innings. The outcome was a drawn match, and a tied series.

With Women's Test cricket now being played by Australia, England, India, Ireland, Netherlands, New Zealand, Pakistan, South Africa, Sri Lanka and the West Indies, in 1958 the International Women's Cricket Council [IWCC] was launched, with the objective of coordinating the women's game.

In February of that same year, in an amazing Test match against England held at the Melbourne Cricket Ground, the Australian cricketer Betty Wilson became the first player, male or female, to record a century and take ten wickets in a game. Batting at fourth wicket down in her opening innings, Betty's contribution of a skimpy dozen runs was the highest score in the Australian first innings total of 38, with the left-arm Mary Duggan [1925-1973] capturing 7 of the Australian wickets for just six runs off 14.5 overs. Even so, England fell three runs short of the meagre target set by Australia, recording the lowest score ever registered in a women's Test match in Australia. With Betty Wilson collecting 7 wickets at a cost of 7 runs in 10.3 overs. Her contribution of 100 runs on next outing with bat helped *the 'Southern Stars'* to a second innings total of 202 for 9 declared. England failed to reach the 206 runs required for victory in the time allocated and the match was declared a draw. In the England second innings the dynamic Wilson added another 4 wickets to her overall tally for 9 runs. A total of 11 wickets at a cost of 16 runs in 29.3 overs, which included 18 maidens.

Baroness Rachael Heyhoe-Flint OBE, DL [née Heyhoe] [1939-2017]:

Rachael Heyhoe-Flint is fondly remembered as a true heroine of women's cricket, one of the most pioneering women cricket has ever known.

She played for England from 1960 to 1982, and in all probability best remembered by devotees of cricket for her 12 year term as captain of the England women's cricket team from 1966 to 1978. Throughout her tenure of six Test series she never lost a match, including the momentous spell in 1973 when she led her country to World Cup glory.

Born in the Staffordshire city of Wolverhampton, Rachael was the daughter of Geoffrey and Roma Heyhoe [née Crocker]. Her parents first met at college in Denmark, before becoming teachers of physical education in Wolverhampton. Her father Geoffrey later became the Director of Physical Education for the Staffordshire County Council.

Rachael was educated at the Wolverhampton Girls High School, where her passion for sport was initially inspired, although there can be little doubt it was greatly stimulated by her sporting parents. Until 1960, Rachael enjoyed a brief spell at the Dartford College of Physical Education, now recognised as the North Kent College. The college was purchased in 1895 by Martina Sofia Helena Bergman-Österberg [née Bergman] [1849-1915], a Swedish-born physical education instructor, who developed the college as a physical training academy, specialising in gymnastics for girls and young women. It matured to become a benchmark in the sporting history of women, providing the country with countless physical training teachers. A passionate advocate of women's suffrage, Madame Bergman-Österberg spent most of her working life in Britain. Where, she played a key role in the early development of netball as a sport for women. It is said, she is also credited with the introduction of the use of gymslips for women playing sport. Shortly before her death in 1915, Madame Bergman-Österberg bequeathed the training college as a gift to the nation, and left its care and administration in the hands of a management committee. It became the Dartford College of Physical Education in 1945 until 1960, with physical education continuing on the campus until 1986.

As a school girl Rachael excelled at hockey, netball and rounders. Her interest in cricket was not ignited until 1954, when she went on a school trip to Edgbaston to watch the New Zealand women's team play. Her instinctive flair with bat in hand was quickly confirmed, and not long afterwards a school cricket team was formed, from which she swiftly progressed to represent Staffordshire Women's County cricket.

Before moving to teach physical education at the Northicote School in Wolverhampton, from 1960 to 1964 Rachael was a teacher at the Wolverhampton Grammar School, which was founded in 1512 and originally known as the Wolverhampton Boys Grammar School.

Rachael took leave from work when she was selected as a member of the England women's team to tour South Africa in the winter of 1960-1961. Batting at number five in the order, Rachael made her first half-century at the Wanderers cricket ground in Johannesburg, in the second of three drawn Test matches. In her innings of 51, she spent 71 minutes at the crease, knocking up five boundaries, before being bowled by Pamela Hollett. Rachael took the ball in South Africa's second innings, and bowled six overs, which included four maidens, at a cost of three runs. England won the four match series 1-0, with three drawn games.

At the time women's international cricket remained rather disorganised, with global tours somewhat fragmented. As a consequence the England women's team did not play again until two years later when in 1963 it journeyed to Australia and New Zealand.

Even at international level, women's cricket was a poorly funded affair, and for the tour of Australia and New Zealand in 1968-1969, no doubt fuelled by her unrelenting enthusiasm and energy, Rachael herself had to resort to the task of fundraising. Her fervour, assisted by a crumb of good fortune, led her to enlist the help of her close friend, Sir Jack Arnold Hayward OBE [1923-2015], an English businessman and philanthropist, and President of Wolverhampton Wanderers Football Club. Moreover, no doubt generously supported by Hayward's cheque book, and her indubitable organisational skill, Rachael was instrumental in putting together a strategy which led to the first women's cricket World Cup. Two years before the inaugural men's cricket World Cup ! She captained the England side in the tournament, and contributed a half-century in the final, when the England women triumphed against Australia at Edgbaston in July 1973.

Rachael eventually abandoned the teaching profession in favour of journalism, when she became a correspondent with the *Wolverhampton Express and Star*. In 1967 advanced her status when she launched a 23 year association with the *Daily Telegraph* and the *Sunday Telegraph* as a freelance sports writer.

Rachael married Derrick Flint [born 1924] in November 1971, and immediately began using the double-barrelled surname Heyhoe- Flint, also assuming the role of stepmother to Flint's three children, Simon, Hazel and Rowan. Born in Creswell, in Derbyshire, her husband was a right-arm leg-spin and googly bowler, who played ten first-class matches for Warwickshire CCC in 1948-1949. He was the son of Benjamin Flint [1893-1959], a right-arm fast bowler, who made thirteen first-class appearances for Nottinghamshire from 1920 to 1921. Rachael and Derrick's only son Ben [born 1982], who also enjoyed playing cricket, moved to Singapore at the age of 19, where he runs a sports related and entertainment businesses.

An astute business woman and philanthropist, the multi-talented Rachael continued her work as a journalist and broadcaster after retiring from cricket. Frequently making regular appearances on the BBC Home Service panel show *'Petticoat Line'*, an all-woman panel show, during which the letters and problems of its listeners were discussed.

Media coverage of women's cricket in the early-1970s was minute, as indeed it was for most forms of women's sport. By then Rachael was acknowledged as one of the nation's most outstanding sportswomen, and was recognised with the award of an MBE in 1972, a just compliment to her flair for publicity. She was also very much admired as an award-winning public speaker, and when selected by the Guild of Professional Toastmasters as its leading after dinner speaker in 1973, she could hardly contain her delight. Nonethe less, in the sme year she embarked upon a career move as televisions first woman sports presenter with ITV *World of Sport*, which would ultimately prove to be one of her less successful ventures.

Before she was married, Rachael played squash, and hockey, turning out as the goalkeeper for the England national field hockey team. She was also an extremely accomplished single-figure handicap golfer and represented the Staffordshire Ladies.

From 1997 to 2003 she served on the board of directors of the Wolverhampton Wanderers Football Club, alongside her friend Sir Jack Hayward OBE, before her appointment as an *'ex officio'* Vice-President of the club.

A right-handed batswoman, and occasional leg-spin bowler, Heyhoe-Flint played in 22 women's Test matches from December 1960 to 1982, her debut coming in the opening Test in the series against South Africa at Port Elizabeth. Although she collected only three Test wickets in her career, her best bowling figures being one wicket for three runs. With the bat she amassed a cumulative total of 1594 runs from her 38 Test innings, in 22 Test matches, including three Test centuries, at an average score of

45.54. She also appeared in 23 Women's One Day Internationals, scoring 643 runs with a batting average of 58.45, and a top score of 114.

The England women's cricket team were invincible in the 1960s, sailing through fourteen Test matches without loss. The women's team captain then was the right-handed Worcestershire bat Mary Beatrice Duggan [1925-1973], who hit the first century by a woman in the summer of 1963, posting a score of 101 not out against Australia at the Oval. England won the match by 49 runs and claimed the much coveted Ashes, in what subsequently turned out to be England's last win against Australia for 42 years. But once again it was still the irrefutable Rachael who stole the show, when she spanked the ball high over the ropes to become the first ever woman to hit a six in a Test match, a shot which she herself described as *'a hoick to leg'*. By the end of that summer Rachael had been appointed captain and scored her first century.

During the sweltering summer of 1976, Rachael proudly led the first England women's team out into the sun on to the sacred, immaculately prepared, turf at Lord's, for a historic one-day international match against Australia. Until that day, with the notable exception of the annual visit of Her Majesty the Queen, women had always been barred from the Long Room at Lord's. The importance of the first women's match to be staged at the game's ancient headquarters was not lost on Rachael, who confessed to feeling overcome with emotion as she set foot on the outfield. However, it proved to be no more than a momentary distraction, and she soon resumed the serious business of leading her team to an eight-wicket victory. And fittingly, she was at the crease when the winning runs were hit.

Rachael recorded her top score of 179 not out in 1976, a world record at the time, when she batted for more than 8½ hours in a drawn-out, match-saving Test against Australia at the Oval to earn a draw for England in the Women's Ashes and save the series.

She was replaced as the England captain in 1977, and played her last Test match in July 1979 at Edgbaston, Birmingham against the West Indies. The *'Windies'* captain, all-rounder Patricia Whittaker, won the toss and put England in to bat. In its first innings England declared on a total of 214, scored in 63 overs, for the loss of 4 wickets, with Rachael contributing 35 not out. The West Indies knocked up 188 runs in its first visit to the crease. In England's second innings response of 164 all out, Rachael put on 8 runs before being bowled by Jasmine Sammy. In its second visit to the crease the West Indies managed to score 166 in 68.4 overs and England ran out winners by 24 runs.

During her reign as captain Rachael never lost a match, however her sporting significance did draw some bitterness. In 1977 she was dismissed as captain by the WCA, and dropped from the team for the World Cup in the following year. The decision hurt Rachael bitterly, and although she never regained the captaincy, she continued to play on until she was 42 years of age, and the 1982 Hansells Vita Fresh Women's World Cup hosted for the first time by New Zealand.

When Rachael was at her peak women still played in skirts, and it is said that once the Duke of Edinburgh mischievously enquired if the players wore coconut shells in their bras for protection, which the fun-loving Rachael thought highly amusing.

That famous fortress of male cricketing privilege, the MCC, was not easily breached. It would take decades of campaigning before women were allowed to become members, and it was Heyhoe-Flint who was in the vanguard of that revolution. She first applied for membership in 1991, and the crusade that was to follow accurately characterised her qualities of persistence, persuasion and passion. For in 1999, Rachael was one of the first ten women to be admitted to the MCC as an honorary member. Five years later she was elected a full committee member, and ultimately her appointment as a Trustee.

In 2001 she was elected, and served for 10 years, as the President of the fundraising charity, the Lady Taverners, many of which hail from the world of sport and entertainment. The Lady Taverners owe its foundation to the late Baroness Thatcher. Founded in 1950 at the Tavern pub at Lord's Cricket Ground, it is quite usual for each male Prime Minister to be made a member of the Lord's Taverners, the election of the first Lady Prime Minister set the previously all-male club a bit of a challenge. Being ever inventive they decided to form the Honorary Lady Taverners and in early 1980 Baroness Thatcher [1935-2013] was invited to become the first Honorary Lady Taverner. Fortunately she agreed !

The Lord's Taverners President, the late celebrated comedian and national treasure, Eric Morecambe [1926-1984], immediately invited 23 other ladies to join, which included amongst its number Rachael Heyhoe-Flint. Published in 1978, by Pelham Books, Netta Rheinberg authored the autobiography '*Heyhoe*', which included a foreword by the former President of the Lord's Taverners, the amiable cricket-lover Eric Morecambe.

Rachael, who never completely lost her *'Black Country'* accent, was appointed one of a number of Deputy Lieutenants of the West Midlands in 1997. Appointment to the position is conferred for life, unpaid and calculated according to the size of the population. Those chosen are required to undertake such tasks as may be requested by the Lord-Lieutenant, the sovereign's non-political representative.

In 2010 Rachael became one of the first female directors of the England and Wales Cricket Board [ECB], and in November the same year, in recognition of her wider work as a charity fundraiser, was ennobled and took her place in the House of Lords as a Conservative Party working peer. *'I was completely taken by surprise when I took the call from the Prime Minister in September,'* she said. *'Obviously I am really thrilled at my appointment but still very humbled at the thought of joining such a historic institution. My background in sport, journalism, charity and community work will I hope stand me in good stead, and I hope I can make a positive contribution as a working peer. I will certainly look forward to the commute from one Lord's to another Lords.'* She was subsequently invested as a life peer in January 2011 taking the title of Baroness Heyhoe-Flint, of Wolverhampton in the County of West Midlands. In April that year she was granted the freedom of Wolverhampton.

According to Scyld Berry [born 1954], the noteworthy cricketing correspondent of the *Sunday Telegraph*, and former editor of *Wisden Cricketers' Almanack*, *'She was, among other achievements, the Dr. W.G. Grace of women's cricket. The pioneer without whom the game would not be what it is.'*

Like the bearded doctor, she was an energetic trailblazer. Although the legendary former England captain Sir Leonard Hutton [1916-1990] was not quite so gracious when he remarked, *'A woman trying to play cricket is like a man trying to knit'.* A gritty opening bat, Hutton rose to fame after making 365 runs against the celebrated Sir Donald George Bradman's [1908-2001] Australian test side at the Oval in 1938. Often referred to as 'Bradman is widely acknowledged as the greatest batsman of all time, and his career Test batting average of 99.94 is repeatedly cited as one of the greatest achievements by any sportsman in any major sport.

Baroness Rachael Heyhoe-Flint OBE, DL died aged 77, in January, 2017, following a short illness. On the way to the St Peter's Collegiate Church, in Wolverhampton, for a service of thanksgiving, members of the public lined the streets in tribute as the limousines passed by Molineux, the Wolverhampton Wanderers football ground. Flags were flown at half-mast at Lord's and the Molineux stadium.

In the Reverend David Wright's address to the mourners, he said *'Rachael's death is a painful loss and it leaves a gap that no-one else could ever fill. Rachael was unique, one of a kind'.*

Amongst those who paid tribute to Rachael was the BBC cricket correspondent, Jonathan Agnew [born 1960], who said, *'Very sad news about Rachael Heyhoe Flint. A great champion of women's cricket, and one of life's real enthusiasts'.*

Clare Connor [born 1976], the ECB's Director of women's cricket, said, *'She was so special, so ever-present and now she has gone. But her impact can never be forgotten. Rachael was one of our sport's true pioneers and it is no exaggeration to say that she paved the way for the progress enjoyed by recent generations of female cricketers.'*

Matthew Fleming [born 1964], the President of the MCC, which remains as the guardian of the laws and spirit of the game, said, *'Heyhoe-Flint was the first global superstar in the women's game and her overall contribution to the club, cricket, and sport in general, was immense'.*

Batting and fielding averages:

Tests:	Innings:	Not out:	Runs:	Highest score:	Average:	100:	50:	Caught:
22	38	3	1594	179	45.54	3	10	13
ODI Matches:	Innings:	Not out:	Runs:	Highest score:	Average:	100:	50:	Caught:
23	20	9	643	114	58.45	1	4	6

Bowling averages:

Tests:	Innings:	Balls:	Runs:	Wickets:	Average:	Economy:	SR:
22	15	402	204	3	68.0	3.04	134.0
ODI matches:	Innings:	Balls:	Runs:	Wickets:	Average:	Economy:	SR:
22	2	18	20	1	20.0	6.66	18.0

Enid Bakewell [née Turton] [born 1940]:

Enid Bakewell remains one of England's finest women cricketers of all time. She was the leading run-scorer, accumulating the grand total of 264 runs, in the inaugural Women's World Cup tournament in 1973 which England won. She contributed 118 runs in the final against Australia at Edgbaston, and took 2 wickets for 28 in 12 overs. During the afternoon, as the Australian team came out to bat, HRH Princess Anne arrived to enjoy the game, and stayed to present the cup at the end of the day.

Born in the Nottinghamshire mining village of Newstead, Enid was attracted to game of cricket from an early age. Although she confesses she still unable to remember exactly when she first took up a bat, it is said when she was only nine years old, she joined some local boys who were playing cricket on a rough field of ankle-high grass on a hilltop opposite a cemetery close to her home. It was there, together with some local boys, she would play her cricket, *'for there were too few girls available'*. After being chased off the outfield of the village cricket club, *'We had hedge shears and scissors and cut out a pitch just big enough for a wicket, because the long grass had slugs and you used to lose the ball in it. It helped me. With that sort of surface, you daren't let the ball pitch so I used my feet, and that helped me get the confidence to play.'*

As an only child of a non-cricketing family, her parents encouraged her enthusiasm and provided her with all the essential equipment. At her primary school in Newstead, Enid soon became more proficient at cricket than all the boys, and when she graduated to the Brincliffe County Grammar School in Nottingham, the boys used to borrow her gear.

Following a brief spell with the Nottinghamshire Casuals Women's Cricket Club, Enid was selected to play for the Nottinghamshire county women's team at the age of 14. Even then she was a quiet, steady, right-hand opening bat, whose primary aim was not to give away her wicket. Those early lessons of awareness and concentration provided her with a sound basis for the future, enabling to score easily and stay at the wicket.

Enid Turton's notable batting ability first became noticed in the summer of 1957 when, as a 16 year old, she made an encouraging start to her cricketing career against Leicester, scoring 43 not out in an innings total of 101. In the return match the following month she knocked up a further 56 not out.

When asked if she had ever received any coaching from anyone, she replied, *'Oh no. At senior school we weren't allowed to play cricket, it was considered to be too 'unladylike'. In fact, whistling was too 'unladylike' then. But I managed to join a team in Nottinghamshire because the PE teacher knew someone who played for them. I didn't have any coaching.', 'I went to Lilleshall when I was 18,'* she continued, *'but I was a natural player and just loved playing. We played virtually every evening until we lost the ball, or it got dark, or we were too hungry to stay out.'*

Enid also went to the Dartford College of Physical Education, where she graduated in 1959, that same year she was chosen to tour Holland with a WCA team of young up and coming players. At this point in her cricketing development Bakewell, who is still strongly regarded as one of the best all-rounders the English women's game has ever produced, did not take her bowling seriously, preferring to concentrate her attention on developing her batting skills. It was only later that she was encouraged to cultivate her slow left-arm spin bowling technique by the former club President, Edna Valentine, and Eileen White, the Honorary Secretary of the County Association. She modelled her bowling style along the lines of the left-arm spinner Tony Lock [1929-1995], even to the extent of taking the same number of paces in her run up around the umpire.Lock played in 49 Tests for England, taking 174 wickets for an average of 25.58. She later confessed that *'as a Nottingham girl I was torn two ways. When I went to watch Nottinghamshire play Surrey I admired Tony Lock's bowling and was delighted by Peter May's batting [1929-1994], so I sometimes hoped Surrey might win'.*

Enid was first considered for possible Test selection against Australia in 1963, who were touring England at the time. *'My first feelings were of excitement and surprise, tempered somewhat on seeing the full list of names'*. However, she disappointed not to secure her place, moreover she was not selected in 1966, when the New Zealand women's team toured England, as she had subsequently married and was pregnant at the time with her daughter Lorna.

However, Enid would eventually be rewarded with the opportunity to make her first Test appearance in 1968-1969, when she did battle against the Australian and New Zealand cricketers in the four-and-a-half-month Test tour. Although Enid would be the first to modestly acknowledge there may well have been several others before her who had registered significant success in first-class cricket, but whose achievements had for the most part remained unpublished and gone largely unnoticed.

The rest of her story is one of consistent and amazing success. Enid joined the tour, and played in all six Test matches. She opening the batting on her debut against Australia, and made a confident century, but that was the easy bit. The trauma of leaving her two-and-a-half-year-old daughter behind was far more difficult to bear. Bakewell had to pay her own way, but her husband Colin, who worked for Rolls Royce as an electrical engineer, and her parents, who were most understanding and stepped in to help, and look after her two year old daughter Lorna while she was away. *'I had to raise £603 for the air fare,'* she said. *'So I went back to work teaching, I sold paperback books, I sold potatoes out of the garden, we had a coffee morning, and I wrote round locally to anyone who had any money who might be a benefactor. Eventually I raised it.'*

The 1968-1969 Test tour is now confined to history, and set the tone for Bakewell's illustrious international cricketing career. Slight of build and small in stature, Enid was described as a *'diminutive and tiny blonde, small, but athletically built, quick-witted and alert'*. On her first Test appearance against Australia she opened the innings for England scoring 113 runs. As an opening batsman, in the first and second Tests against New Zealand, she scored two consecutive centuries, 124 and 114. Moreover, in addition she scored six half-centuries throughout the tour, and took 10 catches. She also collected 50 wickets with her venomous left-arm spin, including eight wickets in an innings on three occasions, once in Australia and twice in New Zealand, and five wickets or more on nine other occasions. Enid's record on the tour is well chronicled, and the reputation she earned through the consistency of her performance with both bat and ball gathered deserved respect. Headlines in both the Australian and New Zealand press revelled over her sparkling ability. Her top score of 59 against Victoria, followed by the demolition of seven batsmen for 28 runs, was described in an Adelaide newspaper, *'English girl does a Sobers'*. Another newspaper, in an article describing the same performance revealed, *'Bakewell routs Vic'*.

England won its second Test match in Christchurch, New Zealand by seven wickets, in which Enid's achievements were so outstanding the Test was designated as *'Bakewell's match'*. In the first innings she scored 114 runs and claimed four wickets at a cost of 68 runs, which she followed up in the second innings with 66 not out, and took a further five wickets for 56. Amid much excitement, with just four minutes remaining before the end of the match, she most appropriately nicked the single required to secure England's first victory against the *'White Ferns'* since 1954.

Following this outstanding performance Enid was rated as the world's best woman all-rounder. With many varied comments surpassing each other in praise of her prowess, *'Mainstay of an aggressive English knock was Enid Bakewell who played as correctly as any male Test player might have as she moved relentlessly towards her century'*, contrasting with *'an audacious batsman, fast between wickets, who uses her feet better than many Plunket Shield cricketers'.* Since the 1906–1907 seasons, New Zealand ran a domestic first-class cricket championship known by its original name of the Plunket Shield. Meanwhile, her orthodox left-arm spinners were bowled throughout the series with skill and consistency, although the Enid modestly claimed spin bowlers were only as good as the batsmen make them look.

On her return home to England, Enid was accorded a Civic Reception by the Nottingham County Council, where she was presented with numerous gifts, including a cheque as a contribution towards her expenses, and an engraved silver salver bearing a record of her achievements. She was also presented with an engraved silver cup by one of the men's teams which she played against the previous season when raising money to fund the tour. When the local council gave her a gift of a dressing-table set, her three-year-old daughter, commented loudly and cheerily, *'And what have we got this time? '* But to this day, amongst her most prized possessions is the ball, mounted and inscribed, which was used in *'Bakewell's match'.*

Enid managed to dislodge *'the pebble from her shoe'* with her 1968-1969 tour performance, which to this day remains a challenge to women cricketers wherever they might play.

A nonsensical situation almost occurred in the 1970s as England and Australia prepared for a women's Test match at Lord's. As the all-rounder Enid enlightened a BBC reporter, *'It wasn't until 1976 that Lord's let us have a televised match there, and when we first went there I don't think they were going to allow a woman in the score-box'*. The pavilion, with its revered Long Room, was for the use of men only, and the Lord's players wondered how they would actually walk onto the field. *'We didn't know if we could use the changing rooms, and we certainly didn't know if we could go through the Long Room. The Aussies didn't know about the tradition of the Long Room, so they walked through and we followed them.'*

Throughout an international career, spanning the period 1968-1979, Enid played a total of twelve women's Test matches for England, and 22 innings, four of which she carried her bat. She amassed a total of 1078 runs, including four centuries, and seven half-centuries, at an average of 59.9, including a top score of 124. She bowled 2697 balls in Test cricket, collecting 50 wickets with her deadly left-arm spin for an average of 16.6. Her best bowling figures being 7 wickets for 61 runs. In addition, she also made 23 appearances in One-Day International matches, knocking up 500 runs at an average of 35.7, including two centuries and two half-centuries, her top score being 118. She took 25 wickets from 1313 balls bowled, and recording a bowling average of 21.1, her best figures being 3wickets for 13 runs.

In her final Test against the West Indies at Edgbaston in 1979 Enid scored 112 runs not out in an England innings which only assemble a total of 164, notching up a tally of 10 wickets for 75 runs. The Australian Betty Wilson is the only other woman cricketer to have since matched that feat.

In 2012 she became only the third woman cricketer to be inducted into the ICC's hall of fame after Rachael Heyhoe-Flint and Belinda Clark [born 1970], and in 2014 was named in Wisden Cricketers' Almanack as one of the five greatest female players of all time.

A qualified ECB coach, Bakewell continued to play cricket for the East Midlands into her 50s, and when in her 60s opened the bowling for her club the Redoubtables in Surrey.

Enid still lives in the cricketing county of Nottinghamshire, in the village in which she grew up, barely a mile from the school where the great bowler Harold Larwood [1904-1995] was educated.

In 2018 the story of *Enid Bakewell, The Coalminer's Daughter*, written by Simon Sweetman and published through the Association of Cricket Statisticians and Historians.

Batting and fielding averages:

Tests:	Runs:	Highest score:	Average:	100:	50:	Caught:
12	1078	124	59.88	4	7	9

ODI Matches:	Runs:	Highest score:	Average:	100:	50:	Caught:
23	500	118	35.71	2	2	7

Bowling averages:

Tests:	Balls:	Wickets:	Average:	Best Bowling:	5 wkts:	10 wkts	Econ:	SR:
12	2697	50	16 62	7 for 61	3	1	1.85	53.94

ODI matches:	Balls:	Wickets:	Average:	Best Bowling:	5 wkts:	10 wkts	Econ:	SR
23	1313	25	21.12	3 for 13	0	0	2.42	52.52

Chapter 7

The Pittwater Picnic

Australian women enjoy a long history as lovers of cricket, even since the early settlers are known to have eagerly joined in games whenever they were given the opportunity. Even though cricket was still not generally considered a game suitable for ladies, towards the end of the nineteenth century.a number of regional areas had formed their own all-women teams. As a growing number of young women had become accustomed to playing cricket as children alongside their brothers, a number would later develop as outstanding cricketers.

The first recorded Australian women's cricket match was an informal affair, which took place in 1874 in the Victorian gold town of Bendigo, said to have sat above the world's richest goldfields. The match generated a sum of money equivalent to around £300, which was donated to the Bendigo District Hospital. It was reported, '*Several of the players exhibited remarkably good form, and one young lady proved herself to be a round-arm bowler who would have been an acquisition to any team*'.

However, the first officially organised women's cricket match was not held until several years later, in March 1886, between the Fernleas and the Siroccos, at the Association Ground, which is now the Sydney Cricket Ground. The Fernleas team was captained by Nellie Gregory, and the Siroccos by her cricketing sister Lily. A crowd of around 600 animated spectators attended the game, which had been arranged to raise money to be donated to the Bulli Relief Fund, a charitable organisation formed to financially assist the poor and impoverished. Although the match failed to initiate the more frequent organisation of regular women's cricket matches, it claims precedence over the first English women's cricket club, the White Heather Club, which was formed in Nun Appleton in Yorkshire in the following year. Although women's cricket in England can be accurately traced back to a report in the *Reading Mercury* of the 26 July 1745, which relates to the well documented cricket match that took place at Gosden Common near Guildford, Surrey, '*between eleven maids of Bramley and eleven maids of Hambledon*'.

As a nation Australia has always been known for its enthusiasm, and for the fervour of its spectators of cricket, and the Australian women were soon to demonstrate they were equally keen when on the field of play. For several decades the popularity of cricket waxed and waned, and it was still considered by some an unseemly sport in which ladies should engage. Even so, in the last decade of the nineteenth century, teams and clubs for women and girls began to emerge, and the first competitive inter-colonial, now inter-state matches, were arranged. This eventually led to the formation of the Australian Women's Cricket Council [AWCC] in 1931, with the stated objective of promoting and supporting the sport, and which in due course resulted in the first series of international matches between England and Australia.

The start of the summer season of 1934-1935 was cool and wet in Sydney. It also heralded the beginning of international women's cricket. A number of Australian women players welcomed an excited English team as it docked in Sydney, after completing a long, tiresome voyage aboard the SS Orion, a coal-fired ship built in Sweden, measuring just 32 metres [105 feet] by 6 metres [20 feet], and boasting seven cabins, two salons, three mess halls, a galley, shower facilities and a cargo hold.

On the opening day of the inaugural international match the Sydney Cricket Ground was at its eye-catching best, after weeks of rain and wind the weather had taken a turn for the better, and two days of brilliant sunshine beamed down on the players. Looking elegant and neat, the teams turned out wearing divided white skirts, short-sleeved blouses, long white stockings, and canvas shoes. The English players wore smart white hats, matching their attire, while most of the New South Wales team opted for white caps, or white linen hats lined with blue. Those fortunate enough to witness that very first women's international match on that glorious Saturday in Sydney, were unlikely to ever forget the exciting closing moments when the English women snatched victory from the New South Wales women's side.

All the same the Sydney Cricket Ground Committee drew some criticism for insisting the women change under the Sheridan Pavilion, instead of the old Members' Stand from which male players would generally parade out to the field of play. Yet the women soon clearly demonstrated they were just as capable of skilfully handling a cricket bat and ball, and of honouring the revered traditions of the game with a cheerful respect.

The crowd of around 5,000 celebrated skilful strokes and competent catches with modest bursts of applause. Be that as it may, several spectators arrived armed with portable radios in order that they might listen to a commentary on the horse racing from the Royal Randwick Racecourse. A few additional feminine touches were introduced by the ladies too, for when the lemon squash was brought out at the drinks interval, they had no hesitation in dispensing drinks to the parched umpires. A courteous gesture which no one had witnessed before, which the crowd appreciated, marking its approval with a generous round of applause.

Drinks break !

Many Australians commented on the English-women's dark suntan acquired during their sea voyage to Australia. *'It's just as well we got in ahead of the Sydney sun,'* said one of the English team. *'I hate to think how sunburned we would have all been when we resumed play to-morrow.'*

Guest of honour at lunch, was The Governer, Lieutenant General Sir John Northcott KCMG, KCVO, CB, KStJ [1890–1966], who served as Chief of the General Staff during World War II, and commanded the British Commonwealth Occupation Force in the occupation of Japan.

At the end of the opening day's play the New South Wales team was all out for 146, with the English touring team losing one wicket for a score of 40. England's eventual victoryon the second day of play was made possible by the New South Wales captain, Margaret Elizabeth Maynard Peden, who announced a second innings declaration by the State side, leaving the visitors half-an-hour to knock off the 57 runs needed to win. Although New South Wales might well have played for a draw, Miss Peden's momentous sporting gesture afforded the visitors a slim chance of success, and they took it. Excited at having achieved their first win in Australia, the English girls were the first to acknowledge Miss Peden's action, and all agreed, *'What a sporting declaration on the part of New South Wales. It was a wonderful match.'*

On Monday, 17 December 1934, the English team were entertained to a picnic at the renowned Palm Beach, Pittwater, known for being one of the places to visit. It was quite common for every conceivable type of organisation to wend its way to Palm Beach for the occasional *'picnic outing'*. For it was known as being the very essence of relaxed enjoyment of the Australian outdoors, and frequently compared with that of the Palm Beach in Florida, USA. So even though it had been a cool start to the Australian summer, escorting the English team to spend a little time relaxing on its delightful beaches would have been a must.

Although it was not unusual for the occasional cow to wander aimlessly across the picnic rugs, the weather was ideal for the pleasant picnic beach party Emma Linda Palmer Littlejohn [1883-1949], of the United Associations of Women [UA], had organised a for the visiting cricketers. Thirteen members of the England team, including the English captain, Molly Hide, and the New South Wales captain, Mary Clouston 'Mollie' Dive [1913-1997], were driven along the headlands, and took lunch at Whale Beach, at the home of Mrs. A.L. Holt, a member of the New South Wales Hockey Association. Afterwards the team journeyed on to Palm Beach, where they sampled one of best *'surfs'* of the whole tour.

Emma Linda Palmer Littlejohn was an extremely gifted lady. A writer, journalist, radio broadcaster, and advocate of women's rights and autonomy, she was considered as being one of the most radical, politically forceful Australian feminist groups of the mid twentieth century. The UA was formed in 1929 and active during the 1930s and 1940s, when it sought to bring political pressure and draw attention to the rights and needs of Australian women. It was created by Emma Littlejohn, together with Jessie Mary Grey Street [née Lillingston] [1889 –1970] commonly known as Lady Street, a Jewish community leader, Ruby Sophia Rich [1888-1988], and Adela Constantia Mary Pankhurst Walsh [1885 –1961], the daughter of the British suffragette Emmeline Pankhurst [1858-1928], Adela was born in Manchester, England, and was a British-Australian suffragette, political organiser, and co-founder of the Communist Party of Australia.

The picnic at Whale, and the surfing at Palm Beach, may have been seen as an opportunity for Littlejohn to garner the support of the English women for more recognition of women's rights or, perhaps less cynically, it may simply have been a feast for all their senses, a lovely afternoon where like-minded ladies might spend time dwelling on the beauty of Pittwater.

The Women's Supplement in the *'Sydney Morning Herald'* reported, *'Now come down to Palm Beach, Sydney, for a breath of salt sea air and a week-end in the caressing sunshine on a warm, sandy beach, with the song of the Pacific continually lapping the shore, in your ears, and with a vista of bush and beach mostly as Nature made it, with here and there a bungalow jutting out of the hillside, almost apologetically, as if realising that man's hand must do nothing to spoil the entrancing work of Nature. To be sure, we have our Florida-road at Palm Beach, but no millions of dollars have been spent to put it there. It meanders along the hillside, dodging round corners, and going off its course here and there for the convenience of some bungalow owner who has required an entrance for his garage It is a dirt road-or rather a rocky one, with a little dirt here and there to hold it together, but it serves its purpose picturesquely. But down on the beach society plays in the sand under multi-coloured beach umbrellas, like a crop of mushrooms, and sun and surf provide the only entertainment necessary free, gratis, and for nothing. Most of the summer cottages are open for the season now, which will continue until after Easter and, indeed, so warm and mild are the days on beach and golf links that many people go down regularly every week-end almost throughout the year.'*

The following afternoon the England team were scheduled to play against the Wollongong and District Women, at Wollongong, and the Women's Cricket Association arranged for the team to be transported there and back by car, allowing them the opportunity to see some of the Australian South Coast. Often referred to informally as *'The Gong'*, the seaside city of Wollongong is the third-largest city in New South Wales and is located some 50 miles [80 kilometres] south of Sydney. After the match they were entertained at a dinner by the Mayor of Wollongong, and early the following morning left for the return journey to Sydney. On the Wednesday morning they caught a flight for Newcastle in time to play a match there before continuing their onward journey to Brisbane. '*Wherever we have gone we have brought the fine weather,*' said Helen Elizabeth *'Betty'* Green [died 1956], the player manager of the English team, *'but this is the hottest day we have experienced.'* However, her Australian colleagues, gently reminded her they had not experienced summer so far, and the day in question was really quite mild. The prospect of hotter days to come did nothing to cheer Betty, for her team of English girls were thoroughly exhausted when the match ended, after spending nearly all day in the field.

1935. Second women's match at the Sydney Cricket Ground.
Anne Palmer [New South Wales] bowled out, with Spear, Snowball and Partridge [England] looking on.

The 1935 sporting year for the women of New South Wales opened on January 4 with the second of the matches played at the Sydney Cricket Ground, between the women's teams of England and New South Wales proving to be one of the tour's most appealing. It provoked enormous interest, not only among the women enthusiasts, but also with the male cricketing community. With many coming along to watch, perhaps with the aim of confirming their doubt, that the women did not possess the ability to properly play the game. However, if there were any in doubt at all, it seems they were soon to be persuaded otherwise and ultimately won over, since they stayed to record their appreciation.

A decade later another English women's cricket team was also entertained to a picnic in the Palm Beach and Whale Beach areas.

Chapter 8

The Colwall Festival of Cricket

In the early spring of 1926 the nation celebrated the birth of HRH Princess Elizabeth of York, later to be proclaimed Queen Elizabeth II at the age of 25 in February 1952, following the death of her father King George VI [1895-1952].

In the summer of that historic year, a fervent group of friends gathered together in the village of Colwall to enjoy several days of cricket. They could hardly have imagined their few days of fun would lead to the foundation of the Women's Cricket Association, and the popular annual Festival of Women's Cricket which continues to this day. The group, who were all members of the All England Women's Hockey Association [AEWHA], met at the Park Hotel situated at the centre of the peaceful village of Colwall, midway between Great Malvern and Ledbury. Graced by beautiful and spacious grounds, with footpaths leading directly onto the slopes of the Malvern Hills, the country house hotel was owned by Mrs. Scott Bowden, one of the most influential members of the UEWHA.

The initial launch of the annual Colwall Cricket Festival was blighted somewhat by a short period of political upheaval, coinciding as it did with the General Strike called by the General Council of Trade Unions Congress [TUC] in an futile attempt to prevent the reduction of wages and the worsening of working conditions of 1.2 million British coal miners. The Conservative government, led by Stanley Baldwin [1867–1947], was appropriately prepared, enlisting the help of numerous middle class volunteers to maintain essential services, which led to a short period of military control during which martial law was temporarily enforced. Eventually the beaten miners were compelled to give up their fight and concede defeat.

In spite of this unrest the AEWHA launched the popular cricket festival at the Colwall Cricket Club on the Herefordshire side of the Malvern Hills. It's stated objective being to provide an opportunity for adult women to enjoy the game of cricket and develop their cricketing skills.

The first official *'Cricketing Week'* was held in Colwall the following year, organised by the WCA in its first season, and was soon to become acclaimed as an annual Festival of Women's Cricket in which players of all ages, and all levels of ability, might participate and suitably enjoy. However, members were required to be able to afford to take a full week away from work, meet their respective travel and accommodation costs, and stump up a deposit of 10 shillings [50 pence]. Consequently, less than 8 per cent of the early members of the Association ever attended *'Cricketing Week'*. Despite which, in subsequent years the September issue of '*Women's Cricket*' reported the event extensively, which led to one outraged member writing to the journal to express some concern regarding accommodation. Even if a member was able to afford the cost of attending *'Cricketing Week'*, *'What constitutes the right to stay at the*

Park Hotel. Is it reserved for the Committee, and for want of a better word the 'Grandees' ? ' The criticism brought forth an incisive response from Marjorie Pollard, the editor of '*Hockey Field*' and '*Women's Cricket*', '*It is foolish to think that it is reserved for 'Grandees' and I think that it would be an immense pity to let such a feeling grow'.* It was predictable this feeling of bitterness continued to rankle amongst some of the membership of the WCA for some time to come.

Nevertheless, in 1928 a total of 48 eager women cricketers descended upon Colwall to take part in the festival, with the village's charitable residents offering hospitality for the players on a bed and breakfast basis. In the early years, around a dozen teams would usually compete, with matches arranged every day, and entertainment organised to take place during the evenings. Each team was randomly selected, and was usually captained by an England international, or a seasoned County player, the remainder of the side was more often than not made up of experienced players including a few beginners. With a number of local cricket grounds situated in close proximity to Colwall used to stage the matches. Not only was the popular annual cricketing festival an opportunity to savour a fun-filled week of competitive matches between teams of experienced players, it was renowned for its fellowship. Especially the celebration on the final evening before departure, and what a celebration it was too ! Players dressed up, sang and danced in the Horse and Jockey public house, their frolics proving most entertaining to the village population.

Apart from the period spanning the 1939-1945 years of war, the festival has been held annually in August in Colwall, which has since become known to many as *'the birthplace of women's cricket'*. Devoted women cricketers from all over the country descend upon Colwall, keen to engage in the nation's summer sport. Amongst the frequent pre-war supporters of the popular cricketing jamboree were such legendary players as Betty Snowball, Myrtle McLagen, Molly Hide, and Helen Elizabeth *'Betty'* Archdale, the educationalist and former captain of the first England women's cricket team on its victorious tour of Australia and New Zealand in 1934-1935. The grand-daughter of Emmeline Pankhurst, Betty was herself a suffragette, serving a brief period of incarceration for breaking windows in Whitehall.

During the late 1980s and early 1990s, teams which included many of the England squad players, assembled to play matches in both Colwall and Malvern, on the cricket grounds of Malvern College, the Elms, the Downs and Colwall CC, which boasted the best pitches available at the time. The England cricketing luminary and member of the ICC Hall of Fame, Enid Bakewell regularly attended *'Cricketing Week'*. Amongst the more recent cricketing stars to give their support was the first woman to be named a *'Wisden'* Cricketer of the Year, Samantha Claire Taylor MBE [born 1975], a top-order batsman who represented England women on more than 150 occasions, and was the mainstay of England's batting during the first decade of the 21st century.

Born in New Zealand in 1950, Gillian Elizabeth McConway, the former ECB Director of Women's Cricket and slow left-arm England international bowler contends, *'Cricketing Week has a special place in the women's cricket calendar. It provides everyone with a chance to play the game, take some time out in a beautiful part of England in summer, make new friends and enjoy themselves'*.

Audrey Toll Collins OBE [1915-2010] was one the most esteemed figures of English women's cricket. She was born in Mussoorie, in the United Provinces of British India, and came to England with her Australian mother, following the death of her father in the Great War.

Her career in cricket began at the age of 12, from which she progressed to represent Middlesex and the South. Audrey played for England in her one and only Test match against Australia, at the Oval in the 1937 Women's Ashes. Batting at number 8 she scored 27 runs, putting on 54 in a half hour partnership with Betty Archdale, after the pair had been admonished and instructed to *'get on with the job'*.

She taught chemistry at St Albans Girls' Grammar School in Hertfordshire, for 35 years from the 1940s, and there is now an Audrey Collins Cup awarded to girls' cricket teams in Hertfordshire.

After the World War II she played cricket for the East, and became Secretary and later Chairman of the WCA, serving from 1983 to 1994. Her term as President of the WCA was the longest in the history of the organisation. Although all her work with the WCA was conducted on a voluntary basis, she is credited with steering it through the most difficult times, and it was her dogged determination which helped underpin the foundation which enables the women of today preserve their love for the game of cricket.

Audrey was one of the first ten female members elected to the MCC, when the ban on female members entering the Long Room was eliminated in 1999.

Fondly remembered by those who continue to support the Colwall Cricketing Week, Audrey Collins attended regularly, and even helped with the scoring, until her death in Shrewsbury, Shropshire in 2010 at the age of 94.

On her 90th birthday Audrey was thrilled to be presented with a cricket bat signed by the England women's team. Audrey, who was awarded the OBE for her services to the game of cricket, was a founder member of the Radlett Women's Cricket Club. And the following heartfelt tribute was published on the ECB website following her death, *'Bless you Audrey, you are very much loved and missed by your fellow players at Radlett Cricket Club [The Vagabonds]. We have all benefited from your commitment and your love of the game. Your scorebook was never to be forgotten, even when you used light yellow pencil too. We have lovely memories of your last indoor game with us in 2007, batting, you tripped, the hall went silent, you picked yourself up to run again before the ball reached the stumps. If only others were made of the same stuff Audrey! We won the indoor league this year, and dedicate that win to you.'*

At the time of her passing the England team which was on tour in India, wore black armbands during the second one day international, with both teams observing a minute's silence as a mark of respect before the beginning of the play.

A memorial match honouring Audrey was held at the Colwall Cricket Festival in 2010. With cricket bats held aloft, the players formed a guard of honour flanking Audrey's nephew Christopher, and the England women's captain Charlotte Edwards [born 1979], together with representatives of the WCA. Her ashes were scattered beneath a tree, planted in her memory between the two grounds at Colwall.

It is through the generosity of such enthusiastic volunteers as Audrey Collins, whose only reward was the personal satisfaction they achieved through the game of cricket, that the vision of the development of early women's cricket was conceived and delivered. The organisation of matches, whether for club or county, or at international level, either at home or abroad, became an outstanding and well developed feature of the work of this precious group of committed women.

Fabulous times are still enjoyed at Cricketing Week, and enduring friendships are still being made. How inspired it was that the WCA had the initial foresight to take it under its wing, and that this great annual festival of cricket continues to thrive.

Chapter 9

The Women's Cricket Association

Following the cricketing holiday in the Worcestershire spa town of Colwall, the concept of a Women's Cricket Association [WCA] was conceived by the group of ardent cricket enthusiasts which gathered there. As a consequence the WCA was founded on the 4 October 1926, at a meeting held in the Ex-Service Women's Club, Buckingham Gate, Victoria, London, at which the former President of the All England Womens Hockey Association [AEWHA], Mrs. Alice Heron-Maxwell [1860-1949], took the chair. The proposition *'That a central association for women's cricket be formed'*, was put before the meeting by Miss K. Doman [Kent], a games tutor at the eminent Dartford Physical Training College, who declared that such an association would *'be a help to existing clubs, a boon to those keen cricketers who had no club to join and a stimulating influence to the game in schools and colleges'*. The motion was seconded by Mrs. Scott Bowden [Hertfordshire], and was formally carried by 14 votes to 2. Among those attending were 18 cricket enthusiasts representing 12 English counties, 3 physical training colleges, and by a group of 20 others who, although unable to be present at the meeting, pledged their written support for the proposal.

Shortly after the formation of the WCA, a report was recorded in *The Times* which read, *'Women's Cricket. English Association formed. For some years there has been a demand for an organisation to foster and encourage cricket amongst women, such as exist in the games of hockey, lacrosse and netball. A meeting of cricket enthusiasts from all over the country was held in London recently, and it was unanimously decided to form an association'.*

The women who served on the original Executive Committee of the WCA originated from society's upper and upper-middle class, the majority of which were residing in the Home Counties. Indeed, even six years later in 1932, not one of the twelve Committee members lived further north than Hertford. Mrs. Heron-Maxwell owned the 17 century manor and Great Comp estate in Kent, comprising four and a half acres of land frequently used to host cricket and hockey matches. Mrs. Scott- Bowden owned the Park Hotel in Malvern, invariably occupied by the majority of those attending the annual Colwall Cricket Festival. And Mrs. Arthur Moores, the President of the Northern Counties WCA, who was comfortably able to host the entire Australian cricket team in her home for three days during its 1937 tour.

In the short-term it was agreed the Association would primarily serve as an exploratory organisation, identified as *'The Women's Cricket Association'*, serving as an inspiration to schools and colleges to promote the sport, and wherever possible to providing assistance to committed women cricketers with opportunities to join an established club.

It is a well known fact that women had been playing cricket for some time prior to the formation of the WCA, predominantly in girls' schools, colleges and universities. Consequently, during the early years the Association limited the circulated of information to fee-paying schools and colleges which provided an education for middle and upper-class girls. The WCA presented them with the fundamental essentials of cricket, which at the time was in direct competition to the sport of tennis, which girls were taught from an early age and could be played casually amongst friends.

There is persuasive evidence to suggest competitive women's cricket was being played as early as 1898 in the small town of Brighouse, four miles north of Huddersfield in West Yorkshire, its most famous resident being the Reverend William Booth [1829-1912], the founder of the Salvation Army. The Brighouse Ladies Cricket Club, one of the few women's teams in the North of England, was regrettably compelled to disband temporarily as interest in the ladies game subsided. However, it was in Manchester, the other side of the Pennines, that the first significant evidence of working-class women playing cricket was documented. In April 1913, the *Manchester Evening Chronicle* announced what appears to be the first reference of the formation of a women's cricket league in Britain. Observing that although the league had only one division of eight clubs, its growing popularity suggested there would be a second tier developed in the following season. Meanwhile, the first known working-class women's cricket team formed after the Great War, was at Hey's Brewery in Bradford in 1926, coincidentally the same year the WCA was inaugurated. Although it is unclear who the brewery team competed against prior to its affiliation to the Bradford Women's Evening Cricket League which came into being five years later. In the following year in Doncaster, South Yorkshire, the Dearne Valley Women's Cricket League was also formed. The league, which included six teams, was supported by the local newspaper, the *Mexborough and Swinton Times.*

The formation of a governing body for women's cricket reflects the struggle for social changes in society taking place at the time, with more and more women presented with an opportunity to transcend the borders of private life, work, sport and leisure. Even though interest in women's cricket was showing signs of growth, and it had become better organised, the number of women who played the game rarely, if ever, exceeded 5,000.

Women in Britian had still not been granted the right to vote in 1903. Although in 1918, women over the age of 30, who met certain property qualifications, were given the right to vote in public. Ten years later in 1928, the right to vote was broadened to include all women over the age of 21. In many other parts of the world women had already been conditionally granted entitlement to vote in elections, and the following table shows the year in which other countries first allowed women the vote.

Year Country	Year Country	Year Country
1893 New Zealand	1902 Australia *	1906 Finland
1913 Norway	1915 Denmark	1917 Canada **
1918 Austria, Germany, Poland, Russia		1919 Netherlands
1920 United States of America		1921 Sweden
1928 Britain ***	1931 Spain, Ireland	1934 Turkey
1944 France	1945 Italy	
1947 Argentina, Japan, Mexico, Pakistan		1949 China
1950 India	1954 Colombia	1956 Sri Lanka
1957 Malaysia, Zimbabwe	1962 Algeria	1963 Iran, Morocco
1964 Libya	1967 Equador	1971 Switzerland
1972 Bangladesh	1974 Jordan	1976 Portugal

1988 Namibia	1990 Western Samoa	1993 Kazahkstan
1994 South Africa	2005 Kuwait	2006 United Arab Emirates
2011 Saudia Arabia		

* Australian women, with the exception of aboriginal women, won the vote in 1902, although aborigines, male and female, did not have the right to vote until 1962.
** Canadian women, with the exception of Canadian First Nation women, won the vote in 1917. Canadian First Nation, male and female, did not win the vote until 1960.
*** In 1918, British women over the age of 30 were given the vote, subject to specific property qualifications. In 1928, the Conservative government approved the vote for all women over the age of 21, on equal terms with men.

Historical opinion amongst some scholars remains divided as to whether the militant policies of the suffragette movement of the late nineteenth and early twentieth centuries, helped, or hindered, the specific cause of women in general. British suffragettes, led by the political activist Emmeline Pankhurst, were generally made up of women from upper and middle-class backgrounds, frustrated by their social and economic circumstances. Born in Moss Side, Manchester to politically active parents, Emmeline Pankhurst was introduced to the women's suffrage movement at the age of 14, and in 1999 was named by *Time* magazine as one of the *'100 Most Important People of the 20th Century'*, asserting that *'she shaped an idea of women for our time, and shook society into a new pattern from which there could be no going back.'* Pankhurst later decided that in order to become truly effective the movement would need to become more radical and militant. As a result their crusade became increasingly hostile, leading to property damage and hunger strikes. Which in turn were resisted by the authorities through the introduction of terms of imprisonment and force-feeding. The movement was eventually put on hold, in support of the British Government's stand against the *'German Peril'*, and the outbreak of the 1914-1918 war.

In its first year the WCA concentrated its attention on the development of the women's game through the creation and development of clubs, with the intention of promoting the expansion of county and district organisations at a later date. The Committee were also mandated to keep in mind the prospect of establishing a future national team. At the time no official Constitution for the Association was created, and the rules and regulations under which the WCA would operate were confined to a minimum, until sufficient time had elapsed to enable it to determine the overall appeal of women's cricket, and an elected Committee deputed to expand the early rules as deemed fit.

Mrs. Patrick Heron-Maxwell CBE, an organiser of the Women's Land Army, and first chair of the Women's Institute, was elected to serve as Chairman, and Miss Vera M. Cox CBE, a hockey player and former secretary of the West Kent Land Army, appointed to act as Honorary Joint Secretary and Treasurer, along with a Miss Hatton, about which little is known. A further eight ladies were voted to serve on the Committee, including Mrs. Scott Bowden and Miss K. Doman, which was given the authority to co-opt additional members as deemed necessary.

The first Committee Meeting was held at the Ex-Service Women's Club on the 24 November 1926, when the annual membership subscription for an individual player was initially set at five shillings [25p]. Prospective members were required to be over the age of sixteen, and be officially proposed and seconded by persons approved by the WCA.

To encourage the formation of cricket clubs, the WCA chose to replicate the structure employed by the AEWHA, which had proved so efficient in encouraging the growth of hockey as a women's sport. One year after the formation of the WCA, encouraging signs indicated women's cricket was growing in size and popularity, with the Association reporting it had recruited 347 members, mainly from the South East of England, with 10 affiliated Clubs, 28 schools, 6 colleges and 2 business houses. Forty-nine matches were also organised in its first season, along with the popular annual cricket festival at Stowe Lane in Colwall. Perhaps even more noteworthy was the fact that through its concept and creation, the WCA had delivered a structure and central form of administration which would become the foundation for the future of the women's game.

The WCA became responsible for the organisation of women's cricket throughout England, and through its administrative system resulted in the advancement of women's cricket year on year. Annual reports were published, which included detailed advice in relation to dress code, training and coaching courses, and educational courses for umpires and scorers. Indeed, every effort was made in ensuring women were aware of the laws of the game, and how it was to be played.

The expansion of the WCA was quite significant, and by the start of its second season, ten clubs had become affiliated, and by 1928 membership had swelled to number 21 clubs, 6 colleges and 32 schools. By 1934 the figure had reached 80, and by 1938 climbed to reach 123. At its peak it had accumulated a total of 208 affiliated clubs and 94 school and junior teams.

At the outset, an appropriate form of standardised cricketing attire was not approved by the WCA until a number of suitable designs had been carefully considered. Until such time club players were free to wear what they thought fit, although players chosen to represent the WCA were asked to wear *'tunics of a sort most suitable to the game'*. Eventually an approved WCA dress code was defined which directed teams to play in white or cream, with white hats and knickers. Dresses, or tunics, must not be shorter than *'touching the ground'* when kneeling. And sleeveless dresses and transparent stockings were not allowed. Shoes with spikes or nails were permitted. Nonetheless, the WCA repeatedly experienced insurgence from its more belligerent members, especially in relation to what was considered *'appropriate'* clothing.

In 1936 the Australian born sisters Betty [1905-1981] and Barbara Peden [1907-1984] toppled the specified requirement of wearing stockings along with an inconvenient suspender belt. While Mrs. Alice Heron-Maxwell and Miss Vera Cox were away enjoying a summer holiday, Betty talked club members into turning out wearing knee-high hose, which at the time were considered stockings. On their return Betty later recalled *'the furious elders reacted as if we were ruining the whole image of cricket'*. Marjorie Pollard was also critical of the younger set and their laid-back approach towards the designated clothing, and expressed her frustration and that of a number of other senior members of the WCA, in a publication of *'Women's Cricket'*. Meanwhile, *The Times of India* also ran an article on the uprising claiming, *'the long white stockings forced upon them by the Women's Cricket Association are a thorn in the side of British women players, it seems from heated views I have heard expressed this week. Some women want bare legs. Others want socks, but the Association is sticking to stockings'.*

During the formative years of the WCA there was some resentment expressed towards the development of the women's game, and in a determined attempt to lessen the hostility the WCA actively promoted the women's game as being wholly detached and somewhat different to that of the men's game. In an article written in the 1930s by its founder member, Marjorie Pollard OBE, who firmly asserted, *'We always recognised our limitations, no one tried to bowl too fast. We wanted cricket of our own, we did not want to play cricket like the men. We wanted to play women's cricket.'*

The first WCA representative match was held in 1929 three years after its inauguration, at the Beckenham Cricket Ground, in a game between *'London and District'* and the *'Rest of England'*. A small crowd, which included a selection of scholars from ten local schools, paid an admission fee of sixpence [2 ½ p] to access the ground. The Beckenham Cricket Club generously covered the cost of all other expenses in addition to providing the use of the pitch and facilities free of charge. The match was hailed a success, and resulted in two new clubs affiliating to the WCA. *The Times* confidently reporting the Association as *'carrying on their excellent pioneering'*, and *The Cricketer* asserting, *'if any mere man visited the*

Beckenham ground last week in the expectation of seeing a series of amusing and unpremeditated antics ... he must have been considerably surprised'.

The earliest of the WCA's County Associations were formed by 1931, when County Durham played a combined Cheshire and Lancashire XI, and within the next four years England had been sub-divided into five Regional Associations comprising the East, Midlands, North, South and West.

Two years later the Yorkshire Women's Cricket Federation [YWCF] was approached by the Littleborough Cricket Club. Situated on the border between Yorkshire and Lancashire, the club, which had been formed in 1839, expressed its aspiration to form an affiliated women's team. Recognising the growing appeal of cricket by working-class women in Lancashire, the YWCF helped its neighbouring county create the Lancashire Women's Cricket Federation [LWCF], which progressed to become equally as popular as that of the red-rose County. The establishment of the LWCF eventually led over time to the fiercely competitive county matches between the YWCF and the LWCF for the *'Hannah Drake Trophy'*.

At a general meeting held at the White Hart Hotel in Todmorden, Lancashire, in April 1934, a proposition was tabled and subsequently approved, in that the Yorkshire and Lancashire Women's Cricket Federations combine to form the English Women's Cricket Federation [EWCF]. However, little is documented about the working women who played under the EWCF, since most of the names published in match reports remain untraceable, consequently it has been difficult to establish why such women elected to play cricket. It is said one anonymous player maintained it was the *'done thing'* for women who worked at the mill to play cricket, recalling her auntie and several women *'up her street'* had also played in their youth. And because, *'its good exercise and strenuous, and it is such a thrill to knock up fifty, and if you are a bowler, it is nice to see wickets falling down'*..

Unlike the WCA which had a minimum age requirement of sixteen years before a player could gain affiliation, membership of the EWCF was open to all women who were skilled enough to play, with the majority of the players in their teens and early twenties, and yet there were reports of exceptional players being as young as twelve years old. This was quite a common occurrence in other sports catering for working-class women, such as hockey, netball and women's football, which frequently included players as young as eleven years of age.

Although it was not without its critics, working-class women's cricket never quite experienced the negative attention as women's football. Yet from the outset, J.J. Booth, the President of the Bradford Cricket League expressed his disapproval of women's cricket, remaining unyielding in his opinion that cricket was a man's game, and women playing impeded the men's game. However, he was not opposed to cricket clubs having women's sections. It was his firm opinion that *'those clubs which did well for the men were those which had a fine battalion of women on the grounds providing teas and refreshments and using their sweetness and charm to counteract the possible bad dispositions and bad language of the men'*.

Arguably the acceptance of women's cricket was as likely as not because male cricket clubs had become an important part of working-class life. Wives and girls friends played an important role within the men's clubs by fulfilling what was seen as traditional women's work. They served teas during men's games, washed and mended the kit and cleaned the pavilion. More often than not clubs formed a ladies committee, which assumed responsibility for the social element of the cricket club. They would also raise additional funds for the club, organising events at which the women would serve on stalls selling homemade goods and refreshments which they had produced. The money raised would often be required to help the survival of clubs throughout the closed season.

In the beginning, the WCA took the view that men should not be allowed to become members of the organisation, or hold any position of authority. Insisting the Association should be run by women, for women. However, understandably the WCA remained dependent from time to time upon male assistance, and were quite willing to engage their support where deemed necessary. Primarily when the WCA required help in obtaining the use of suitable grounds on which to hold its matches. The WCA habitually needed men to serve as umpires, since during the early years there was a distinct shortage of the female variety. As a result it was not long before the Committee agreed to modify its rules and recruit men into the organisation, and in 1927 it allowed them admission in honorary positions.

Yet the relationship between the WCA and men was not without controversy. Many men continued with their unyielding disapproval of women's cricket, convinced that the women who engaged in what was traditionally considered a masculine activity, did so because men played it. In the first monthly publication of the WCA's magazine, '*Women's Cricket*', several letters and disparaging comments were submitted and published.

One group of men calling themselves, *'The Shades of the Great Cricketers of the Past'* declared, *'It could not really be true that another field of male activities was to be usurped by the fair sex! Women seriously betaking themselves to the greatest of all British games ? Why it is a sacrilege !'* Another irritable gentleman wrote confirming his personal judgement that, *'Cricket for females is a preposterous idea. I felt sorrow and dismay at the idea that another field of male activities was to be usurped by the fairer sex, cricket is degraded ... let us have this one spot to ourselves ... let us pray women never gain admittance to the Pavilion at Lord's.'*

However, not all the articles printed were of a negative nature, with the *Hull Daily Mail* commenting in an article printed in 1927, *'Cricket is rapidly capturing the enthusiasm of the modern girl and I don't see any reason why they should not make a success of it. Now what is Hull going to do about it ? Surely we are not to be left out. I should like to know if it is anyone's intention to start a cricket club for girls'*. The following year the *Cheltenham Chronicle* maintained *'those who have watched the ladies play on the Victoria Ground, Cheltenham, must have been surprised at the skill with which some of them wielded the willow'*.

In spite of conflicting debate, the WCA continued to blossom throughout the 1930s, alongside New Zealand which in 1928 was the only other nation to have formed a Women's Cricket Association. Although there were no other cricketing governing bodies formally operating at the time, information is available to suggest women were playing cricket in South Africa, India and Holland.

In 1931, as the Association began to feel more secure, a formal constitution was at last affirmed. In which the primary objective was stated as, *'The main purpose of the WCA is to provide an organisation for the furtherance of women's cricket'.* Its Terms of Membership confirmed that, in the first year, prospective members were expected to join individually, either as playing or associate members, with an age limit regulating membership to those over the age of 16. Without wishing to inflict restrictions which might unreasonably limit or restrict membership numbers, it was nevertheless agreed sufficient information be provided with the application in order to confirm the suitability of all applicants. The affiliation fees and terms of membership, which were due on for payment by April 1 were set at:

Associate Members [non-playing]: 10 shillings and 6 pence [52½ p];
Umpires and scorers: 5 shillings [25p];
Playing members: 5 shillings [25p] - entrance fee - 5 shillings [25p];
Members of affiliated clubs and schools: 2 shillings and 6 pence [12½p], no entrance fee;
Life Membership: 5 guineas [£ 5.25p];
Schools, Colleges and Clubs : 5 shillings [25p].

All classes of membership were encouraged to add a little more to their respective subscription if they chose to do so.

Cricket clubs boasting more than 10 members were also allowed to join the WCA for an annual subscription of 4 shillings each [20p].

There was also a proposal made to offer Honorary Life Membership to men upon payment of a fee of 3 guineas [£ 3.15p].

Just prior to the beginning of World War II nineteen counties had formed an Women's Cricket Association, and inter-county matches were taking place on a regular basis. The WCA Committee conceding *'if there was time to spare, there seemed no reason why one county team should not meet in a friendly way a team from a neighbouring county'*. However, the Committee strongly disapproved of the use of the term *'County cricket'* in order to avoid direct comparison with the men's game, and pronounced such matches be labelled *'County Association matches'*. Prior to which the Association's friendly matches had been confined to school and village grounds, but by arranging matches featuring more proficient women cricketers, it was anticipated the profile of women's cricket would be raised. With Pollard claiming, *'It was no good playing games in secret and hoping that new players would be attracted that way'*. Consequently, the public and press were encouraged to attend in order to draw attention to the quality and ability of the players and encourage the creation of more clubs.

Just eight short years after its formation, the WCA embarked on one of the high points in the evolution of women's cricket. In 1934 it received an invitation to send a touring team to Australia, which was eagerly accepted, and the WCA enthusiastically began to plan the first cricketing tour of Australia and New Zealand. The AWCC had generously offered to cover all expenses while the WCA team were guests in Australia, but was unable to meet the cost of travelling expenses. Similarly a cable received from New Zealand stated, *'delighted at prospect of English visit, can guarantee billets, entertainments, matches, but regret no travelling expenses, writing fuller details, trust satisfactory'*. Consequently, the WCA ruled that any player wishing to participate would have to pay their own fare, and in April 1934 a letter was sent to every member of the Association by Miss Vera Cox, informing the potential players would be required to meet their own expenses, and fund the individual costs themselves. Clearly suggesting those playing at this level were, for the most part, wealthy enough to meet the expensive costs of travel.

As a result, the England side selected was under-representative, with some of the better players, who could not afford the estimated cost of £80 for the six-month trip, missing out. Married women were also excluded, as it was considered inappropriate for them to contemplate spending so much time away from home.

Those that were fortunate enough to be able to gather together sufficient funds to meet the considerable expense included a combination of seven school teachers, two secretaries, two art students, a lawyer, an army auxiliary, and two *'ladies of leisure'*. Until 1997, when the WCA merged with the ECB, international players were still required to contribute to tours and blazers.

With an average age of twenty-four, the players selected for the tour came mostly from the South East of England. In preparation the women played a match at Old Trafford, the first time women had used an authentic Test ground. As they prepared to set sail from Tilbury in October on the SS Cathay, the young women viewed the tour as an exciting adventure, and the reserve wicketkeeper, Grace Morgan [1909-1996], who was employed in the Ministry of Heath, kept a diary throughout the tour in which she recorded the thrills and adventures experienced by the cricketing pioneers. Having pledged not to smoke, drink or gamble or *'be accompanied by a man'*, the players and officials made their own fun throughout the voyage, playing deck cricket and table tennis against the officers, and posing for photographs.

However, the women's game was still battling to be taken seriously, as to a lesser extent it still does today, with the ground-breaking tour failing to meet with widespread approval. *The Times* was acutely ungracious, commenting *'It does not seem nice to think that they are future mothers charged with the responsibility of setting an example of gentleness, refinement and restraint to the coming generation'.*

The newspaper wasn't the only cynic, and it was only retrospectively the women were acknowledged as pioneers. And it took a woman wielding a bat, the indubitable Molly Hide, to change opinion. *Wisden* recognising and acknowledging, *'her batting had a strength as well as a style that astonished sceptical male spectators, many of whom in her era thought women's cricket was like a dog on its hind legs'.*

Even though provincial cricket in Australia had been established for several years, it was still in its infancy on a national scale. Similarly, the game of cricket had been played in New Zealand for almost half-a-century, ever since eleven Marahua girls challenged eleven Riwaka girls to a match *'any time they like. Dinner and dance provided.'* It was clear to those fortunate enough to have made the trip, the AWCC had devoted an immense amount of time organising a generous and entertaining tour for the English women. And the fun did not stop when the English girls reached Australia. During the tea interval in the town of Deniliquin, in the Riverina region of New South Wales, close to the border with Victoria, the girls were amused by a display of boomerang throwing and singing by the aboriginals, who presented the tourists with boomerangs and flowers made from feathers. And Betty Green recalled, *'the greatest fun of all was the kangaroo hunting. We chased them in motor-cars over rough country, and it was rather like speed boating, only with more bumps'.*

Although England was under strength they were by far the strongest of the trio of nations competing. Centuries were hard won, as there were no boundaries, and players had to run for all the runs scored.

Following the first Test, held on the 28- 31 December, at the Exhibition Ground in Brisbane the England captain Betty Archdale observed that an England victory, *'brought victory but no blaze of glory, for nerves and spin combined to make the cricket on both sides less good than it might have been.'* Australia was dismissed for 47, with England's Myrtle Maclagan, collecting 7 wickets for 10 runs.

Venue:	Exhibition Ground, Brisbane, Australia - 28-31 December, 1934	
Umpires:	F.J. Bartlett [Australia] & J.A. Scott [Australia]	
Result:	England won by 9 wickets	
First Innings:	Australia 47	England 154
Batting:	K.M. Smith 25	M.E. Maclagan 72
Bowling:	M.E. Maclagan 7 for 10	A. Palmer 7 for 18
Second Innings:	Australia 138	England 34 for 1
Batting:	E.M. Shevill 63	E.A. Snowball 18
Bowling:	M.F. Spear 5 for 15	P. Antonio 1 for 20

Betty Archdale

Helen Elizabeth 'Betty' Archdale captained the English Women's cricket team in 1934-1935, and led the first English women's team to tour Australia and New Zealand. The tour did much to raise the status of women's cricket and repair some of the damage done to Anglo-Australian cricket relations following the bodyline tactic, or fast, leg-bowling theory devised and employed by the English cricket team in the 1932–33 Ashes tour of Australia. Perceived by many as being overly aggressive, and even unfair, the method ultimately threatened diplomatic relations between the two countries, before the situation was eventually calmed with the assistance of the ladies in 1934-1935. Born in London, Betty was the daughter of Helen Alexander Archdale [née Russel] [1876–1949], a journalist, leading British feminist and a suffragette, who was imprisoned for smashing windows at Whitehall.

England won the second Test held at the Sydney Cricket Ground, Sydney, on the 4-8 January1935, which included a duck for the Australian batsman Essie Mabel Shevill [1908-1989] after enduring a gruelling 47 minutes at the crease. England's response included another first for Myrtle Maclagan. Having already taken the first wicket in a women's Test match, she followed that by crafting the first Test century notching up a total of 119 runs in an opening 149-run stand with the renowned Betty Snowball.

Venue:	Sydney Cricket Ground, Sydney, Australia – 4-8 January, 1935	
Umpires:	Puffet [Australia] & Simpkins [Australia]	
Result:	England won by 8 wickets	
First Innings:	Australia 162	England 301 for 5 dec.
Batting:	K.M. Smith 47	M.E. Maclagan 119
Bowling:	M.E. Maclagan 4 for 33	K.M. Smith 3 for 42
Second Innings:	Australia 148	England 34 for 1
Batting:	E.M. Shevill 36 not out	E.A. Snowball 4 not out
Bowling:	J.E. Partridge 6 for 96	E.A. Shevill 1 for 2

The third Test, in Melbourne was held at the Melbourne Cricket ground on the 18-20 January, 1935, and resulted in a draw. England won the toss and elected to bat first with Maclagan contributing 50 runs.

Venue:	Melbourne Cricket Ground, Australia - 8-20 January, 1935	
Umpires:	H.E. Nichols [Australia] & W.R. Wettenhall [Australia]	
Result:	Match drawn	
First Innings:	Australia 150	England 162
Batting:	A. Palmer 39	M.E. Maclagan 50
Bowling:	M.F. Spear 3 for 21	P. Antonio 6 for 49
Second Innings:	Australia 104 for 8	England 153 for 7 dec,
Batting:	J.P. Brewer 31	E.A. Snowball 83 not out
Bowling:	M.E. Maclagan 4 for 28	A. Palmer 3 for 17

The tour did a great deal to assist the development of women's cricket in Australia, greatly enhancing the acceptability and respectability of the women's game in the eyes of the public and the press. At the farewell dinner given by the Victorian WCA at the close of the tour, the English women were congratulated and informed their *'visit has been thoroughly appreciated and has helped Australia women's cricket considerably'*. The teams had demonstrated cricket was a sport suitable for women. And the players were well aware their performance and behaviour, both on and off the field of play, would be subjected to close scrutiny, and would be of crucial importance for the future reputation of women's cricket.

The day after the third and final test in Australia, the English side set sail from Melbourne for New Zealand aboard the trans-Tasman passenger liner Waganella, eagerly anticipating the opening Test to be played at Lancaster Park in Christchurch. It was the only Test match played between England and New Zealand on the tour, and it soon became evident the English side was vastly more experienced than the *'White Ferns'*. Although scheduled as a three-day match, it was memorably forgettable for the host's first showing in a Test match, and soon clear the match would not last the course.

New Zealand won the toss and elected to bat, but were skittled out for a first innings total of 44 runs within 30 overs. England declared on 503 for 5, with the batting honours going to Betty Snowball, who set a new Test match record with her score of 189 runs, knocked up in 222 minutes. New Zealand's attack lacked penetration and Molly Hide also added an impressive century. New Zealand could only add a meagre 122 runs in its second visit to the crease, and England romped home by an innings and 337 runs. Despite the result, the English team's visit was invaluable in helping further the development of the women's game in New Zealand.

Venue:	Lancaster Park, Christchurch - 16-18 February, 1935
Umpires:	R. Coleman [New Zealand] & J. McGuinness [New Zealand]
Result:	England won by an innings and 337 runs

First Innings:	New Zealand 44	England 503 for 5 dec.
Batting:	M. Hollis 24	E.A. Snowball 189
Bowling:	M.MacLagan 5 for 22	R.E. Symons 2 for 71
Second Innings:	New Zealand 122	
Batting:	M.C. Bishop 27	
Bowling:	J.E. Partridge 4 for 60	

The overall schedule for the inaugural tour of Australia and New Zealand was made up of a total of fourteen matches, which included three Test matches against Australia, and one against New Zealand, resulting in three victories for England and one drawn game. The *'mythical women's ashes'* against Australia were easily won by the superior England side. Although not at its strongest, it plainly exposed weaknesses in the Australian Women's Cricket Council [AWCC] side, undoubtedly due to its relatively recent formation only four years earlier in 1931. In recent years the Women's Ashes has been decided by one Test match which, according to some, is considered a backward step for the women's game.

Despite the ensuing euphoria generated by the women's cricketing tour to Australia and New Zealand, considerable hostility was caused within the WCA. For although the invitation to tour Australia initially received an enthusiastic welcome,, and was notionally open to all its members, all but an elite few were not able to come close to affording to meet the cost of the tour. In reality only those members who were in a position to raise price of the return fare, and leave their home, or jobs for six months, were able to apply to the Selection Committee for a place on the tour. Consequently, the financial costs proved problematical for all but the wealthiest individuals, and suggestions were made that the Committee had shown bias towards its wealthier members. One member, D. Macpherson alleged the travel expenses alone were the equivalent of forty-three weeks of her salary, and

Miss E. M. Child, chose to resign from her job at Queen Ethelburga's School in Yorkshire in order to attend the tour as they wouldn't sanction the time off. To add insult to injury, those individuals who demonstrated they could afford both the cost of travel, and take time away from work to participate in the tour, were called upon to face the Selection Committee, which shamelessly selected players based primarily on their social suitability, rather than cricketing ability. A good many members of the WCA had little awareness of what constituted an average wage at the time. With Betty Archdale, the England women's captain recording, *'As regards personal finance, some of us arrived home penniless. But when one thinks of the many thousands of miles we travelled for the official round-the-world fare of £ 91.8 shillings, it is surely a sound investment. Naturally we have had to pay a good deal in tips, current expenses, presents, side trips in New Zealand, and above all photography, which raised the bills ... without exception we were all students or in jobs ... we were nice people, with nice manners, but had no money at all'.*

The decision to select Betty Archdale as the England captain was not at all well received within the general membership of the WCA. The strength of feeling was the honour should have been awarded to Molly Hide, a far superior player and an experienced captain. Archdale conceded her appointment as captain was not based upon her experience or cricketing ability, but that her law degree would be beneficial when called upon to prepare and deliver speeches. *Women's Cricket* recorded *'Archdale has been chosen captain. She is an experienced and travelled person. Sane, sensible, level headed and broad minded. A good bat, a willing field and an enthusiast'.*

Despite the rather late formation of the Australian National Governing Body, there is evidence to suggest women's cricket was being played *'down-under'* as early as 1855, when a small number of convicts were still being deported to Western Australia from England. Between the years 1788–1868 a total of around 164,000 convicted criminals were transported to the Australian colonies on board 806 convict ships. Australia was transformed economically, politically and demographically following the discovery of gold in New South Wales in 1851, and the newly formed colony of Victoria. For the duration of that decade *'gold rushes'* followed hard on the heels of a worldwide economic depression, during which about two per cent of the population of Britain and Ireland emigrated to New South Wales and Victoria.

Throughout the 1934-1935 series of matches played in Australia and New Zealand, England enjoyed playing its Test matches on such prominent grounds as Brisbane, Sydney and Melbourne, something which it had struggled to accomplish back home. Suggesting the acceptance and support for women's cricket, perhaps supplemented by candid male support, may have been more forthcoming in Australia than in the United Kingdom. As a result the WCA were encouraged to become increasingly critical of the opportunities and facilities offered to women's cricket in England. Despite its persistence, women were not allowed to play matches at Lord's until 1976. In fact, the MCC remains infamous for its practice of excluding female members until 1998. Epitomising just how much the male sex continued to dominate cricketing structures in the United Kingdom for so long.

The visit to Australia by the England women's team had undoubtedly been a tremendous success for the host nation. Keen to replicate the benefits the visitors had enjoyed, and before the English side had set sail on its return voyage home from New Zealand, the WCA delivered an invitation to host an AWCC representative side during the summer of 1937. A wounded Australian team paid a visit to England to play a return series of matches two years later. Stronger and fitter, the sixteen members of the WCAA side arrived in England in May 1937, accompanied by their manager Mrs. Olive Peatfield, who immediately proceeded to parade her squad of players up and down the country, out-playing the English county sides at will. Setting the tone for the challenges the England team had yet to face. The average age of the players was twenty-two, and when asked how they preferred to be addressed, they insisted they should be referred to as *'girl cricketers'*, rather than *'women cricketers'*. Husbands and friends were not allowed to travel with the players, all forms of alcoholic drink, smoking, and gambling were strictly forbidden, and players were required to be tucked up in bed by 10 p.m. On the long and tiresome crossing team members were required to take part in physical drills on deck every day at 7.15 in the morning ... except on Sunday. Although the reason for the decision remains unclear, players were not allowed to write articles on the subject of cricket. Perhaps the reason being it is implied they were encouraged to focus solely on playing the game, and avoid the possibility of any negative publicity. Suggesting that, even though the amateur spirit of the game prevailed and some concern was shown for female propriety, such sporting excursions were becoming much more structured and organised in a professional manner. The majority of the Australian team were working-class women, drawn from a wide variety of occupations, ranging from architect to a cardboard box machinist. Most of which experienced severe difficulty in raising the money to meet the cost of the tour, which included the sum of £75 for fares, and in the region of an additional £50 towards the cost of clothing, equipment and pocket money. However, the WCAA did make a contribution of £300 to help players meet the travel costs, which it had raised through the 1934-1935 tour. School teacher, Sue Summers, along with the help of her family, was only able to raise £30 towards the sum required. Yet when the former international Australian bowler Arthur Alfred Mailey [1886-1967] heard of her plight, he set about recruiting the help of other first class cricketers and arranged a benefit match against a South Australian women's cricket XI at the Unley Oval, and Sue's travelling expenses was raised in full. Various friends and organisations helped supply the funding required for clothing and other incidental expenses. Peggy Antonio, whose fearsome spin bowling had tested the English side in 1934-1935 Test series, also received external help to fund her tour, with a director of the Victorian Stevedoring Company generously contributing £75 as a gesture of respect for Peggy's late father, a former employee of the business.

A motor coach was chartered for the use of the *'Southern Stars'* throughout the entire tour, during which the social aspect was not over-looked. A full social calendar was arranged, which included a visit to Warwick Castle, the 12 century Cistercian monastery Fountains Abbey in North Yorkshire, Lake Windermere, Oxford, the coronation ceremony of George VI and Elizabeth Bowes-Lyon [1900-2002] at Westminster Abbey, and tea at 10 Downing Street with the Prime Minister's wife, Lucy Baldwin, the notable ex-cricketer and member of the legendary White Heather Club.

In the series of Tests that followed the English team faced a vastly improved Australian side which, following the defeats suffered during the 1934-1935 tour, had clearly devoted a great deal of time honing its game. Prompting the English captain, Molly Hide, to observe, *'the Australians showed evident signs of intensive coaching and practice backed up by tremendous keenness and enthusiasm, the result of this was the Australians took a much shorter time to reach the same standard as English women'.*

Subsequent press reports compared the strength of the Australian team with that of the English team, observing *'we may have been able to teach the Australians something in 1934-1935 they are now repaying us, plus a thumping interest'.* Some correspondents reported that they had expected to be *'bored',* or find *the 'play substandard',* but were agreeably surprised. *The Times* conceded, *'these matches have drawn attention to the extent to which cricket has become a woman's game and have given a final answer to those who had, in their inexperience, supposed that women were incapable of playing a game that, until a few years ago, was man's universal province'.* The innovative cricket writer Sir John Frederick Neville Cardus CBE [1988-1975] was also explicit about the women's game, when he concluded, *'their play must have convinced the most stubborn die-hards that women cricketers can be as skilful and as natural as tennis or hockey players'.*

The discipline and self-awareness demonstrated by the Australian team in preparation for the tour was self-evident, and a similar approach was subsequently taken by the officials of the WCA. Which demonstrated a keenness to organise the women's game along similar lines to that of the men's game, emphasising the value and importance of amateur status, playing fairly, and exhibiting courteous and *'gentlemanly'* conduct. In all probability such values had no doubt been used throughout sport to distinguish upper and middle-class awareness from those of the working-class. Besides which, women who were already engaging in what were usually considered typically male sporting activities, were thought to be challenging Victorian standards of femininity, and did not wish to be seen as further disturbing the gender order.

For the 1934-1935 series it was resolved the home side accept the responsibility of providing the umpires for the matches, as such the responsibility fell to the Australians, the outcome being that all the matches were umpired by men. The decision set the pattern for all subsequent tours abroad, when the umpires were always men. Conversely, when the Australian women's team made a visit to the United Kingdom for the first home tour, by contrast the umpires selected were all women, including M. Bryant, K. Doman, P. Drake, F. Hardcastle and C.A. Partridge. An umpiring tradition which, for women's home Tests, and later One Day Internationals, would continue until 1996.

It is not clear how the early umpires learned their trade, since there were no formal qualifications available at the time. It wasn't until 1953 that the Association of Cricket Umpires was founded, which would later add the suffix *'and Scorers'* to its title [ACU&S]. The primary objective of the ACU&S primary was to raise the standard of umpiring, for the most part at club level, by improved methods of training and examination. Initially there were only a small number of members, but the Association grew rapidly, and by the end of the decade the names of a number of women began to appear amongst its list of members. The first woman to qualify was Doris

Mildred Coysh [née Turner] [1908-1986], who played in all four of the Test matches played on the WCA's first tour of Australia and New Zealand in 1934-35. She became the first female cricket umpire in 1959, later progressing to umpire two women's Test matches. Her first in 1963 was the second Test between England and Australia, and her second the third Test between England and New Zealand in 1966. Other women umpires quickly followed, including Netta Rheinberg MBE. Although Netta only played in one Test match for the England Women's team, she was a prominent figure within the women's game as an administrator and journalist. The celebrated former England captain, Rachael Heyhoe-Flint, said of Netta's role as an administrator, *'Netta was an action girl. We had very few people then, and she galvanised activity, partly just by having a great personality and a sense of humour.'* Shortly after her death in 2006 at the age of 94, the award-winning sports journalist and leading cricket writer, Rob Steen, put on record that, *'For a north London Jew, playing cricket for England and being one of the game's most important administrators is about as well-trodden a career path as prime minister or bacon-buttie salesman. That Rheinberg happened to be a woman made her accomplishments all the more admirable'.*

The ACU&S established a sub-committee responsible for:

1: Maintaining the Registers:

Which involved collecting, and assessing, the recommendations made by the cricketing counties, and gathering together the comments and observations of players.

In 1965 the ACU&S divided the now comprehensive list of qualified umpires into two categories A and B. To be included on the A list of umpires, a person had to be recommended by the relevant regional association, and be willing to travel to regional matches, which could on occasions prove extensive. By the World Cup year of 1973, there were 14 on the A list, of which only 10 were fully qualified. On the B list there were 6, with only one suitably qualified. With a further 35 names listed in a register of scorers.

Although the ACU&S operated in all the major cricketing countries throughout the world, in 1973 it was revealed that apart from England, Ireland was the only other country that included a number of suitably qualified women umpires.

Until Jack Hayward, encouraged by Rachael Heyhoe-Flint, generously dug deep into his amply filled pockets to sponsor the 1973 World Cup, umpires and scorers could not even claim expenses, let alone receive any remuneration. Not only did they have to meet all their personal travel costs, they were frequently called upon to find, and pay for their accommodation, as well as stumping up for their meals and refreshments when on duty, which more often than not seemed to be the case when officiating at the most important matches. Umpiring a Test match could be an expensive business ! What is more, the players were in the same boat ! As sponsorship gradually became more readily available, some funding was made available to assist players and officials meet their costs, although it was rarely the full amount. And yet, even then there were those who elected to waive all or part of what they were offered.

2: To appoint umpires and scorers to preside over high-level matches:

These included matches held in each of the five designated regions of the country, namely the North, South, East, West and the Midlands. And in addition all national tournaments and competitions, along with Test matches when there was a home tour. As national competitions began to increase in number, there was a corresponding increase in the need for umpires and scorers, which from time to time was provided by additional help from committed locals. As recompense for these dependable volunteers, they were rewarded with the opportunity to stand alongside one of the fully qualified women umpires, who would in turn be required to provide commentary on their field performance, an essential requirement on route to the final stage of qualification.

3: To write the Rules for matches:

Both home and away national tours had to be negotiated and agreed between the two participating countries, and an appropriate set of rules established. This was not always as straight forward as might be imagined. For a home tour, a sub-Committee of the ACU&S would generally organise a one day pre-tour conference for umpires and scorers. When an agreement on the rules had been reached, separate guidance notes would be written and distributed amongst match organisers, captains, umpires and scorers. Such notes might include an explanation of how to manage an intricate system which may need to be implemented. For example, should, the number of overs be reduced due to excessive rain.

Although umpiring and scoring has on the whole been considered satisfactory at the highest levels of the game, the standard at lower levels has been inconsistent. With only the well established clubs able to boast a qualified, or part qualified member, willing to perform official duties at their matches. Although for a period of several years, one West London club enjoyed the luxury of having three fully qualified women umpires, most women's teams had to compete for the service from a completely inadequate stock of umpires available for non-professional cricket. Only the highest divisions of the leagues had *'proper'* umpires. On the other hand, the ostensibly less demanding role of scoring was nearly always competent.

In 1954, the concept of forming an organisation to deal with international women's cricketing matters was first contemplated by one of the founder members of the WCA. Subsequently a special committee was formed to assume responsibility for preliminary preparations, and making an opening approach to countries which had expressed initial interest. It was suggested the purpose of the organisation should be to:

- further cricket among women and girls at international level;
- promote international tours;
- provide a liaison between countries between tours;
- legislate on problems which could not be mutually resolved

In January 1956, upon the completion of all the necessary preparatory work, a draft Constitution and Rules were drawn up and despatched to the national governing bodies of the countries which had expressed initial interest for their further consideration.Two years later, in February 1958, the WCA attended an inaugural meeting held at the Victoria Cricket Association House in Melbourne, Australia, with all the countries which had expressed interest in the original concept in attendance. After due consideration, the draft Constitution was approved and adopted, and the International Women's Cricket Council [IWCC] came into being. With the following officers proposed and duly elected, President, Miss E.W. Stevenson [England]; Vice-President, Miss M. Robinson,[South Africa], and Honorary Secretary, Miss N.P. Whitehorn [England]. The founding members of the IWCC included the five cricketing nations of Australia, England, the Netherlands, New Zealand, and South Africa, later to include the nations of India, Denmark, and several of the West Indian islands.

The first meeting of the Council was held the following day, when it was agreed that in order to provide a communicative link between meetings a newsletter would be published and circulated to all the participating nations at six monthly intervals. The first newsletter was issued a year later, but due to a lack of items of interest, the publication was quickly abandoned.

After a period of 26 years, the WCA surrendered the organisation and running of women's cricket in England to the England and Wales Cricket Board [EWCB] in 1998. And following the eighth Women's World Cup in 2005, the IWCC was formally incorporated within the International Cricket Council [ICC], and an ICC Women's Cricket Committee formed to consider all matters concerning women's cricket. In total the IWCC held a series of 18 meetings throughout the 47 year period since its formation, it's final meeting was convened in April, 2005, in Pretoria South Africa, where at a Special General Meeting the dissolution of the IWCC was unanimously approved, and its subsequent merger with the global governing body for cricket the International Cricket Council [ICC] agreed. Nominations for the ICC Women's Committee were also agreed, and under the Chairman; Betty Timmer [The Netherlands]; also included Africa-Joan Edwards [South Africa]; the Americas-Ann Browne John, [West Indies]; Asia-Shubhangi

Kulkarni [India]; Europe-Gill McConway [England]; East Asia Pacific-Catherine Campbell [Australia]; and a co-opted member: Belinda Clark [Australia].

England's first delegate to sit on the ICC Women's Committee, was Gillian Elizabeth McConway. Born in New Zealand in 1950, Gillian was a slow left-arm orthodox bowler, who turned out for England in 14 Test matches, and 23 Women's One Day Internationals.

The ninth Women's World Cup was the first to be convened under the full support of the ICC, and was hosted by Australia in March 2009. Eight teams competed over 50 overs, including Australia, England, India, New Zealand, Pakistan, South Africa, Sri Lanka and the West Indies. With England's Women becoming the first English cricket team of either sex to win an ICC competition.

Conscientious administration, together with thoughtful consideration for detail, is essential in ensuring the success of any organisation. And these were the foundation of the accomplishments of those early pioneers of the WCA, in order to successfully overcome the countless issues it faced relating to the development and improvement of the sport to which they were so passionately devoted. Without the complex structure of organisational levels created and monitored so efficiently by the WCA, covering every aspect of the game, both on and off the pitch, the development of women's cricket in England would have undoubtedly been seriously prejudiced.

Chapter 10

Integration

From its inception the aim of the WCA was to establish an autonomous organisation, run by women for the benefit of women. It's prime objective being to seek to improve the opportunities and facilities available for girls and women who previously had little prospect of continuing to play cricket after leaving school. In so doing, its members remained acutely aware of the risk of being too outspoken, and of the intrinsic danger of being seen as contesting the supremacy of men's cricket. Tension, for the most part created by long-standing male tradition, regarding the development of the women's game, threatened to hinder the expansion of the WCA. Perhaps justifiably leading the WCA to become concerned it might result in the loss of essential male support and co-operation. Consequently, it was hardly surprising that in 1927 it was proposed and adopted that men be offered the opportunity to take up Honorary Life Membership of the WCA although they were not allowed a vote until 66 years later in 1993.

Despite the international success of the England women's cricket team, women's involvement was by and large still marginalised, with the media choosing to focus its attention primarily on men's competitions. With the enduring notion cricket was essentially a *'man's sport'*, coupled with a deficiency of adequate press coverage of the women's game, it is hardly surprising the women's game has struggled to become truly acknowledged within the world of cricket, continuing to remain *'a pebble firmly lodged in the cricketing shoe'* of women.

For the most part historical reports are inclined to record the early struggles women experienced during Victorian times, while the significance and global development of the women's game in the early 20 century is fitting of closer examination, including the effects of the merging of the WCA with the ECB in 1998.

Marjorie Pollard OBE was one of the founder members of the WCA. A prolific writer her candid comments published in the WCA journals of 1976 were well-known for her observations on social class and gender, and the adverse impact they had upon the participation of women in cricket. *'We stuck to the simple principles,'* she observed. *'Strict order and decorum. No official cricket with, or against, men. And no official games on Sunday'*. Pollard insisted it was imperative women should not offend the male cricketing fraternity. Stressing women's cricket, to a large extent, very much depended upon *'the good faith and support of men'*, particularly if they wanted to continue to use their cricketing facilities.

It was self-evident masculine dominance, coupled with the much sounder financial support structure it enjoyed, required women to repeatedly rely upon male backing. Despite the on-going development of the women's game, it would remain influenced for some time by male supremacy, both on and off the pitch. It was commonplace at the time for forceful views to be expressed questioning the role of women in society. In particular their physicality, since they were still generally regarded as being the *'weaker sex'*.

Former England International and Chair of the WCA, Catherine 'Cathy' Mary Mowat [b.1952] observed women's cricket as being *'either staying static or holding its own, depending on how you look at it'*. For in spite of the glittering years the women's game had enjoyed in the 1970s under the captaincy of Rachael Heyhoe-Flint, cricket remained almost non-existent as a sporting activity in girls' schools, and even struggled to maintain a place on the sporting curriculum in a considerable number of boys' schools. Even though the National Cricket Association provided the services of qualified coaches, and the Lord's Taverners generously made some funding available, the women's game suffered a quieter period. During which women's clubs were called upon to inspire and tutor their own junior sections in the rudiments of the game.

More often than not players were still required to meet the cost of the expenses they incurred, even when representing their country in international matches. Women umpires, even when officiating at first-class matches, were also required to serve without financial recompense. As John Featherstone [1939-1998], the cricket enthusiast and editor of the Yorkshire club newspaper the *'White Rose'* reasoned, *'Playing at international level means finding money for flights, clothing and equipment, perhaps taking unpaid leave of absence, or even giving up one's job. However, the cricketers are all amateurs, playing for the love of the game and the pleasure they gain from it. Long may it continue'*. A former secretary of the Council of Cricket, and also the WCA, Featherstone died from a heart attack aged 59 on his way to a football match.

Throughout the years women's cricket has frequently been in need of institutional help, with young women who represented the universities of Oxford and Cambridge at cricket, subsequently awarded with half-Blues as a consequence, sadly regarded by some as being a reward for determination rather than dexterity. Be that as it may, Cyril Coote BEM, [1910-1990], regarded as one of the most widely respected groundsmen in the Country, and responsible for the perfection of the famous wicket at Fenner's from 1935 to 1980, willingly let the Cambridge women play there when he was asked. In spite of an old soccer injury which left him lame, the incomparable Coote was much more than a groundsman, he served as mentor, counsellor and friend to all Cambridge undergraduates who sought to dip into the innermost depths of his cricketing knowledge. The charitable Coote thoroughly understood all the stages of pitch preparation, and was entirely convinced no young cricketer could be expected to develop into a first-class player unless they were given the chance to play shots on a surface which had both pace and a reasonable bounce. He died at the wheel of his car in Cottenham, a dormitory village about five miles north of the city of Cambridge, in January 1990, aged 80.

Women have been allowed the use of the nets at Lord's since 1976, when Rachael Heyhoe- Flint successfully convinced the MCC it should allow women cricketers to tread its hallowed turf. Since then the WCA's relationship with the MCC has remained fundamentally cordial, and nowadays the England women's team are allowed the use of its pitch for Test matches.

Several bright career women now occupy senior administrative positions within the game, although initially their elevation to the upper ranks of first-class cricket provoked some male misgiving. By way of example, Lisa Pursehouse MBE [born 1969], remains a driving force at the Trent Bridge ground since joining Nottinghamshire as its Sales and Marketing Manager in 2000, following a short spell working with the Yorkshire County Cricket Club. Lisa was promoted to the position of Chief Executive of the Nottinghamshire County Cricket Club in April, 2012. And upon her appointment Lisa remarked, *'This role is the greatest honour and the biggest challenge that I have ever faced but I have a clear vision and I am relishing the road ahead.'* She was awarded an MBE for her services to Sports, Charity Engagement and Community Development in the Queen's Birthday Honours List of 2017.

In 1985 a simple ten-year study was initiated by an English county club, which explored the incidence, nature, and site of acute sports injuries sustained by professional cricketers. Prior to which there had been a scarcity of evidenced based research. A sample of injuries sustained by 54 cricketers who had played in the first team in any, or all, of the seasons in that decade, which resulted in the player needing to seek medical attention were investigated. With injury defined as being the onset of pain, or a disability resulting from either training or playing cricket. It was discovered that an acute injury rate of just over 57 injuries per 1000 days of cricket played occurred. Most injuries were sustained during April, the month in which the least number of days of play took place. The lower limb was found to be the region most vulnerable to injury, accounting for 45% of all injuries, followed by the upper limb recorded as being 29%, the trunk 20%, and the head and neck 6%.

The conclusion reached was that there was a need to develop a national cricketing injury database in order to assist in predicting and reducing injury at all levels of the game. No doubt influenced by the findings of such research numerous clubs began to engage the support of physiotherapists in an attempt to combat sports injuries, a vast number of which were skilled women physiotherapists, sourced from a plentiful supply of female physiotherapy students. The Nottinghamshire County Cricket Club is particularly well accustomed to the use of female physios, having profited from the use of them from as far back as 1975, with Sheila Ball MCSP formally appointed as the club physiotherapist ten years later in 1985. In spite of running into early problems gaining access to the Lord's Pavilion with her team for the 1985 NatWest final, Sheila remains well regarded, for her exceptional work.

Diana Fram Edulji [born 1956], a former captain of the Indian Women's Test team, was similarly outraged when she was barred from entering the pavilion at Lord's when the Indian men's team were playing England in the summer of 1986, at the same time as the Indian Women's Test team was touring England. *'I was shocked at the male chauvinism which has survived,'* she remarked angrily. *'I had to sit in the Tavern stand. The MCC should change their name to MCP [sic. male chauvinist pigs]'.* Said to be the greatest Indian woman cricketer of all time, Diana was born in Mumbai, formerly known as Bombay, and was drawn to sport at an early age. She played basketball and table tennis as a junior at national level, and grew up playing cricket with a tennis ball in the railway colony near to where she lived. Despite losing her four front teeth when playing cricket, she eventually settled and devoted the rest of her sporting life to the game. Diana progressed to join and represent the Railways CC, before later being elevated to the Indian Women's national cricket team as a lucrative orthodox slow left-arm bowler. She played her first series in 1975, and made her Test debut the following year against the West Indies women at the Chinnaswarmy Stadium, Bengaluru, bowling a total of 39 overs, including 6 maidens, collecting 3 wickets in all at a cost of 96 runs. Three years later Diana was made captain of the Indian Women's team. *'Cricket is extremely popular in India'*, Edulji revealed, *'where it is widely played'*. When a Young England side toured there in 1980-81, major matches were attended in some centres by crowds of upwards of 20,000 to 25,000. In 1983 Diana was awarded India's greatest sports honour, the *Arjuna Award*, for her outstanding achievement in a national sport. And in 2002 the Government of India awarded her, the *Padma Shri* award, one of the highest of India's civilian honours. Announced annually on Republic Day it is conferred upon citizens of India in recognition of their distinguished contribution in various spheres of activity, including sports.

Another keen and prominent follower of Indian women's cricket was Mrs. Indira Priyadarshini Gandhi, [née Nehru] [1917-1984], who served India as its Prime Minister for three consecutive full terms, and from 1980 in a fourth term in office until her assassination in 1984.

By and large antipodeans are recognised for their sporting fortitude. Especially those who waged a hard-fought campaign seeking the acceptance of women's cricket throughout Australia since the launch of its first women's cricket league in 1894. It was considered a great achievement when the celebrated spin bowler, Peggy Antonio, was nicknamed the *'Girl Grimmett'* by the Australian press after capturing 6 English wickets for 49 runs in the third Test at Melbourne in 1934-35. Her emphatic achievement subsequently inspired Sir Neville Cardus CBE, a self-educated writer and one of the foremost critics of his generation to pose the question *'Suppose one day the greatest slow left-handed bowler in England is discovered to be a woman, will any male selection committee at Lord's send her an invitation?'* Born and raised in a working class suburb of Melbourne, Peggy's father was a Chilean docker of French and Spanish descent who died when she was just 15 months old. As a young girl she learnt her cricket playing alongside the boys in her neighbourhood streets, before finding work in a shoe factory in the industrial suburb of Collingwood. The factory fielded a women's cricket team and the young Peggy soon drew the attention of Eddie Conlon, a club cricketer with an encyclopaedic knowledge of the game. With Conlon's help, Peggy developed a rare mix of leg spin and off spin, including a top spinner and a *'wrong'un'*. At the tender age of 17 Peggy was selected to represent Australia in the inaugural women's Test match against England at the Brisbane Exhibition Ground in 1934. Although she was out for a *'duck'* in her first visit to the crease in a Test match, caught Joy Evelyn Partridge [1899-1947] off the bowling of Mary Isabella Taylor [1912-1989], she became the first Australian to take a wicket in women's Test cricket, dismissing Betty Snowball for 15, caught by Essie Mabel Shevill. She was invited to tour England in 1937, but the £75.00 fare required to meet the cost of the passage was far beyond the means of a shoe factory worker. However, thanks to the benevolence of a local businessman, a former acquaintance of her late father, a campaign was launched to raise the necessary funds to allow the *'Girl Grimmett'* to take her place in the Australian squad.

Clarence Victor Grimmett [1891-1980] was a profound influence on the young Peggy Antonio, as it did on thousands of devotees of cricket who were fortunate to see him play. Born in New Zealand, a sign-writer by trade, Grimmett was quite simply a cricketing legend. Bowling to a marked area in his backyard, helped by his faithful fox terrier which he trained to retrieve the ball, he made himself as accurate as a machine. Never once believing he knew it all, he mastered all the many variations of spin bowling. Wonderfully accurate he was endowed with a physical co-ordination not even the most infinite practice could be developed to reach his international class. His unprecedented skill and temperament secured him a permanent place in Australian cricket history. It is said he was only once taken by surprise when his captain Monty Noble [1873-1940] remarked, *'Do you think you're the only one playing in this game ?'* When Clarrie enquired how he had come to cause offence, Noble responded, *'Don't you know there is a bowler on at the other end ?' 'Yes,'* said Clarrie, *'but what's that to do with me? '* Only to be informed the fast bowler at the other end hardly had time to put his sweater on before he had to take it off again. Grimmett was taking just one-and-a-half-minutes to bowl a six-ball over ! Dutifully rebuked, the little man was instructed to walk back more slowly to his mark.

Now long since retired, Rose Fitzgibbon was also a dominant force in the development of women's influence in English first-class cricket. She was made Assistant Secretary at Old Trafford in 1978, after beginning her career there as the Principal Private Secretary. She would later become the Cricket Secretary, one of her duties being to *'deputise for the chief executive'*. It took some time before the resolute Rose was wholly accepted by everyone at the club during her term in office, with many said to have declared she ran the Lancashire CCC. Nevertheless, in common with many other women, even after 40 years of service in cricket administration, it is said she felt she did not receive the recognition her contribution truly deserved.

In common with members of so many notable cricket clubs, the Lancashire Club members were traditionally thought a conservative bunch. And it was not until its Annual General Meeting in December 1989, that it was proposed the Club admit women to full membership. During the heated discussion which followed, one enraged member threatened to alter his will if women were admitted to membership. Whereas the author and Methodist Minister, the Reverend Malcolm G. Lorimer, expressed his support for *'the preservation of tradition were it worth preserving'*, but *'if the Church of England could move towards women Priests, and Eastern Europe could make such changes as had been seen in recent weeks, then Lancashire CCC could also change'*. The debate eventually progressed to earn the Club a brief period of dubious repute, when one of its members, Mr. Keith Hull, otherwise known as Stephanie Lloyd, informed the meeting that since he had previously undergone a sex-change operation, by a legal technicality he *was 'the Club's first full female Member'*. Full membership for women was finally accepted by the necessary two-thirds majority, and after an uncertain start, the Club was seemingly happy with the arrangement. The next step, Rose FitzGibbon interjected, is a seat for ladies on the Club Committee and *'maybe, in time, it will have a lady President'*.

By and large members and administrators of English cricket clubs have benefited enormously from having women amongst their numbers, many of which took a rather pitying view of the MCC, who unsurprisingly chose to vote in favour of defending their age-old traditions. The Secretary of the MCC at the time, Lt-Col. John Robin Stephenson CBE [1931-2003], stressed that the decision relating to the admission of women members lay with its members, but held the view that women would probably be admitted to membership eventually, possibly even before the end of the next century !

With the MCC on the verge of attaining its double centenary, John Stephenson would steer the Club through some of its most challenging times. A retired Lieutenant Colonel, he took over the role as Secretary of the MCC in 1987, at a critical point in its history, having previously served eight years as its Assistant Secretary. Although cherishing the history of the game, he did not seek to preserve cricket in a time warp. And when Lord's had a streaker, he was heard to remark to a groundsman, *'Much better looking than the one at Twickenham. But if you do see anyone stripping off, jump on them ! If you see what I mean.'*

Obvious signs were emerging which characterised women's cricket as becoming increasingly international. In 1948, shortly after the end of the Second World War, the England women's team embarked on another tour of Australia and New Zealand, captained by the great Molly Hide. And there were also budding signs the women's game was developing in other countries too.

In 1953 the South African and Rhodesian Women's Cricket Association was inaugurated, and five years later the international development of women's cricket was duly commemorated. Five of the most influential of women's cricketing nations, England, Australia, Holland, New Zealand and South Africa, got together in 1958 and founded the International Women's Cricket Council [IWCC]. Its principal purpose being to co-ordinate women's cricket throughout the world relieving the WCA of the responsibility, which to all intents and purposes had been doing the job since its creation.

Although at its inaugural meeting it was agreed a *'newsletter'* would be produced, the project failed since those involved with the organisation and administration of the IWCC were volunteers, who in the main were fulfilling roles within their own national governing bodies. As a consequence communication between the member nations of the IWCC was challenging and difficult to sustain.

Limited funding severely influenced the growth of the organisation, despite which it persevered and continued its struggle. Efforts were made to promote development through meetings during which future tour schedules were specifically debated and planned. With the arrangements and orchestration of international tours delegated to the individual IWCC host member countries, although little, if any, financial or practical support was forthcoming.

Initially, membership of the Association was limited to the governing bodies of cricket from within the British Empire where Test cricket was played. And in the summer of 1909, at a meeting of cricketing representatives from the member nations of England, Australia and South Africa, held at Lord's, the *Imperial Cricket Conference* was formed. In 1926 India, New Zealand and the West Indies, were elected as full members of the Association, doubling the number of Test playing nations to six. In the same year a change in the conditions of membership was agreed, which allowed the election of members to be extended to include the *'governing bodies of cricket in countries within the Empire to which cricket teams are sent, or which send teams to England'*.

The United States of America applied for membership of the IWCC at the time the new rules came into being, but as its application did not properly meet the qualifying criteria membership was denied. Pakistan was granted membership in 1947, following the division of British India which resulted in the two independent dominions of India and Pakistan set down in the Indian Independence Act. It was given Test status in 1952, and became the seventh IWCC Test-playing nation.

Eight years later, in 1960, the South African government, the affirmed republican Afrikaner-dominated right-wing National Party, which regarded Queen Elizabeth II as its head of state, a relic of British imperialism. A referendum was subsequently organised, in order to decide whether the Union of South Africa should become a republic, and the vote, which was restricted to whites, was narrowly approved by the voters. Resulting in the constitution of the Republic of South Africa in May of the following year, consequently South Africa left the Commonwealth, and at the same time lost its membership of the IWCC.

In 1965 the organisation was renamed the International Cricket Conference [ICC] and additional rules were adopted which would lead to its further expansion, when it was agreed the election of countries from outside the Commonwealth as Associate Members would be permitted. Sri Lanka was admitted as a full member in 1981, restoring the number of Test playing nations to seven.

In 1989 a number of new rules were introduced, and the organisation was once again re-named, with the current name of the International Cricket Council coming into being. The ICC generates income from the tournaments it organises, primarily the cricket World Cup which, together with additional amounts accrued from sponsorship and television rights, is distributed largely between its members. From its inception the ICC has occupied offices in the *'Clock Tower'* building at the Nursery End of the Lord's Cricket Ground.

South Africa was re-instated as a full member of the ICC in 1991, following the eventual collapse of apartheid, the Afrikaans descriptive name given by the ruling white South African Nationalist Party to the country's harsh, system of racial segregation, which eventually led to the formation of a democratic government in 1994.

Zimbabwe was admitted to the ICC as the ninth Test-playing nation in 1992, and in the millennium year 2000, Bangladesh received Test playing status.

The IWCC finally combined with the ICC in 2005, to form a single unified organisation with the objective of assisting the overall management and development cricket. And in 2017, at a full council meeting of the ICC held at The Oval, the Afghanistan Cricket Board and Cricket Ireland were both unanimously confirmed as full members.

Women's cricket has been played internationally since the inaugural women's Test match between England and Australia in 1934. In the following year the New Zealand women joined the global ranks, with South Africa re-elected a quarter of a century later in 1960. India and the West Indies joined the group of nations in 1976, followed by Pakistan and Sri Lanka in 1998. Ireland swelled the ranks further when it joined in the Millennium year. And in 2007 the Netherlands women became the tenth women's Test nation, making their debut against the South Africa women's team.

Limited over Women's One Day Internationals [ODIs] were launched in 1973, as part of the first Women's World Cup held in England. Since then the popularity of this format has escalated so quickly that it has become the current focus of women's international cricket.

England has played more international matches, including around 100 Test matches, and 320 ODI matches. The 1,000 women's ODI took place in South Africa against New Zealand in 2016, which New Zealand won by 9 wickets at the Diamond Oval in Kimberley.

The even shorter format of women's international cricket, Twenty20, was introduced in 2004. In Twenty20 each team plays up to a maximum of 20 overs. The first match was played at the County Ground in Hove between England and New Zealand, six months before the first Twenty20 international match was played between two men's teams. A strong New Zealand side won the game by the narrow margin of 9 runs. Initially, very little women's Twenty20 cricket was played at international level, with only four matches having been played by the end of 2006. However, in the following three years the format grew quickly, with six matches played in 2007, ten in 2008 and thirty in 2009.

That same year heralded the inaugural ICC Women's World Cup between New Zealand and England at the North Sydney Oval, Australia. On a gloriously sunny, despite conditions conducive to swing bowling, the New Zealand's captain, Haidee Maree Tiffen [born 1979], chose to bat first after winning the toss. New Zealand amassed a total of 166 in 47.2 overs, with Lucy Rose Doolan [born 1987] the best performer for the *'White Ferns'* with both bat and ball. England knocked off a winning score in 46.1 overs to win by 4 wickets. Nicola Jayne Shaw [born 1981] was awarded the accolade of player of the match following her tally of 4 wickets in 8.2 overs at a cost of 34 runs, and her contribution with the bat of 17 not out.

Chapter 11

The Women's World Cup

Arsenal had defeated Liverpool 2-1 in an exciting FA Cup final at the Wembley Stadium. The UK had agreed terms for its proposed membership of the European Economic Community [EEC]. And the Conservative Party's Education Secretary, Margaret Thatcher's proposal to end free school milk for children aged over seven years was backed by a Parliamentary majority of 33 MPs.

Yet it all began on a warm summer day in July 1971, when an England XI took the field in a representative cricket match against a Young England XI at the Victorian sea-side resort of Eastbourne, East Sussex. The philanthropic businessman and keen supporter of cricket, Sir Jack Hayward OBE, in conversation with Miss S.M. Swinburne, the Chair of the Women's Cricket Association, proposed a women's cricket World Cup competition be staged in England organised by the WCA, pledging his personal support by donating the substantial sum of £40,000 in order to help get the project off the ground. A former president of the Wolverhampton Wanderers Football Club, Sir Jack Hayward was well-known amongst English women cricketers, and a close personal friend of Rachael Heyhoe-Flint. He was equally as well known in the Caribbean too, having previously sponsored an unofficial WCA tour to the British colony of Jamaica in February of the previous year.

Among the WCA squad of 15 players who made the trip were:

Rachael Heyhoe[Flint] – Captain -16 Test matches. Batting at number 3. Close fielder.
Lesley Clifford – Vice-captain - 9 Test matches. Opening bat. Left-arm seam bowler.
Ann Sanders - 10 Test matches. All rounder. Off-spin bowler.
Heather Dewdney - 2 Test matches. Middle order bat. Leg-spin bowler.
Jean Clark - 1 Test match. Lively bat. Seam bowler.
Pam Ferdinand - Fast lively bowler.
Marilyn Reid – Wicket keeper.
Lesley Judd – Middle order bat.
Linda Beresford – Medium pace attacking bowler.
Isobel Crocker – All rounder. Left-arm spin bowler.
Alison Hall – Opening bat.
Wendy Williams- Fast swing bowler. Tail-end bat with run-scoring ability.
Dawn Francis – Medium fast bowler. Unorthodox lusty bat.
Pat Sheringham – Steady, number 5 or number 6 bat.
Bonnie Russell – Medium pace bowler.

The philanthropic cricketing devotee also helped fund the first official tour of the West Indies, the Bahamas and Bermuda in the following year, and was instrumental in establishing a Triangular Tournament between England, Trinidad and Jamaica. In the late 1970s women's cricket had begun to slowly decline in popularity in the Caribbean, since school-teachers who had previously come from the United Kingdom, bringing with them a passion for cricket, were being replaced by teachers who had been trained in the United States. Teachers with little knowledge of the game of cricket, who tended to promote track and field, baseball and softball instead, with lucrative offers of sports scholarships in colleges in the United States tending to lure potential players away from cricket.

Without doubt the primary point of the discussion which took place that sun-drenched afternoon in Eastbourne, would have cautiously crossed the minds of copious numbers of women cricket administrators and players previously. But for the first time, this was a positive proposal ! And at the Annual General Meeting of the WCA held in London in November 1971, a most important proposal was ratified when the Committee agreed to go ahead in 1973 with the inaugural Women's Cricket World Cup competition. During the following two years the Association co-ordinated and liaised with other countries, especially those upon which the responsibility for future World Cup matches would ultimately fall. Creating an administrative set-up which would become the basis of the inaugural women's World Cup.

An unremitting publicity campaign and a drive to attract suitable sponsorship deals was set in motion without delay, and before long the cricketing bodies, general public, press, radio, television and commercial institutions were obliged to consider, and confirm or otherwise, whether women's cricket at international level was worth backing.

The Country's leading players who were likely to be considered for selection in the England teams, were also required to shoulder considerable responsibility for the successful promotion of the WCA's World Cup plans. Since their performance and personal image would be subject to public scrutiny all through the build up to the competition. By the early Spring of 1973 considerable interest and backing had been roused, with introductory plans well in hand, everything seemed set fair for the first Women's World Cup.

In addition to the official England women's team, the WCA decided it would also enter a Young England team, and in order to be seen as fair-minded, invited all the other competing countries to send additional players to make up an International Invitation XI.

However, a blow was delivered which threatened to rock the boat! When, sensitive to current world political opinion, the WCA had deliberately avoided despatching an invitation requesting the South Africa & Rhodesia Women's Cricket Association send a team to participate. As an alternative preferring to invite five individual South African players to form the basis of what would become known as the International XI. But at the eleventh-hour, when it became too late to agree any other suitable course of action, the WCA was compelled to withdraw the invitations, in order to firmly secure the reassurance of the other countries which had previously agreed would take part in the competition.

Significantly encouraged by the former England captain, Rachael Heyhoe-Flint, and aided by the generous support of the kind-hearted patron Sir Jack Hayward OBE, the Women's Cricket World Cup was officially inaugurated. And on an extraordinarily hot summer's day, the 14 June, 1973, with Jack Hayward's striking solid silver trophy on display for all to see, and the competing nations resplendent in their colourful team uniforms, the first ever women's World Cup Cricket Competition was officially launched and took up its rightful place in the history of the sporting world.

Held two years before the first limited over World Cup for men, it was the first tournament of its kind, and included teams from England, Australia, New Zealand, Trinidad and Tobago, and Jamaica, supplemented by an International XI and a Young England side. The seven teams competed for the World Cup in a series of 60 over one-day international matches, played throughout England wherever first-class grounds and suitable amenities were available. Bringing the intriguing spectacle of women's cricket to towns and communities, which had never before had the opportunity to see the game played at national level.

Having been tempted into a false sense of security by a fortnight's pre-competition heat wave, the English weather reverted to normal summer standards immediately the competition started, with some members of the WCA fearing the event might be wrecked. The first match never even started, and five other matches were affected by rain. However, it was perhaps the England team that fared the worst of the bunch, with four out of their half-dozen games turning out to be irrefutably sodden. Nevertheless, firm in the belief that Australia and England would most probably emerge as the two strongest teams in the competition, the final match was scheduled to be played between the pair at the Edgbaston Cricket Ground, Birmingham. Home to the Warwickshire County Cricket Club, the Edgbaston ground had hosted the first Test match in the Ashes series against Australia in 1902, when the club erected a permanent stand, along with a range of other facilities, at a total cost of £1,500. Even though Warwickshire's eventual financial share of the tour funds was only £750.

The WCA prediction proved to be accurate and national interest increased when it became increasingly evident this would not only be the deciding match, but the match in which the first holder of the Women's World Cup would be determined. Consequently, the final round-robin match was held on the 28 July, and won by the hosts England, who defeated Australia by 92 runs. It was notable for the authoritative total of 118 runs made by Nottinghamshire's Enid Bakewell, together with the contribution of 64 runs made by the team captain Rachael Heyhoe-Flint, formed the foundation of England's imposing total score of 279 for the loss of 3 wickets from its 60 overs. Constrained by tight England bowling and some sharp, accurate throwing from the deep, Australia fell well short of their target, scoring 187-9.

At the presentation ceremony after the game the World Cup, a handsome Georgian Silver Chalice, was presented to the winning captain by HRH the Princess Anne.

Inaugural Women's World Cup Final

England v Australia

Venue: Edgbaston Stadium, Edgbaston, Birmingham - 28 July, 1973
Umpires: Jane Ayres [England] & Sheila Hill [England]
England won by 92 runs.

England Women Innings [60 overs maximum]:

E. Bakewell	lbw	b Knee	118
D.L.Thomas	st. Jennings	b Knee	40
R.Heyhoe-Flint [Capt]	c Wilson	b Thompson	64
C.J.Watmough	not out		32
J.E.Cruwys	not out		18
H.M.Dewdney	did not bat		
L.J.Clifford	did not bat		
M.Pilling	did not bat		
J.Moorhouse	did not bat		
S.Hilliam	did not bat		
S.A.Hodges [Wicket]	did not bat		
Extras	[1 b, 1lb, 5nb]		7
TOTAL	60 overs – Run Rate 4.65		**279**

Australian Bowling:	O	M	R	W	Econ.
T.MacPherson	12	2	51	0	4.25
S.A.Tredrea	7	0	28	0	4.00
R.Thompson	12	1	45	1	3.75
P.May	9	0	44	0	4.88
M.Knee	11	0	53	2	4.81
D.A.Gordon	2	0	13	0	6.50
W.Blundsen	7	0	38	0	5.42

Australia Women Innings [60 overs maximum]:

B. Wilson		b Moorhouse	41
J. Potter		b Bakewell	57
M. Jennings [Wicket]	run out		0
D.A. Gordon	lbw	b Hilliam	10
M. Knee [Captain]		b Hilliam	1
E.J. Bray	run out		40
R. Thompson	c Hodges	b Pilling	0
T. Mac Pherson	c Bakewell	b Pilling	14
S.A. Tredrea		b Bakewell	0
W. Blunsden	not out	3	
P. May	not out		6
Extras	[3 b, 7lb, 5nb]		15
TOTAL	60 overs – Run Rate 3.11		**187**

England Bowling:	O	M	R	W	Econ.
M. Pilling	12	1	41	2	3.41
L.J. Clifford	8	0	20	0	2.50
J. Moorhouse	9	3	13	1	1.44
E. Bakewell	12	2	28	2	2.33
S. Hilliam	9	0	34	2	3.77
D.L. Thomas	9	0	29	0	3.22
R. Heyhoe-Flint	1	0	7	0	7.00

Standings:

Team	**Pld**	**W**	**L**	**T**	**NR**	**A**	**Pts**
England	6	5	1	0	0	0	20
Australia	6	4	0	0	1	0	17
New Zealand	6	3	2	0	0	1	13
International XI	6	3	2	0	1	0	13
Trinidad & Tobago	6	2	4	0	0	0	8
Jamaica	6	1	4	0	0	1	5
Young England	6	1	5	0	0	0	4

Pld =Played; **W** =Win; **L** =Loss; **T** =Tie; **NR** No result; **A** =Abandoned; **Pts** =Points

Second Women's Cricket World Cup 1978

The second Women's World Cup tournament was hosted in India during January 1978, four years after the inaugural event held in England. It was originally planned South Africa would host the tournament, but this proposal was abandoned in order to conform with the sporting boycott placed on South Africa due to the system of institutionalised racial segregation and discrimination in force from 1948-1991. Consequently, the Women's Cricket Association of India [WCAI] made a successful bid, and was chosen to act as the primary organiser, with the International Women's Cricket Council [IWCC] providing limited administrative supervision.

Initially India, which was making its debut in the event, was joined by five other national teams, including Australia, England, the Netherlands, New Zealand, and the West Indies. However, the Netherlands and the West Indies, both of which would also been participating for the first time, were compelled to withdraw for financial reasons. With the number of teams now reduced to four in total, it was initially felt the tournament might not be financially viable and was almost cancelled. But after careful thought, the decision was taken that the tournament should go ahead since the host country India was the only one likely to draw sufficient crowd support. As there would now only be four teams competing, fewer than the number which competed in the inaugural year, it was agreed the event would be played in a round-robin format, without a final, with each team playing three matches. And since it was agreed the Australian and England women's teams were by far the two strongest teams competing, it was settled that the final match would be played between featuring those two teams.

This was not the only controversial issue to plague the troubled second World Cup. Rachael Heyhoe-Flint, who was undeniably extremely influential in initiating the inaugural Women's World Cup, and arguably one of the greatest female cricketers of all time, was dropped from the England squad, as it was alleged she was becoming *'too popular'* which was undeniably causing some discomfiture amongst administrators and selectors.

Fielding eleven debutants, the Indian women, had a catastrophic start in its campaign against the defending champions, at Eden Gardens, Kolkata, formerly known as Calcutta. Widely acknowledged as being one the most iconic cricket stadiums in the world Eden Gardens is often regarded as India's *'home of cricket'*, and has been spoken of as *'cricket's answer to the Colosseum'*. Bowled out for a meagre 63 runs in 39.3 overs, the England Women chased down the target set with 9 wickets intact. The hosts lost again to the New Zealand Women at Patna in the state of Bihar on the southern bank of river Ganges, and although on this occasion they did manage to reach a score of 130 for 9. The Kiwis, under no pressure, won the match by 9 wickets with 6 overs to spare.

Meanwhile, the Australian women opened their campaign with an easy win over New Zealand at the multi-purpose Keenan Stadium, in Jamshedpur. Batting first the Aussies put on 177 with Wendy Hills [born 1954] contributing 64. Sharon Tredrea [born 1954], a rare female bowler classified as *'fast'*, opened the Australian bowling attack alongside Raelee Thompson [born 1945], a right-handed batswoman and right arm fast-medium bowler. The pair finished with figures of 9 runs for 2 wickets in 10 overs, and 11 runs for 2 wickets in 10 overs respectively. The New Zealand women were seized in an inescapable iron-grip and could only muster 111 for 8 wickets in reply.

In Australia's next match against India in Patna, Sharon Tredrea excelled once again, but this time with the bat, knocking up 56 runs in the Australian women's total of 150 for 9. In India's opening partnership in reply Fowzieh Khalili [born 1958], who held the record for the most dismissals as a wicket-keeper in a Women's Cricket World Cup series, combined with Shobha Pandit [born 1956] and contributed 31 runs. But Peta Verco [née Cook] [born 1956] with bowling figures of 9 wickets for 3 runs was crucial in dispensing with the Indian batting challenge for an overall total of 79 runs.

Meanwhile, in Hyderabad, the capital of the southern state of Telangana, Barbara 'Barb' Lynette Bevege [1942–1999], knocked up a total of 57 to reinforce the New Zealand women's total score of 157. Their opponents England got off to an excellent start and went on to win comfortably by 7 wickets with 57 balls to spare.

The final fixture was decided as agreed between England and Australia, the finalists from the previous World Cup. Though not technically a final, it became acknowledged as being equivalent to one.

Cheshire born Mary Pilling [born 1938] won the toss for Australia and elected to field. The wicket of Megan Lear [born 1951] fell to Sharon Tredrea without scoring. While Derryth Lynne Thomas [born 1939] paired with Christine Joy Watmough [born 1947] added a plodding partnership score of 21 for the second wicket, which turned out to be one of the high points of the England innings. The Welsh cricketer Lynne Thomas had opened the batting for England in the1973 Women's Cricket World Cup, and would later became the first woman to score a century in One Day international cricket. In addition, batting alongside the legendary Enid Bakewell the pair combined to create a record for the highest opening run partnership in women's cricket World Cup history with a score of 246, which would stand until 2008.

An inspired spell of bowling from Sharon Tredrea, yielded 4 wickets for 25 runs, helped by some valuable assistance from Peta Verco, the pair collectively steered the England women to a collapse with 28 for the loss of 6 wickets. Shirley Hodges, the wicket-keeper, then strolled out to join Lynne Thomas at the crease, and the pair struggled to add another 22 for the seventh wicket, before Sharyn Hill [née Fitzsimmons] [born 1954] picked up two more wickets. At 60 for the loss of 8 wickets things began to look desperate for England, and the focus now turned to batting out the 50 overs. Glynis Hullah [born 1948] joined Shirley Hodges and together they put their heads down and survived to post a final score of 96 runs without further loss.

Despite the easy target set for Australia, Hullah started in spectacular style, clean bowling the left-hander Lorraine Hill [born 1946] for two, before trapping Wendy Joan Hills [born 1954] leg-before-wicket for a duck. With the Australian score on 6 for 2 wickets, things began to look a little more hopeful for England. That is until Janette Tredrea [born 1956], the younger sister of Sharon Tredrea, joined her captain wicket-keeper and right-handed batswoman Margaret Jean Jennings [born 1949] at the crease. The trivial total set for Australia left the pair in no hurry, as they calmly closed in on the target. With Jennings finishing an unbeaten innings on 57 at the close, with the young Janette Tredrea also carrying her bat to contribute a creditableof total 37 runs.

The Australian women won the match by 8 wickets with 111 balls to spare, and saw the series out undefeated, to lay claim to its first title under its skipper, Margaret Jennings, the leading run-scorer in the tournament, while team-mate, Sharyn Hill claimed the title for the highest haul of wickets taken in the tournament.

Second Women's World Cup Final

England v Australia

Venue: Lal Bahadur Shastri Stadium, Hyderbad - 13 January, 1978
Umpires: V.K. Ramaswamy [India] & A.N.Other [India]

Australia won by 8 wickets with 111 balls remaining

England Women Innings [50 overs maximum]:

D.L.Thomas	c Jennings	b Fitzsimmons	19
M.A.Lear	c Thompson	b S.A.Tredrea	0
C.J.Watmough	c Jennings	b S.A.Tredrea	12
H.M.Dewdney		b S.A.Tredrea	0
J.M.Court		b S.A.Tredrea	1
R.Heggs	c Jennings	b Verco	1
M.Wilks		b Verco	0
S.A.Hodges [Wicket]	not out		26
M.Pilling [Captain]	c Farrell	b Fitzsimmons	8
G. Hullah	not out		18
C.M.Mowatt	did not bat		
Extras	[1b, 4lb, 6nb]		11
TOTAL	50 overs – Run Rate 1.92		**96**

Australian Bowling:	O	M	R	W	Econ.
S.A.Tredrea	10	1	25	4	2.50
R.Thompson	9	2	18	0	2.00
P.Verco	8	3	9	2	1.12
S.Fitzsimmons	10	3	14	2	1.40
L.Hill	7	2	9	0	1.28
M.J.Cornish	6	4	10	0	1.66

Australia Women Innings [50 overs maximum]:

L.Hill		b Hullah	2
M. Jennings [Capt. &W'ket]	notout		57
W.J.Hills	lbw	b Hullah	0
J.Tredrea	not out		37
S.A.Tredrea	did not bat		
R.Thompson	did not bat		
R.Verco	did not bat		
S.Fitzsimmons	did not bat		
M.J.Cornish	did not bat		
V.Farrell	did not bat		
E.J.Bray	did not bat		
Extras	[1b, 3lb]		4
TOTAL	31.3 overs – Run Rate 3.17		**100**

England Bowling:	**O**	**M**	**R**	**W**	**Econ.**
G.Hullah	6	1	9	2	1.50
M.Pilling	3 1	12	0	4.00	
J.M.Court	5	1	12	0	2.40
R.Heggs	7.3	1	17	0	2.26
D.L. Thomas	5	0	23	0	4.60
C.M.Mowat	3	1	12	0	4.00
M.Wilks	2	0	11	0	5.50

Standings:

Team	**Pld**	**W**	**L**	**T**	**NR**	**A**	**Pts**
Australia	3	3	0	0	0	0	6
England	3	2	1	0	0	0	4
New Zealand	3	1	2	0	0	0	2
India	3	0	3	0	0	0	0

Pld =Played; **W** =Win; **L** =Loss; **T** =Tie; **NR** =No result; **A** =Aband; **Pts** =Points

Third Women's Cricket World Cup 1982

Sponsored by Hansells Vita Fresh

The third Women's World Cup was hosted by New Zealand, four years after the World Cup held in India. The tournament commenced play on the 10 January and ran through until the final match held on the 7 February 1982 at the Lancaster Park Stadium in Christchurch, subsequently to become known as the Jade Stadium, and more recently the AMI Stadium.

A total of six teams were invited to participate in the tournament, which was played as a triple round-robin, and was the longest in terms of duration and number of matches played.

Once again, South Africa and its policy of institutionalised racial segregation cast a gloomy shadow over the tournament, as the organisers remained idealistic about the division between sport and politics. The West Indies opted to make a late withdrawal, choosing to register a protest against the decision made the previous year by New Zealand when it hosted a tour of the *'Springbok'* rugby team. For less political reasons, the Netherlands replicated its decision of 1978 and withdrew due to financial concerns. In order to avoid another World Cup with only four teams of players participating, the organisers chose to repeat the earlier successful initiative of including an International XI made up of a combination of global players.

Having learned a great deal from the 1978 World Cup, the International Women's Cricket Council [IWCC] decided to take a more active role in the organisation of the competition, although it still left the majority of the fundamental duties to the host nation to fulfil. It took the best part of 18 months to make detailed preparations for the tournament, and frequently resulted in several of the host country's players being called upon to help with the groundwork, including a number of those who were eventually selected to play in the New Zealand team. As a result of the hard work of the players, the tournament benefited from the appointment of the iconic food group Hansells Vita Fresh as its first commercial sponsor, largely due to the stering efforts of Patricia 'Trish' Frances McKelvey CNZM, MBE [born 1942], who later became the first woman board member of New

Zealand Cricket, and 'Barb' Bevege, who set the record as the oldest woman to score a maiden century in women's ODI history at the age of 39.

In spite of the two previous World Cup tournaments being played in a league format, which by a stroke of good fortune both provided a suitable final, the 1982 event featured an authentic final encounter for the very first time. Overall the tournament included a total of 30 matches, with each of the five teams playing each other three times over a period spanning less than a month. The amount of cricket played was also increased, as the event was staged as contests of 60 over duration, whereas the World Cup games held in India were all 50 over matches. Consequently, this was undoubtedly the most extensive and most exhaustive women's cricket tournament ever played for its time.

In order to fit in so many matches into such a compact time period, fifteen venues, from Auckland to Dunedin, shared the role of hosting matches. The Basin Reserve in Wellington, commonly known as *'The Basin'* and the oldest Test cricket ground in New Zealand, hosted most of the games, a total of six in all, with the final and only match held at Lancaster Park, Christchurch. Other venues used included:

Basin Reserve, Wellington – 6 games
Cornwall Park, Auckland – 3 games
Fitzherbert Park, Palmerston North – 3 games
Pukekura k, New Plymouth – 3 games
University of Canterbury, Christchurch – 3 games
Christ's College, Christchurch – 2 games
Eden Park,Auckland – 2 games
Logan Park, Dunedin – 2 games
Cooks Gardens, Wanganui – 1 game
Dudley Park, Rangiora – 1 game
Hutt Recreation Ground, Lower Hutt – 1 game
Lancaster Park, Christchurch – 1 game
McLean Park, Napier – 1 game
Seddon Park, Hamilton – 1 game
Trafalgar Park, Nelson – 1 game

Australia was undefeated in all 13 of its matches on the way to its second successive World Cup win, defeating arch rival England in the final at Lancaster Park, to extend its number of matches undefeated to 24 throughout the period from 1978 to 1985, and creating a ODI record for the time.

The Third World Cup was blighted by low scoring, with only one of the five competing teams managing to register an innings score in excess of 250 runs. Two of the games ended in a tie, a first for women's international cricket, both of which matches featured England, the first against New Zealand, and the second against Australia.

Throughout the series England's elegant and doggedly determined opening bat, Jannette Ann Brittin MBE [1959-2017], notched up 391 runs in her 12 visits to the crease, her highest score being 139 not out, to lead the tournament as the player accruing the most runs scored. Brittin's cricketing career overlapped an era when one-day cricket was considered the customary type of game most suitable for women. She played in 27 Tests and 63 ODI matches, 36 of which were in Women's World Cup matches. She collected a total of 10 centuries along the way, and finished as leading run-scorer on two occasions. The Australian slow left-arm spinner, Lyn 'Lefty' Fullston [1956-2008] led the tournament for the number of wickets taken, bagging 23 for a total of 276 runs from 123 overs, her best bowling figures being 5 wickets for 27 runs.

Third Women's World Cup Final

England v Australia

Venue: Lancaster Park Stadium, Christchurch - 7 February, 1982
Umpires: Dickie Bird [England]: Fred Goodall [New Zealand]
Australia won by 3 wickets with 6 balls remaining

England Women Innings [60 overs maximum]:

J.A.Brittin		c & b Lutschini	17
S.Goatman [Captain]		b Fullston	29
C.J.Watmough	c Kennare	b Fullston	9
J.Allen	c Fitzsimmons	b Tredrea	53
R.Heyhoe-Flint	c Fullston	b Tredrea	29
G.Hullah	not out		1
E.Bakewell	not out		0
C.A.Hodges [Wicket]	did not bat		
J.C.Tedstone	did not bat		
S.A.Hodges	did not bat		
A.M.Starling	did not bat		
Extras	[5b, 7lb, 1w]		13
TOTAL	60 overs – Run Rate 1.92		**151**

Australian Bowling:	**O**	**M**	**R**	**W**	**Econ.**
S.A.Tredrea	12	2	36	2	3.00
R.Thompson	12	2	34	0	2.83
D.Martin	12	2	31	0	2.58
M.J.Cornish	12	6	17	1	1.41
L.A.Fullston	12	3	20	2	1.66

Australia Women Innings [60 overs maximum]:

P.Verco	c Goatman	b Starling	2
S.Fitzsimmons	c Goatman	b Starling	12
J.Kennare	run out		4
K.Read	c Southgate	b Tedstone	32
S.A.Tredrea [Captain]	c S.A.Hodges	b C.A.Hodges	25
J.M.Jacobs	run out		37
M.J.Cornish	not out		24
R.Thompson	run out		8
L.A.Fullston	not out		0
D.Martin	did not bat		
T.J.Russell [Wicket]	did not bat		
Extras	[2b, 3lb, 2nb, 1w]		8
TOTAL	59 overs – Run Rate 2.57		**152**

England Bowling:	O	M	R	W	Econ.
J.C.Tedstone	12	4	24	1	2.00
A.M.Starling	11	3	21	2	1.90
G.Hullah	11	0	35	0	3.18
E.Bakewell	12	3	26	0	2.16
C.A.Hodges	12	1	33	1	2.75
C.J.Watmough	1	0	5	0	5.00

Standings:

Team	Pld	W	L	T	NR	A	Pts	RR
Australia	12	11	0	1	0	0	46	3.124
England	12	7	3	2	0	0	32	2.988
New Zealand	12	6	5	1	0	0	26	2.534
India	12	4	8	0	0	0	16	2.296
International XI	12	0	12	0	0	0	0	2.034

Pld=Played; **W** =Wins; **L**=Losses; **T**=Tied; **NR**=No result; **A**=Abandoned; **Pts**=Points; **RR**=Run rate

Women's Bicentennial Fourth Cricket World Cup 1988

Sponsored by Shell

The 1988 Shell Bicentennial Women's World Cup was hosted from the 29 November to the 18 December 1988. The first time by Australia as part of its Bicentenary celebrations. Sponsored by Shell, the fourth Women's Cricket World Cup was held six years after the 1982 World Cup tournament held in New Zealand.

Organised by the International Women's Cricket Council [IWCC] the initial entries included Australia, England, India, New Zealand the West Indies, along with Ireland and the Netherlands both of which were making their tournament debuts. Unfortunately both the West Indies and India were forced to pull out, the latter after failing to secure sufficient sponsorship funding.

Once again the matches were contested over 60 overs, and Australia won the tournament for the third consecutive time, defeating England by eight wickets in the final, at the Melbourne Cricket Ground. The final was broadcast live on radio and ABC Television, and although the ground had the capacity to hold over 90,000 spectators, only around 3,000 turned up to watch the match. Jan Brittin later described the venue as having *'wall-to-wall seating with no one sitting in them'*, making it *'a very large and a very lonely place'*.

New Zealand defeated Ireland by 60 runs in the third-place playoff, while the Netherlands, the only other team competing in the tournament, were placed fifth and last after failing to win a single match.

The Australian right-arm opening bat Lindsay Reeler [born 1961] led the tournament with the highest number of runs scored collecting a total of 448 from 8 innings, and the slow left-arm bowler 'Lefty' Fullston took the honours for the number of wickets taken, amassing 16 from 86.1 overs. The English all-rounder, Carole Hodges [born 1959], won the award for the overall *'player of the series',* marking her achievement of taking 12 wickets from 83 overs bowled, and an overall runs tally of 336. Hodges was presented with a Waterford Crystal trophy, donated by the Irish company R and A Bailey.

A *'Golden Oldies'* tournament, scheduled to be held following the series of World Cup matches, was seriously disrupted due to the cold, wet weather.

Fourth Women's World Cup Final

England v Australia

Venue:	Melbourne Cricket Ground, Melbourne - 18 December, 1988
Umpires:	Robin Bailhache [Australia]: Leonard King [Australia]

England won the toss and elected to bat.
Australia won by 8 wickets with 91 balls remaining.

England Women Innings [60 overs maximum]:

C.A.Hodges		b Larson	23
W.A.Watson	c Annetts	b Fullston	17
J.A.Britten	not out		46
J.Powell [Captain]	c Matthews	b Larson	1
K.Smithies		b Fullston	5
J.C.Tedson		c & b Fullston	2
J.M.Chamberlain	run out		14
P.A.Lovelll	lbw	b Goss	4
S.J. Kitson	not out		1
L.Nye [Wicketkeeper]	did not bat		
G.A.Smith	did not bat		
Extras	[4lb, 10w]		14
TOTAL	60 overs – Run Rate 2.11		**127**

Australian Bowling:	O	M	R	W	Econ.
Z.J.Goss	12	4	33	1	2.75
K.M.Brown	12	2	15	0	1.25
S.A.Tredrea	12	1	24	0	2.00
L.A.Larson	12	1	22	2	1.83
L.A.Fullston	12	3	29	3	2.41

Australia Women Innings [60 overs maximum]:

L.A.Reeler	not out		59
R.Buckstein	lbw	b Chamberlain	0
S.J.Heywood	run out		5
D.A.Annetts	not out		48
B.Haggart	did not bat		
S.A.Tredrea [Captain]	did not bat		
L.A.Larson	did not bat		
C.Matthews [Wicket]	did not bat		
Z.J.Goss	did not bat		
K.M.Brown	did not bat		
L.A.Fullston	did not bat		
Extras	[3lb, 14w]		17
TOTAL	44.5 overs – Run Rate 2.87		**129**

England Bowling:	O	M	R	W	Econ.
J.C.Tedstone	4	0	16	0	4.00
J.M.Chamberlain	8	1	23	1	2.87
C.A.Hodges	4	1	14	0	3.50
G.A.Smith	8	4	11	0	1.37
K.Smithies	10	2	23	0	2.30
P.A.Lovell	6	2	23	0	3.83
S.J.Kitson	4.5	0	16	0	3.31

Standings:

Team	Pld	W	L	T	NR	A	Pts
Australia	8	7	1	0	0	0	28
England	8	6	2	0	0	0	24
New Zealand	8	5	3	0	0	0	20
Ireland	8	2	6	0	0	0	8
Netherlands	8	0	8	0	0	0	0

Fifth Women's Cricket World Cup 1993

The 1993 Women's Cricket World Cup was once again organised by the International Women's Cricket Council [IWCC], with the matches played over 60 overs. It was held a little over four years following the previous tournament in Australia, and hosted for the second time by England from 20 July to 1 August 1993. A record number of eight participating nations took part in the tournament, including Australia, England, the Netherlands, India, Ireland, and New Zealand, with Denmark and the West Indies making their tournament debuts.

Sadly, the two-week tournament once again came close to being cancelled due to lack of funding. It wasn't until a few days prior to the start of the event that the Foundation for Sport and the Arts came to the rescue with a generous donation of £90,000, which helped save the day. Established in 1991 by Littlewoods and a number of other football pools companies, the aim of the Foundation for Sport and the Arts was to provide funding for a wide range of sporting and artistic activities. In total the

Foundation provided donations totalling in excess of £350 million to worthy causes. Although following a review of its financial position the Foundation was closed down in 2012, coinciding with the extremely successful London Olympics.

Undoubtedly it was due to the financial support of the Foundation, together with that of several other significant benefactors that the 1993 Women's Cricket World Cup was able to proceed. However due to the lack of adequate funding the matches played were confined to cricket grounds in the southern *'home counties'* surrounding London. Although on this occasion unlike in previous years, there was the advantage of being able to play the matches on some county grounds. Prior to the commencement of the tournament eleven warm-up matches were organised to be played against various other cricket teams. Even so the tournament and its players were still required to face up to, and overcome, some embarrassing problems. By way of example, three days before the final held at Lord's, when the England women defeated the Netherlands at Ealing, the players were obliged to personally roll the pitch and sort out the covers. Accurately described by the England captain Karen Smithies [born 1969] as being *'an absolute disgrace'.*

The bookmakers Coral had made England slight favourites for the final *'on their home ground'* of Lord's, where they faced an unbeaten and very much in-form New Zealand team. The irony of Lord's being considered the *'home to women's cricket'* was not lost on the players, especially the England team coach, and former England wicket-keeper Ruth Prideaux [née Westbrook] [1930-2016]. The 1993 final was the first not to feature the rival teams of England and Australia, for despite the *'home team's* impressive form, Prideaux confessed she much preferred playing New Zealand in the final rather than the *'Aussies'*, even though the *'White Ferns'* had already having taken England down by 25 runs in the earlier qualifying stages of the tournament at the Lloyds Bank Sports Ground, Beckenham. Acknowledging that the atmosphere following England's victory over Australia by 43 runs at Woodbridge Road, Guildford had *'not been pleasant'*.

Lord's seemed hardly fitting as the venue to stage the final of the event, since women's cricket had only been allowed to be played on the sacred sward on the one previous occasion in 1976. And although the MCC would still not allow the women players into the pavilion, on that particular afternoon all that mattered was the cricket, and all prejudice was temporarily cast aside. The BBC revised its sports programming schedule to include coverage in its Sunday afternoon broadcast of Grandstand, yet even so the MCC, who helped underwrite the tournament, totally misjudged the event's attraction, and on the day of the final only opened the Grandstand side of the ground. Paradoxicallly, the decision actually helped create an exciting atmosphere, as the crowd of around 4,500 spectators, including the ardent cricket enthusiast and current Prime Minister of the United Kingdom, John Major, were packed into the one small area of the ground.

The WCA was complimented on its organisation of the final, and in a first for women's cricket, England's victory received extensive coverage in the major national newspapers. Comparisons were drawn with the English men's side, which less than a week earlier brought little joy to the nation's fervent cricket supporters, as Australia clinched the Ashes, in a series which began with low expectations and progressed to prove even more depressing than initially feared. Culminating with the men's captain, the prolific run scorer, Graham Gooch OBE, DL [born 1953], falling on his sword.

In a piece written by the former England women's team vice-captain and cricket journalist Sarah Potter [born 1961], published in the *Times on* the day following the women's final, who observed, *'When a young woman cricketer pushes open the little white gate to step on to the pitch at Lord's, something spidery crawls up the lining of her throat. And the sight of all the nervously flushed faces and twitching limbs brought it all back. There they were again, spilling down the steps in their white skirts, fulfilling the impossible dream.'* Indeed Jan Brittin recollecting the first time she walked out to bat at Lords, *'Never before have I gone out with tears in my eyes, caused by the wonderful ovation from the members who lined our path through the Long Room, followed by the crowd's reception as we walked out to the middle.'*

On the 1 August, Sarah Louise Illingworth, the 30 year-old New Zealand team captain, won the toss and put England in to bat, and from that point on almost nothing seemed to go right for the seemingly composed New Zealand team.

The previous month in the Women's World Cup match against the Australian Women at Beckenham, Illingworth became the first women's wicket-keeper to rack up six dismissals in an innings, which included a total of four catches and two stumped. Sharing the record jointly with the Indian wicket-keeper Venkatacher Kalpana [born 1961], who on the same day, took one catch and stumped five of Denmark's women players, in her final appearance in a Women's World Cup One Day International match at Slough, Berkshire.

New Zealand missed four early chances in the final, including a crucially decisive opportunity to send Jo Chamberlain [née Jordan] [born 1969], a van driver from Leicester, back to the pavilion when she had made only 7 runs after aiming an enormous clout in the direction of the Tavern. Chamberlain eventually fell on 38 to the right-arm medium paced bowling of Julie Elizabeth Harris [born 1960], following a fifth wicket stand of 57. Ambling backwards towards the pavilion, she shook an animated fist at her partner Barbara Ann Daniels [born 1964] encouraging her to press on.

England finished its 60 over innings on 195 for the loss of 5 wickets, leaving the disillusioned New Zealanders chasing a total of 100 runs more than it had in any of their previous matches in the run up to the final. After a reasonable start things soon began to go wrong for the *'White Ferns'* of New Zealand. Chamberlain came into the attack and immediately had the right-hander Kirsty Bond [born 1967] superbly caught at gully by Suzy Kitson [born 1969] when on 12. She followed up by scoring a direct hit from cover to run out New Zealand's leading batsman Debbie Hockley [born 1962], and then took a catch to dismiss the teenage Emily Drumm [born 1974] for a duck, who had earlier in the day been responsible for two costly dropped catches.

With more than half the New Zealand overs gone the English celebrations in the grandstand began early. With only five overs remaining and still 68 runs short of the target set by England, Catherine Campbell [born1963] the Kiwis last batsman, with nothing to lose lofted to ball to deep mid-wicket. As the ball soared towards the grandstand dropping the catch was never an issue for Jan Brittin, who took it cleanly as it came over her right shoulder. Up went her arms in triumph as she hurled the ball in the direction of Swiss Cottage, and galloped off the pitch to greet an ecstatic throng of England supporters. England's women had won the game and the Women's World Cup for the second time, by a margin of 67 runs with 4.5 overs to spare. Even if only briefly, women's cricket made almost all the newspapers, including the front pages of a few, and even the BBC broadcast a report in its evening news bulletin.

The skipper Karen Smithies later revealed the team had received a good-luck message from the England men's side on the morning of the final, and couldn't resist delivering a gentle responsive dig, *'Perhaps they could learn a few things from this,'* she said. *'We hope it might show the way for them with our fielding and our bowling, which was tight and accurate.'*

England's Jan Brittin MBE once again topped the run-scoring table, collecting 410 runs in her total of 8 innings, with a batting average of 51.25, her highest score being 104. Her England colleagues, the right-hand bat Carole Ann Hodges [née Cornthwaite] [born 1959] and Helen Plimmer, who was born in the Solomon Islands in 1965, occupying second and third place respectively with scores of 334 from 8 innings and 242 from 7 innings. The England captain Karen Smithies, led the tournament for the highest number of wickets taken, collecting a total of 15 at a cost of 119 runs from 77 overs, an average of 7.93, her best bowling figures being 3 wickets for 6 runs.

Nevertheless, after all the well deserved celebrations had subsided, the feeling emerged there was need for change. England's success in the final had revealed the significance of the women's game, and the aims it sought to aspire to reach. In order to do so, the WCA would need to demonstrate more resolute and innovative administration. Possibly the most disparaging contribution came from *The Times* correspondent, Sarah Potter, who writing from first-hand authority said, *'Progress has been held back by lack of hard cash and column inches, and buckets of male condescension. The sport in England staggers along in unnoticed crisis. Tours teeter on the edge of humiliating cancellation. Players selected for their country are expected to have deep pockets, sympathetic employers, squeaky-clean shoes and an inordinate patience about the sweet old dears who mostly run the game.'*

Despite temporarily easing the discomfort of the *'pebble in the shoe'*, by way of the international success achieved by the England Women's cricket team, media debate continued to marginalise the women's game. Choosing instead to concentrate its attention mainly upon the men's game, leaving women's cricket remaining for the most part invisible. The significance and accomplishment of the women's game has unquestionably still not received the attention it truly deserves.

Fifth Women's World Cup Final

England v New Zealand

Venue:	Lords Cricket Ground, London - 1 August, 1993
Umpires:	Valerie Gibbens [England]: John West [England]

New Zealand won the toss and elected to field first.
England won by 67 runs.

England Women Innings [60 overs maximum]:

J.A.Britten	c Gunn	b McLauchlan	48
W.A.Watson		b McLauchlan	5
C.A.Hodges	st Illingworth	b Campbell	45
H.C.Pimmer	run out		11
J.M.Chamberlain		b Harris	38
B.A.Daniels	not out		21
K.Smithies [Captain]	not out		10
J.Smit [Wicketkeeper]	did not bat		
C.E.Taylor	did not bat		
G.A.Smith	did not bat		
S.J. Kitson	did not bat		
Extras	[8b, 7lb, 2w]		17
TOTAL	60 overs – Run Rate 3.25		**195**

Fall of wickets:
1-11 [WA Watson, 8.2 overs], 2-96 [JA Brittin, 38.3 overs], 3-114 [CA Hodges, 47.6 overs], 4-118[HC Plimmer, 48.3 overs], 5-175 [JM Chamberlain, 57.2 overs]

New Zealand Bowling:	O	M	R	W	Econ.
J.A.Turner	8	1	32	0	4.00
J.E.Harris	12	3	31	1	2.58
S.McLauchlan	10	2	25	2	2.50
C.A.Campbell	12	2	45	1	3.75
K.V.Gunn	12	5	33	0	2.75
E.C.Drumm	6	1	14	0	2.33

New Zealand Women Innings [60 overs maximum]:

P.D.Kinsella	c Casser	b Taylor	15
D.A.Hockley	run out		24
K.E.Bond	c Kitson	b Chamberlain	12
M.A.M.Lewis	lbw	b Taylor	28
S.Illingworth [Captain]		c & b Smithies	4
E.C.Drumm	c Chamberlain	b Smith	0
K.V. Gunn		b Smith	19
S.McLauchlan	c Brittin	b Kitson	0
J.A.Turner	c Taylor	b Smith	2
J.E.Harris	not out		5
C.A.Campbell	c Brittin	b Kitson	6
Extras	[8lb, 5w]		13
TOTAL	55.1 overs – Run Rate 2.32		**128**

Fall of wickets:
1-25 [PD Kinsella, 10.5 overs], 2-51 [KE Bond, 19.5 overs], 3-60 [DA Hockley, 26.6 overs], 4-70 [SL Illingworth, 32.5 overs], 5-71 [EC Drumm, 33.4 overs],
6-110 [MAM Lewis, 46.1 overs], 7-112 [S McLauchlan, 47.2 overs],
8-114 [KV Gunn, 48.5 overs], 9-120 [JA Turner, 52.4 overs],
10-128 [CA Campbell, 55.1 overs]

England Bowling:	O	M	R	W	Econ.
C.E.Taylor	12	3	27	2	2.25
C.A.Hodges	5	2	11	0	2.20
J.M.Chamberlain	9	2	28	1	3.11
K.Smithies	12	4	14	1	1.16
G.A.Smith	12	1	29	3	2.41
S.J.Kitson	5.1	1	11	2	3.12

Standings:

Team	Pld	W	L	T	NR	A	Pts
New Zealand	7	7	0	0	0	0	28
England	7	6	1	0	0	0	24
Australia	7	5	2	0	0	0	20
India	7	4	3	0	0	0	16
Ireland	7	2	5	0	0	0	8
West Indies	7	2	5	0	0	0	8
Denmark	7	1	6	0	0	0	4
Netherlands	7	1	6	0	0	0	4

Pld=Played; **W** =Wins; **L**=Losses; **T**=Tied; **NR**=No result; **Pts**=Points

Sixth Women's Cricket World Cup 1997

At a meeting of the International Women's Cricket Council [IWCC] held in England during the 1993 Women's Cricket World Cup, it was agreed it would be fitting were the tournament to return to the Indian subcontinent, and it was confirmed India should host the event scheduled for 1997.

The IWCC agreed the organisation of the Women's World Cup tournament was far from a simple affair, with the President of the IWCC, Mary Brito [b.1932] said to have spent more than NZ $ 4,500 on faxes and phone calls, desperately trying to get the Indian organisers to commit to a schedule. However, along with the list of the teams scheduled to participate in the tournament, there was one other constant in the punishing programme Brito was able to pencil in, that being the venue for the final, which would be played in the cricketing cauldron of Eden Gardens, Calcutta.

Mary Brito joined the sporting elite at the age of 85, when she was made an Honorary Life Member of the MCC, an honour that few women cricketers can only dream of bestowed upon her by one of the most conservative sporting bodies in the world. Having fought all her life to help achieve international recognition for the women's game, her love for the game of cricket is remarkable. Mary has missed only one women's cricket World Cup final, since its inauguration in 1973, and that was when India denied her a visa. She grew up in the north of England, playing cricket whenever the opportunity presented itself with a group of young boys from the Yorkshire village in which she lived. One of the boys was Harold Dennis *'Dickie'* Bird [born 1933], who would progress to become one of the most world famous umpires of all time.

Brito became Chair of the New Zealand Women's Cricket Council from 1974 to 1985, after she decided to move to a warmer climate in which to enjoy her cricket.

Initially the 1997 World Cup was to feature a dozen teams, a considerable increase in the number of teams which took up places in previous World Cups. Including amongst the teams was a team from Japan, which was scheduled to make its debut, but the dream was fleeting and Japan was ruled out almost as swiftly as it was written in. A similar fate struck Canada, which was invited to take up the spot vacated by Japan. This left the organisers struggling to find a team to occupy the final slot, and when the New Zealander women's team boarded its flight for India, the understanding was they would be squaring up against Bangladesh in their opening match. However, when they touched down, they discovered Bangladesh would also not be taking part, in spite of being offered playing equipment and reimbursement of its travel costs. Consequently, although the final number of teams participating was now reduced to 11 with New Zealand opening its challenge with a bye, it was still a record number of nations.

Anuradha Dutt, the tournament organiser and secretary of the Indian Women's Cricket Association, whose control of vocabulary was outstanding, was extremely critical of the IWCC for committing to such a large tournament. '*We repeatedly requested them not to have so many teams,*' she grumbled, '*but they would not listen to us and it made life very difficult for us*'.

However, the organisers did have some success in securing Hero Honda, a local motorcycle manufacturer, as the primary source of sponsorship for the tournament, but the company failed to fully cover the tournament's costs, and it became essential additional support was unearthed. Although Eden Gardens provided the use of its facilities free of charge, it is likely the Indian organisers were left with a substantial debt at the conclusion of the event.

Since the passionate Indian cricketing crowds were by and large male-dominated, another pressing facilities issue was quickly revealed. Since the World Cup was expected to draw large crowds of women, and as the ladies had been encouraged to attend the matches by providing free entry to the ground, and many of them bussed to the games, the organising bodies were called upon to exert influence on the Eden Garden officials to allow female spectators the use of suitably assigned male toilets.

The participating teams were seeded into two groups, with 32 matches held in the series overall, played over a total of 25 cricket grounds. In Group A were Australia, England, South Africa, Ireland, Denmark and Pakistan, while in Group B were the teams from New Zealand, India, the Netherlands, Sri Lanka and the West Indies.

After 25 matches had been played the teams from Australia, England, the Netherlands, Sri Lanka, India, South Africa, Ireland, and New Zealand had reached the quarter-finals, while Denmark, Pakistan and the West Indies were eliminated. The opening three matches of the quarter-finals were scheduled to be held on the 9 and 10 December, but torrential rain storms forced them to be cancelled without a single ball being bowled.

The night before the first of the semi-finals in Delhi, the corrugated iron gate leading into the stadium had been decorated with roses, but the start of the match, in which India was scheduled to face Australia on Christmas Eve, was delayed by two and a quarter hours for bad light, resulting in the length of the match being reduced from 50 to 32 overs.

India won the toss and the captain Pramila Bhatt [née Korikar] [born 1969] put Australia in to bat. The Aussies started well, with its awe-inspiring captain Belinda Clark [born 1970], a giant of the Australian women's game, was paired with the left-hander Joanne Broadbent [born1965] in an opening partnership of 66. Earlier in the qualifying series of matches Clark had scored a record number of 229 runs against Denmark in Mumbai. Australia managed to knock up a total of 123 from its 32 overs, during which India suffered a penalty of two overs for slow bowling, which were deducted from its batting innings.

Anju Jain [born. 1974] and Anjum Chopra [born 1977] fell cheaply in India's early reply, and although Chanderkanta Kaul [born 1971] put on 48, only two other players from the Indian side managed to reach double figures. With the last three players all failing to score, India came up short by 19 runs, scoring 104 for the loss of 9 wickets from its 30 overs.

England faced New Zealand in the second of the semi-final matches on Boxing Day in Chepauk, Chennai. Watched by a crowd of around 2,000 New Zealand won the toss, and the captain Maia Lewis [born 1970] elected to bat first. However, they lost the early wicket of Emily Drumm [born 1974] for 4 with just 8 runs on the scoreboard. Opening bat Debbie Hockley [born 1962] was the top scorer for the *'White Ferns'* knocking up 43 before Kathryn Leng [born1973] took a catch off the leg-break bowling of Charlotte Edwards [born 1979]. Hockley was the first women to reach a landmark total of 4,000 runs in ODI events, and the first to play in 100 ODI's. A sizeable sum of 28 extras, including 18 wides, helped New Zealand reach a total of 175 from their 50 overs at the crease for the loss of 6 wickets.

The English side considered this to be its best fielding performance of the tournament, and were thrilled to have contained New Zealand to a score under 180. There was however a twist in the tale, which would shake their confidence. At the end of the New Zealand innings the umpires revealed that England was being penalised an over in their batting innings due to a slow over rate. When the England coach, Megan Amy Lear [born 1951], heard the disturbing news she took the umpires to task, arguing persuasively, although ineffectively, that there had been a number of mitigating factors which had led to the extended innings, not the least being the number of stray dogs that had wandered on to the pitch and had to be chased off.

Needing 176 runs from 49 overs, England reached 100 for the loss of four wickets, with Charlotte Edwards, Jan Brittin and Barbara Daniels [born 1964] collectively contributing a total of 87 runs. Only two other players reached double figures. England wilted to an indifferent total of 155 all out from 47.5 overs, with four players run out, gifting the triumphant New Zealand team victory by 20 runs, and a place in the final against Australia.

The love of cricket in India is intense, and the 1997 final at the Eden Gardens on the 29 December was played in front of a crowd of around 60,000 eager spectators, although the Indian organisers laid claim to a total of closer to 80,000, made up almost entirely of females. Free transport was arranged to transport the excited spectators to the ground in 1,600 buses hired from throughout the Kolkata region, and admission tickets were also distributed free of charge. This inevitably led some to seize upon the prospect of turning a quick dollar, including a traffic warden who was arrested for selling the *'free tickets'* at the gate..

The New Zealand captain Maia Lewis won the toss and once again chose to bat first. Her nervous side got off to a poor start, losing the wickets of Emily Drumm, Shelley Fruin [born 1971], and Katrina Keenan [born 1971] for six, eight and five runs respectively. Australia was supremely confident, and rightly so, and it was only as a result of a master-class in batting delivered by the redoubtable New Zealand opener Debbie Hockley that avoided a complete rout. Debbie held her nerve and stayed at the crease until eventually succumbing to the right-arm pace of Cathryn

Fitzpatrick after posting a score of 79, almost half the combined total of the New Zealand team score, and only one of three New Zealanders to score in double figures. New Zealand eventually reached 164 all out with three balls to spare in its 50 overs at the wicket.

Set with a target of 165 runs to win, Australia enjoyed a sound start to its innings reaching 107 for the loss of two wickets. Joanne Broadbent was caught by the New Zealand skipper off the bowling of Kathryn Ramel [born 1973] for just 15 runs, while Belinda Clark reached a total of 52 before being caught and bowled by Catherine Campbell [born 1963]. Michelle Goszko [born1977] and the left-hand bat Karen Rolton [born 1974] made important contributions with knocks of 37 and 24 respectively. Victory was sealed for Australia in 47.4 overs, for the loss of 5 wickets, three minutes quicker than that of the New Zealand innings. *'When Australia got the winning run, the sound was deafening out in the middle,'* recalled Debbie Hockley. *'It really was like standing beside a jet engine.'*

New Zealand's Debbie Hockley fittingly topped the run-scoring, amassing a total of 456 runs, including two centuries, in her total of 7 innings, for a batting average of 65.1, her highest score being 100 not out. Such was her dominance she was named as New Zealand's Cricketer of the Year. Katrina Keenan [New Zealand] led the tournament for the highest number of wickets taken, collecting 13 in total at a cost of 115 runs from 54 overs, an average of 8.84, her best bowling figures being 4 wickets for 5 runs.

Sixth Women's World Cup Final – Sponsored by Hero Honda

New Zealand v Australia

Venue: Eden Park Cricket Ground, Calcutta - 29 December, 1997
Umpires: Aloke Bhattacharee [India]: S.Choudhary [India]

New Zealand won the toss and elected to bat.
Australia Women won by 5 wickets with 14 balls remaining.

New Zealand Women Innings [50 overs maximum]:

D.A.Hockley		b Fitzpatrick	79
E.C.Drumm		b Calver	6
F.K.Fruin	c Clark	b Calver	8
K.M.Withers	c Price	b Magno	5
M.A.M.Lewis [Captain]	lbw	b Magno	8
K.Ramel	run out		1
C.M.Nicholson	lbw	b Rolton	2
S.McLauchlan	st Price	b Rolton	10
R.J.Rolls [Wicket]	c Calver	b Mason	18
C.A.Campbell	not out		3
K.D.Brown	run out		1
Extras	[10lb, 13w]		23
TOTAL	49.3 overs – Run Rate 3.31		**164**

Fall of wickets:
1-14 [EC Drumm], 2-36 [MK Fruin], 3-49 [KM Withers], 4-87 [MAM Lewis], 5-99 [KA Ramel], 6-104 [CM Nicholson], 7-125 [S McLauchlan], 8-155 [DA Hockley], 9-157 [RJ Rolls], 10-164 [KD Brown]

Australia Bowling:	**O**	**M**	**R**	**W**	**Econ.**
C.L.Fitzpatrick	10	2	22	1	2.20
B.L.Calver	10	1	29	2	2.90
C.L.Mason	9.3	1	32	2	3.36
O.J.Magno	6	1	28	1	4.66
K.L.Rolton	6	1	25	2	4.16
A.J.Fahey	8	1	18	0	2.25

Australia Women Innings [50 overs maximum]:

B.J.Clark [Captain]		c & b Campbell	52
J.Broadbent	c Lewis	b Ramel	15
M.A.J.Goszko		b Withers	37
K.L.Rolton	c Brown	b Ramel	24
M.Jones		b Withers	1
B.J.Calver	not out		7
O.J.Magno	not out		0
J.C.Price [Wicket]	did not bat		
C.L.Mason	did not bat		
C.L.Fitzpatrick	did not bat		
A.J.Fahey	did not bat		

Extras	[8lb, 5w]	13
TOTAL	47.4 overs – Run Rate 4.46	**165**

Fall of wickets:
1-36 [J Broadbent], 2-107 [MAJ Goszko], 3-117 [BJ Clark], 4-153 [M Jones], 5-160 [KL Rolton]

New Zealand Bowling:	**O**	**M**	**R**	**W**	**Econ.**
K.M.Withers	10	2	23	2	2.30
C.M.Nicholson	10	3	26	0	2.60
K.D.Brown	1	0	10	0	10.00
K.A.Ramel	4.4	0	23	2	4.92
C.A.Campbell	10	1	36	1	3.60
S. McLauchlan	9	0	26	0	2.88
D.A,Hockley	3	0	12	0	4.00

Group Stage Standings:
Group A

Team	**Pld**	**W**	**L**	**T**	**NR**	**A**	**Pts**
Australia	5	4	0	0	1	0	27
England	5	4	1	0	0	0	24
South Africa	5	3	2	0	0	0	18
Ireland	5	2	2	0	1	0	15
Denmark	5	1	4	0	0	0	6
Pakistan	5	0	5	0	0	0	0

Group B

Team	**Pld**	**W**	**L**	**T**	**NR**	**A**	**Pts**
New Zealand	4	3	0	1	0	0	21
India	4	2	0	1	1	0	18
Netherlands	4	1	2	0	1	0	9
Sri Lanka	4	1	2	0	1	0	9
West Indies	4	0	3	0	1	0	3

Pld=Played; **W** =Wins; **L**=Losses; **T**=Tied; **NR**=No result; **Pts**=Points

During the summer of 1997 an announcement was made suggesting that in the interests of further developing the women's game, the Women's Cricket Association [WCA] would open formal negotiations with the England and Wales Cricket Board [ECB], regarding the possibility of a merger. The importance of such realignment was viewed by the WCA as an opportunity it could ill afford to ignore. And in April the following year an agreement was reached to integrate the WCA with the ECB, and with it the control of women's cricket.

With its headquarters now firmly established at Lord's, the England and Wales Cricket Board was established on the 1 January, 1997 as the single national governing body for all cricket in England and Wales. The concluding stage of a drive towards creating a unified body responsible for the management and development all forms of cricket for men and women. The formation followed two years of intensive research into how cricket in England and Wales might be better organised, with the objective of attracting more players to the game, raising the standards of play at all levels, and of promoting cricket as a spectator sport.

Seventh CricInfo Women's Cricket World Cup 2000

The seventh Women's Cricket World Cup was the second tournament to be hosted by New Zealand, and was played in Lincoln, a satellite town of Christchurch, located in the Selwyn District, of the Canterbury Region of New Zealand's South Island, from the 29 November to 23 December 2000.

Organised by the International Women's Cricket Council [IWCC], and sponsored by the celebrated cricketing website CricInfo. In another first for women's cricket, the tournament published ball-by-ball text commentary of the matches which were played over 50 overs, along with streamed audio and video coverage.

Australia and New Zealand finished first and second in the round-robin group stage of the tournament, and went on to win their respective semi-finals against South Africa, who Austalia defeated by 9 wickets, and India which New Zealand claimed by a similar margin. To set up a meeting in the final for the second time in succession, on the 23 December at the Bert Sutcliffe Oval, Lincoln, New Zealand. New Zealand won the toss and elected to bat first, but the *'White Ferns'* crumbled and were all out for 184 runs. Right-hand bat Kathryn Ramel [born 1973] was top scorer knocking up 41 runs from 63 deliveries.

In its response Australia lost the early wickets of Lisa Maree Keightley [born 1971] and Karen Louise Rolton [born 1974], but the reliable Belinda Clark managed to remain at the crease, and score 91 runs before being bowled after 42 overs by Clare Nicholson [born 1967]. Nicholson and the right-arm medium pace bowlers Katrina Keenan [born 1971] and Rachel Jane Pullar [born 1977] took two wickets apiece for New Zealand, with Keenan in particularly good form effectively restricting the Aussie run-rate. Australia faced the first ball of the final over requiring five runs to win, but a cheerless Charmaine Lea Mason [born 1970] was caught behind, leaving Australia all out for 180. The Australian skipper Belinda Clark's knock of 91 won her player of the match award after she accounted for half the team score while at the crease.

Rick Eyre, of *ESPNcricinfo,* suggested the match was *'the greatest World Cup final ever'*. With Australia clearly expecting to reach the target, they fell short and New Zealand ran out winners by four runs. It was one of the most memorable days in the 'White Ferns' cricketing history. Australia clearly expected to reach its target, but fell short, and the New Zealand women had won their first World Cup, after finishing runners-up in both the 1993 and 1997 tournaments.

Seventh CricInfo Women's World Cup Final – Sponsored by CricInfo

Australia v New Zealand

Venue:	Bert Sutcliffe Oval, Lincoln, New Zealand – 23 December, 2000
Umpires:	Peter Parker [New Zealand] and Dave Quested [New Zealand]

New Zealand won the toss and elected to bat
New Zealand won by four runs
Player of the match: Belinda Clark [Australia]

New Zealand Women's Innings [50 overs maximum]:

Anna M. O'Leary		b McGregor	1
Rebecca J. Rolls [Wicket]	c McGregor	b Mason	34
Emily C. Drumm [Capt.]	c Price	b McGregor	21
Deborah A. Hockley	lbw	b Fahey	24
Haidee M. Tiffin	c Banbury	b Goss	14
Kathryn A. Ramel	c Clark	b Fitzpatrick 41	
Helen M. Watson		b Fitzpatrick	11
Clare M. Nicholson		b Mason	11
Rachel J. Pullar	not out		9
Katrina M. Withers		b Fitzpatrick	0
Catherine A. Campbell	run out		0
Extras	[9lb, 1nb, 8w]		18
TOTAL	48.4 overs – Run Rate 3.78		**184**

Fall of wickets:
1-17 A.M.O'Leary, 3.4 ov, 2-60 E.C.Drumm, 13.5 ov, 3-60, R.J.Rolls, 14.1 ov, 4-92 H.M.Tiffin, 26.2 ov, 5-121 D.A.Hockley, 37.1 ov, 6-136 H.M.Watson, 40.4 ov, 7-172 K.M.Ramel, 46.6 ov. 8-175 C.M.Nicholson, 47.4 ov, 9-184 K.M.Withers, 48.3 ov, 10-184 C.A.Campbell, 48.4 ov.

Australia Bowling:	**O**	**M**	**R**	**W**	**Econ.**
C.L. Fitzpatrick	9.4	2	52	3	5.37
T.A.McGregor	10	5	26	0	2.60
C.L.Mason	9	2	30	2	3.33
O.J.Magno	6	0	22	0	3.66
Z.J.Goss	4	0	14	1	3.50
K.L.Rolton	6	0	12	0	2.00
A.J.Fahey	4	0	19	1	4.75

AustraliaWomen Innings [50 overs maximum]:

Lisa M. Keightley	c Rolls	b Keenan	0
Belinda J. Clark [Captain]		b Nicholson	91
Karen L. Rolton	run out		1
Cherie A. Bambury	c Hockley	b Pullar	14
Zoe J. Goss		b Campbell	1
Olivia J. Magno		b Keenan	4
Julia C. Price [Wicket]		b Pullar	10
Terry A. McGregor	run out		19

Cathryn L. Fitzpatrick		b Ramel	6
Charmaine L. Mason	c Rolls	b Nicholson	11
Avril J. Fahey	not out		3
Extras	[1 b, 6lb, 12w, 1 nb]		20
TOTAL	49.1 overs – Run Rate 3.66		**180**

Fall of wickets:
1-0 L.M.Keightley, 0.4 ov, 2-2 K.L.Rolton, 2.3 ov, 3-85 C.A.Bambury, 22.4 ov, 4-88 Z.J.Goss, 25.3 ov, 5-95 O.J.Magno, 28.3 ov, 6-115 J.C.Price, 34.4 ov, 7-150 B.J.Clark, 41.1 ov, 8-159 T.A.McGregor, 44.6 ov, 9-175 C.L.Fitzoatrick, 48.1 ov, 10-180 C.L.Mason, 49.1 ov.

New Zealand Bowling:	**O**	**M**	**R**	**W**	**Econ.**
K.M.Withers	10	3	19	2	1.90
R.J.Pullar	10	0	35	2	3.50
H.M.Tiffin	5	1	27	0	5.40
K.A.Ramel	5	0	26	1	5.20
C.A.Campbell	10	2	28	1	2.80
C.M.Nicholson	9.1	1	38	2	4.14

Group Stage Standings:

Team	**Pld**	**W**	**L**	**T**	**NR**	**A**	**Pts**	**RR**
Australia	7	7	0	0	0	0	14	1.984
New Zealand	7	6	1	0	0	0	12	2.008
India	7	5	2	0	0	0	10	0.711
South Africa	7	4	3	0	0	0	8	-0.403
England	7	3	4	0	0	0	6	0.440
Sri Lanka	7	2	5	0	0	0	4	-1.572
Ireland	7	1	6	0	0	0	2	-0.983
Netherlands	7	0	7	0	0	0	0	-2.098

Pld=Played; **W** =Wins; **L**=Losses; **T**=Tied; **NR**=No result; **Pts**=Points; **RR**=Run rate

Eighth Women's Cricket World Cup 2005

The eighth IWCC Women's Cricket World Cup was held in South Africa during March and April 2005. Eight teams competed in the event representing the nations of Australia, England, India, Ireland, New Zealand, Sri Lanka, the West Indies plus the host country of South Africa. The semi finalists were determined after the teams had played each other in a round-robin format with each team allocated an allotted maximum period of 50 overs.

England recorded the highest score in the tournament on its route to the semi-finals, accumulating a total of 284 runs for the loss of 4 wickets against Sri Lanka. After winning the coin-toss, Australia put England in to bat in the first semi-final of the tournament. England's innings ended on 158, but the dependable Beliinda Clark notched up 62 runs to help Australia over the line and reach the required winning score with 5 wickets in hand after 47 overs.

In the second semi-final India played New Zealand, which after winning the toss elected to field. The Indian openers were quickly dismissed, but the situation was soon rescued by Anjum Chopra [born 1977] and Mithali Raj [born 1982] who carried their bats and put on 44 and 91 respectively, on the way to India's eventual tally of 204 runs. New Zealand could only muster 164 in response, and India progressed to the final by a margin of 40 runs.

Before the start of the tournament, Jenny Thompson of ESPN Cricinfo accurately predicted the most likely winners of the tournament would come from Australia, India, England or New Zealand. Australia finished in the runner-up spot in the previous tournament in 2000, and this would be the seventh occasion in which the *'Southern Stars'* had featured in a women's World Cup final. Six of which had been on foreign soil, in contrast with India which was making its debut in a women's World Cup final.

Australia's opening group stage match against England, which was scheduled to be played at the Tshwane University of Technology

Oval, Pretoria, was *'washed out'* after heavy rain lashed Pretoria. Following which Australia went on to record five consecutive victories.

While India's first group stage match against Sri Lanka, also ended with no result. It won its next three matches, and faced it first loss in the tournament by 16 runs against New Zealand. Both finalists were scheduled to face each other in the final match of the group stage, however the match was also abandoned without a ball being bowled.

The final match was played between Australia and India on the 10 April at the SuperSport Park cricket ground in Centurion, Gauteng, South Africa. Formerly known as Centurion Park, it was renamed after the television company SuperSport bought shares in the stadium. Although it was the first time that an Indian team had reached this stage of a women's World Cup, they were unable to take down Australia, which won by 98 runs to secure its fifth World Cup title.

Batting conditions were good, and after winning the toss the Australian skipper Belinda Clark decided to bat first. The Indian bowling attack opened strongly, dismissing Clark caught behind the wicket early on, with Keightley caught out at second slip after 11 overs. Australia reached 100 runs after 34 overs, with vice-captain Karen Rolton, batting at number three, the top scorer for the Aussies, contributing 107 runs not out in an overall total of 215 runs for the loss of 4 wickets in its 50 over spell.

India played a poor innings in reply losing the opening wicket of Jaya Sharma run out in the eighth over for only 5 runs. This set the pattern for India with the bat, as it continued to score poorly, the last of their ten wickets falling for an overall total of 117 at the end of the forty-sixth over. Australia's Karen Rolton was named player of the match, and player of the series.

Eighth CricInfo Women's World Cup Final

Australia v India

Venue:	SuperSport Park, Centurion, Gauteng - 10 April, 2005
Umpires:	Shaun George [South Africa] and Zed Ndamane [South Africa]

Australia won the toss and elected to bat.
New Zealand won by 98 runs.
Player of the match: Karen Rolton [Australia]

Australia Women Innings [50 overs maximum]:

Belinda J. Clark [Capt.]	c Jain	b A.Sharma	19
Lisa M. Keightley	c Dhar	b Goswami	5
Karen L. Rolton	not out		107
Melanie Jones	lbw	b David	17
Lisa C. Sthalekar		c & b Dhar	55
Alexandra J. Blackwell	not out		4
Cathryn L. Fitzpatrick	did not bat		
Julia C. Price [Wicket]	did not bat		
Julie Hayes	did not bat		
Shelly Nitschke	did not bat		
Clea R. Smith	did not bat		
Extras	[2lb, 2w, 4nb]		8
TOTAL	50 overs – Run Rate 4.30		**215**

Fall of wickets:
1-24 B.J.Clark, 7.5 ov, 2-31 L.M.Keightley, 10.3 ov, 3-71 M.Jones, 24.6 ov, 4-210 L.C.Sthalekar, 49.3 ov.

IndiaBowling:	**O**	**M**	**R**	**W**	**Econ.**
J.Goswami	9	2	45	1	5.00
A.Sharma	10	2	39	1	3.90
R.Dhar	6	0	34	1	5.66
N.Al Khadeer	10	1	35	0	3.50
N.David	10	1	39	1	3.90
D.M.Kulkarni	5	0	21	0	4.20

India Women's Innings [50 overs maximum]:

Anju Jain [Wicket]	c Sthalekar	b Smith	29
Jaya Sharma	run out		5
Anjum Chopra	run out		10
Mithali D. Raj [Captain]	lbw	b Nitschke	6

Rumeli Dhar	run out		6
Hemetla Kala	run out		3
Amita Sharma	lbw	b Sthalekar	22
Jhulan Goswami	c sub K.Blackwell	b Fitzpatrick	18
Deepa M. Kulkami	not out		7
Neetu David		b Fitzpatrick	0
Nooshin Al Khadeer		b Nitschke	0
Extras	[2b, 3lb, 1nb, 5w]		11
TOTAL	46.0 overs – Run Rate 2.54		**117**

Fall of wickets:
1-14 J.Sharma, 7.3 ov, 2-39 A.Jain, 15.4 ov, 3-54, A.Chopra, 19.6 ov, 4-59 M.Raj, 21.2 ov, 5-63 R.Dhar, 23.2 ov, 6-64 H.Kala, 24.3 ov,7-93 A.Sharma, 37.4 ov.
8-115 J.Goswami, 42.2 ov, 9-116 N.David, 44.3 ov, 10-117 N.AlKhadeer, 46.0 ov.

Australia Bowling:	**O**	**M**	**R**	**W**	**Econ.**
C.L.Fitzpatrick	8	1	23	2	2.87
C.R.Smith	10	4	20	1	2.00
J.Hayes	10	1	28	0	2.80
S.Nitschke	9	2	14	2	1.55
K.L.Rolton	5	1	9	0	1.80
L.C. Sthalekar	4	1	18	1	4.50

Group Stage Standings:

Team	**Pld**	**W**	**L**	**T**	**NR**	**A**	**Pts**
Australia	7	5	0	0	2	0	35
India	7	4	1	0	2	0	30
New Zealand	7	4	1	0	2	0	29
England	7	3	2	0	2	0	26
West Indies	7	2	3	0	2	0	19
Sri Lanka	7	1	4	0	2	0	12
South Africa	7	1	4	0	2	0	11
Ireland	7	0	5	0	2	0	6

Pld=Played; **W** =Wins; **L**=Losses; **T**=Tied; **NR**=No result; **Pts**=Points:

Ninth Women's Cricket World Cup 2009

The 2009 Women's Cricket World Cup Final was played between New Zealand and England, on the 22 March 2009, at the North Sydney Oval in Australia, where England clinched its third World Cup victory by a four wicket margin, its first win outside England. It was the second time the two teams had faced each other in the final of the Women's Cricket World Cup, the first being at Lord's in 1993 which England also won.

The New Zealand captain Haidee Maree Tiffen MNZM [born 1979] won the toss and elected to put her side in to bat first. It was bowled out in 47.2 overs for 166 runs, with the all-rounder Lucy Rose Doolan [born 1987] batting at number nine, knocking up the highest score of 48. The right-arm fast-medium bowler Nicola 'Nicky' Jayne Shaw [born 1981] took a career-best four wickets for 34 runs for England. Initially Nicky was not included in the England team, but was called up to replace the injured Jennifer 'Jenny' Louise Gunn MBE [born 1986] just minutes before the start of the game, and to her delight was later named the player of the match. Jenny Gunn is the daughter of the former Nottingham Forest FC defender, Bryn Gunn.

England scored steadily and built up an opening partnership of 74 runs in response, from then forward England lost wickets with steady regularity, but managed to reach a winning total with 23 balls to spare, to secure its first World Cricket Cup title for 16 years.

Teams from New Zealand, Australia, England, India, Pakistan, South Africa, Sri Lanka and from the West Indies competed, with six of the eight teams taking part having qualified through a top six finish in the previous tournament held in South Africa in 2005. The two remaining spots were awarded to Pakistan and South Africa. The eight qualifying teams were divided into two groups for the group stage of the tournament. With the traditional rivals Australia and New Zealand drawn together in Group A, alongside South Africa and the West Indies. While in Group B, India and Pakistan were drawn together with England and Sri Lanka.

Following the completition of the group stages, the leading three teams in each group moved forward to the Super Six stage, which was played in the conventional round-robin format, with the half-dozen teams playing only three matches each, rather than five as might have been expected, since each member of the Super Six's results in the earlier representative matches played against each other in the group stages were carried forward in preference to playing against each other again. Consequently, the Super Six table shows five matches played by each team, and includes all the matches played between the Super Six qualifiers, plus those from the group stage. The two top teams in the Super Six final table qualifyied for the final.

Ninth Women's World Cup Final

England v New Zealand

Venue:	North Sydney Oval, Sydney, Australia - 22 March, 2009
Umpires:	Steve Davis [Australia]: Brian Jerling [South Africa]

New Zealand won the toss and elected to bat.
England Women won by four wickets.

New Zealand Women Innings [50 overs maximum]:

K.L.Pulford	c S.C.Taylor	b Guha	8
H.M.Tiffin [Captain]	c S.J.Taylor	b Shaw	30
S.W.Bates	c Atkins	b Shaw	2
A.E.Satterthwaite	c S.J.Taylor	b Shaw	0
S.J.McGlashan	c Greenway	b Colvin	21
A.L.Watkins		b Marsh	13
N.J.Browne	lbw	b Shaw	25
S.J.Tsukigawa	c S.J.Taylor	b Brunt	2
L.R.Doolan	st S.J.Taylor	b Marsh	48
S.F.M.Devine	lbw	b Edwards	0
R.H.Priest [Wicket]	not out		0
Extras	[2lb, 15w]		17
TOTAL	47.2 overs – Run Rate 3.50		**166**

Fall of wickets:
1-26 KL Pulford 7.6 ov, 2-49 SW Bates 11.3 ov, 3-49 AE Satterthwaite 11.4 ov, 4-62 HM Tiffen, 15.5 ov, 5-74 SJ McGlashan, 18.2 ov, 6-92 AL Watkins, 23.2 ov, 7-101 SJ Tsukigawa, 28.6 ov, 8-164 LR Doolan, 45.3 ov, 9-166 SFM Devine, 46.5 ov,

10-166 NJ Browne, 47.2 ov.

England Bowling:	O	M	R	W	Econ.
K.H.Brunt	10	3	33	1	3.30
I.T.Guha	5	0	24	1	4.80
N.J.Shaw	8.2	0	34	4	4.08
H.L.Colvin	10	1	26	1	2.60
L.A.Marsh	10	3	34	2	3.40
C.M.Edwards	4	1	13	1	3.25

England Women's Innings [50 overs maximum]:

S.J.Taylor [Wicket]	c Tiffin	b Doolan	39
C.M.G Atkins	c Devine	b Doolan	40
S.C.Taylor		b Mason	21
C.M.Edwards [Captain]	c Priest	b Doolan	10
L.S.Greenway	c Satterthwaite	b Mason	8
B.L.Morgan	run out		9
N.J.Shaw	not out		17
H.L.Colvin	not out		5
L.A.Marsh	did not bat		
K.H.Brunt	did not bat		
I.T.Guha	did not bat		
Extras	[1lb, 17w]		18
TOTAL	46.1 overs – Run Rate 3.61		**167**

Fall of wickets:
1-74 SJ Taylor, 17.2 ov, 2-109 SC Taylor, 26.2 ov, 3-111 CMG Atkins, 27.2 ov, 4-121 CM Edwards, 31.4 ov, 5-139 LS Greenway,38.3 ov, 6-149 BL Morgan, 41.5 ov.

New Zealand Bowling:	O	M	R	W	Econ.
S.F.M.Devine	9	0	30	0	3.33
K.L.Pulford	3	0	17	0	5.66
N.J.Browne	7	1	24	0	3.42
S.W.Bates	4.1	0	21	0	5.04
L.R.Doolan	10	4	23	3	2.30
S.J.Tsukigawa	4	1	23	0	5.75
A.L.Watkins	9	0	28	2	3.11

Group Stage Standings:
Group A:

Team	Pld	W	L	T	NR	A	Pts	RR
New Zealand	3	3	0	0	0	0	6	2.015
Australia	3	2	1	0	0	0	4	0.714
West Indies	3	1	2	0	0	0	2	-0.655
South Africa	3	0	3	0	0	0	0	-1.777

Group B:

Team	Pld	W	L	T	NR	A	Pts	RR
England	3	3	0	0	0	0	6	1.921

India	3	2	1	0	0	0	4	0.922
Pakistan	3	1	2	0	0	0	2	-0.961
Sri Lanka	3	0	3	0	0	0	0	-1.280

Super Six Stage:

Team	Pld	W	L	T	NR	A	Pts	RR
New Zealand	5	4	1	0	0	0	8	1.180
England	5	4	1	0	0	0	8	1.157
India	5	3	2	0	0	0	6	1.105
Australia	5	3	2	0	0	0	6	0.850
Pakistan	5	1	4	0	0	0	2	-2.589
West Indies	5	0	5	0	0	0	0	-1.559

Pld=Played; **W** =Wins; **L**=Losses; **T**=Tied; **NR**=No result; **Pts**=Points; **RR** = Run rate was to be used as a tie-breaker in the event of teams finishing on an equal number of points.

Standings:

Position	**Team**	**W**	**L**
1	England	6	1
2	New Zealand	5	2
3	India	5	2
4	Australia	4	3
5	Pakistan	2	5
6	West Indies	2	5
7	South Africa	1	3
8	Sri Lanka	0	4

Tenth Women's Cricket World Cup 2013

The 2013 Women's Cricket World Cup was hosted by India for the third time, having previously hosted the event in 1978 and 1997.

Four teams qualified for the tournament through the previous World Cup standings, including teams Australia, England, India and New Zealand, which were later joined by Sri Lanka, South Africa, Pakistan and the West Indies who qualified through the 2011 Women's Cricket World Cup Qualifier held in Bangladesh.

The final of the tenth Women's Cricket World Cup was played between Australia and the West Indies at the Brabourne Stadium in Mumbai, India on the 17 February 2013. The Brabourne Stadium was India's first permanent sporting venue, and is owned by the Cricket Club of India [CCI] and was envisaged as being the Indian equivalent of the Marylebone Cricket Club [MCC].

Once again the top three teams from each of the two group stages moved on to the Super Six stage of the tournament, played as a *'round-robin'* format, with each of the teams competing against the Super Six qualifiers from outside their groups, and carrying forward the result of the games which had already been played against the teams which qualified from its respective group. With the top two teams from the Super Six final table qualifying to compete in the final.

The West Indies were drawn in Group A along with England, India and Sri Lanka and, despite losing to India and England, finished in third place in the group and qualified for the Super Six section, where they won all three of their games to progress to compete in the final. Australia was drawn in Group B together with New Zealand, Pakistan, and South Africa. In its first match Australia defeated Pakistan by 91 runs, won their second match against South Africa by three wickets, and in the final group match beat New Zealand to qualify for the Super Six section of the tournament. They qualified for the final followed a convincing win against Sri Lanka and a narrow two-run victory over England, and ultimate defeat at the hands of the *'Windies'*.

In the final the Australian captain, Jodie Fields [born 1984], won the toss and chose to bat first, which proved to be a shrewd decision as her team accumulated a total of 259 runs for the loss of 7 wickets in its 50 over span. Opening bats Meghann Moira Lanning [born 1992] and Rachael

Louise Haynes [born 1986] put on 52 runs in a first wicket stand, with Haynes progressing to share a stand of 64 with Jessica Evelyn Cameron [born 1989] before falling on 52 to a catch by Kycia Akira Knight [born 1992] off the bowling of seventeen year-old Shaquana Latish Quintyne [born 1996]. Cameron made 75 runs from just 76 deliveries, which included two sixes and eight boundaries, before she was caught by Kyshona Annika Knight [born 1992], the twin-sister of Kycia, off the bowling of Shanel Francine Daley [born 1988]. With just seven overs remaining and 209 runs on the board Australia seemingly lost its momentum adding just 50 more runs off the remaining balls to ultimately record a score of 259.

In response, the West Indies never really got going and were bowled out for 145 in 43.1 overs, securing an easy victory for Australia by 114 runs, the sixth Women's World Cup win for the *'Southern Stars'*. Although the West Indies had defeated Australia in the Super Six group stage, they were outclassed in the final, with the BBC commenting that *'Australia were too clinical for a West Indies side that were sloppy in the field, wayward with the ball and unable to keep up with the run chase'*. The West Indies skipper and wicketkeeper Merissa Ria Aguilleira [born 1985] was top-scorer for her team with 23 in the *'Windies'* reply, but they never looked like threatening the Australian total and were well beaten. Despite the margin of victory, it was stressed that the result was not totally unexpected. *'It was no surprise, and indeed no shame, for the West Indies to be outclassed by a team that lost just one of seven games, and that by only eight runs'*.

In the play-off for third and fourth place England knocked up 222 runs for the loss of six wickets in reply to New Zealand's tally of 220 in 47 overs. Sri Lanka's total of 244 for 7, in the play-off for fifth and sixth place, was enough to comfortably defeat South Africa which could only rack up 156 runs in reply. With the final two places in the standings determined after India sailed passed the Pakistan total of 192 for the loss of seven wickets, with 24 balls to spare.

Tenth Women's World Cup Final

Australia v West Indies

Venue:	Brabourne Stadium, Mumbai, India - 17 February, 2013
Umpires:	Shaun George [South Africa]: Vineet Kulkarni [India]

Australia won the toss and elected to bat.
Australia Women won by 114 runs.
Player of the match: Jess Cameron [Australia].

Australia Women Innings [50 overs maximum]:

Meghann M. Lanning	c Kyshona A. Knight	b Taylor	31
Raechel L. Haynes	c Kycia A. Knight	b Quintyne	52
Jessica E. Cameron	c Kyshona A. Knight	b Daley	75
Alexandra J. Blackwell	c Aguilleira	b Smartt	3
Lisa C. Sthalekar	c Campbelle	b Quintyne	12
Sarah J. Coyte	c Daley	b Quintyne	7
Jodie M. Fields [Capt. & Wicket] not out			36
Erin A. Eastbourne	c Quintyne	b Mohammed	7
Ellyse A. Perry	not out		25
Julie L. Hunter	did not bat		
Megan Schutt	did not bat		
Extras	[3lb, 4nb, 4w]		11
TOTAL	50 overs – Run Rate 5.18		**259**

Fall of wickets:
1-52 MM Lanning 9.6 ov, 2-116 RL Haynes 24.6 ov, 3-126 AJ Blackwell 27.5 ov, 4-181 JE Cameron, 35.5 ov, 5-187 LC Sthalekar, 37.1 ov, 6-190 SJ Coyte, 39.2 ov, 7-209 EA Osborne, 43.2 ov.

West Indies Bowling:	**O**	**M**	**R**	**W**	**Econ.**
S.F. Daley	10	0	43	1	4.30
T.D. Smartt	5	0	43	1	8.60
S.R. Taylor	9	1	44	1	4.88
S.L. Quintyne	10	1	27	3	2.70
A. Mohammed	10	0	61	1	6.10
Kyshona A. Knight	3	0	23	0	7.66
S.A. Campbelle	3	0	15	0	5.00

West Indies Women's Innings [50 overs maximum]:

Kycia A. Knight	lbw	b Perry	17
N.Y. McLean	lbw	b Perry	13
S.R. Taylor		c & b Perry	5
Kyshona A. Knight	not out		21
M.R. Aguilleira [Capt. & Wicket]		b Sthalekar 23	
D.J.S. Dottin		b Sthalekar	22
S.A. Campbelle	c Lanning	b Schutt	11
S.F. Daley		c & b Schutt	2
S.L. Quintyne	c Blackwell	b Osborne	2
A. Mohammed	c Schutt	b Osborne	14
T.D. Smartt	c Sthalekar	b Hunter	0
Extras	[1 b, 8lb, 6w]		15
TOTAL	43.1 overs – Run Rate 3.35		**145**

Fall of wickets:
1-32 Kycia A. Knight, 9.6 ov, 2-38 SR Taylor, 11.4 ov, 3-41 NY McLean, 13.3 ov, 4-88 MR Aguilleira, 26.1 ov, 5-109 DJS Dottin, 30.4 ov, 6- 109 SA Campbelle, 31.1 ov, 7-114 SL Quintyne, 34.1 ov, 8-114 SF Daley, 35.4 ov, 9-141 A Mohammed, 42.2 ov, 10-145 TD Smartt, 43.1 ov.

Australia Bowling:	**O**	**M**	**R**	**W**	**Econ.**
M. Schutt	10	2	38	2	3.80
J.L Hunter	4.1	0	18	1	4.32
L.C Sthalekar	10	3	20	1	2.00
E.A. Perry	10	3	19	3	1.90
E.A. Osborne	7	2	26	1	3.71
S.J. Coyte	2	0	15	0	7.50

Group Stage Standings:
Group A

Team	**Pld**	**W**	**L**	**T**	**NR**	**A**	**Pts**	**RR**
England	3	2	1	0	0	0	4	0.641
Sri Lanka	3	2	1	0	0	0	4	-0.433
West Indies	3	1	2	0	0	0	2	0.276
India	3	1	2	0	0	0	2	0.233

Group B:

Team	**Pld**	**W**	**L**	**T**	**NR**	**A**	**Pts**	**RR**
Australia	3	3	0	0	0	0	6	1.099
New Zealand	3	2	1	0	0	0	4	1.422
South Africa	3	1	2	0	0	0	2	-0.291
Pakistan	3	0	3	0	0	0	0	-1.986

Super Six Stage:

Team	**Pld**	**W**	**L**	**T**	**NR**	**A**	**Pts**	**RR**
West Indies	5	4	1	0	0	0	8	0.941
Australia	5	4	1	0	0	0	8	0.714
England	5	3	2	0	0	0	6	1.003
New Zealand	5	2	3	0	0	0	4	0.694
South Africa	5	1	4	0	0	0	2	-1.131
Sri Lanka	5	1	4	0	0	0	2	-2.477

Pld=Played; **W** =Wins; **L**=Losses; **T**=Tied; **NR**=No result; **Pts**=Points; **RR** = Run rate was to be used as a tie-breaker in the event of teams finishing on an equal number of points.

Final Standings:

Position	**Team**	**W**	**L**
1	Australia	6	1
2	West Indies	4	3
3	England	5	2
4	New Zealand	3	4
5	Sri Lanka	3	4
6	South Africa	2	5
7	India	2	2
8	Pakistan	0	4

Eleventh Women's Cricket World Cup 2017

The 2017 Women's Cricket World Cup was the eleventh of the Women's Cricket World Cup series, the first in which all its players were full professionals. It was the third time the event had been held in England, the previous events being held in 1973 and 1993. It ran from the 24 June to the 23 July, in which a total of eight teams qualifyied to participate.

The ICC announced a panel of thirteen umpires and three match referees to officiate throughout the tournament, all drawn from the ICC's International Umpires Development Panel, four of which were female. Amongst the quartet was Suzanne 'Sue' Redfern [born 1977], born in Mansfield, Nottinghamshire, Sue became the first woman to have played in a Women's Cricket World Cup, and then take on the role as an umpire.

Before the start of the tournament a series of eight practice matches were played. In the group stage, each of the eight sides participating played each other once in a single-league format, a format last used in the 2005 tournament in Australia. Following the group league matches the top four sides progressed through to the semi-finals, with the two winning semi-finalists meeting in the final at Lord's on the 23 July. In the event of teams tying on equal points at the end of the group stage, the final rankings were determined by the number of wins, followed by the calculation of the net run rate. In the event the rankings still remained identical, after applying the determining factors, then a head-to-head deciding match was to be used to determine which team progressed to the semi-finals.

In the first of the semi-finals, played on the 18 July at the Bristol County Ground, South Africa won the toss and elected to bat, scoring 218 runs for the loss of 6 wickets in its 50 overs, with Mignon du Preez [born 1989] scoring 76 not out in her 96 minutes in the middle. England responded with a score of 221 for 8 wickets in 49.4 overs to win by 2 wickets

The second of the semi-final matches, held at the County Ground in Derby, on the 20 July, was reduced to 42 overs per side due to rain. The all-rounder Harmanpreet Kaur [born 1989] scored 171 not out, in just under two hours, assisting India reach its total of 281, for the loss of just four wickets. Australia's valiant run-chase fell short by 36, with the team all out in 40.1 overs. The all-rounder Harmanpreet Kaur [born 1989] was subsequently awarded the Arjuna Award for Cricket in 2017 by the Indian Ministry of Youth Affairs and Sports.

Despite losing to India in the opening match of the series, the England captain Heather Clare Knight OBE, exacted her revenge in the summer when she led her team to victory in front of a euphoric crowd at Lord's, following a remarkable fight back. As a result Heather was awarded an OBE in the Queen's 2018 New Year Honours list.

Chasing a target of 229, India looked well set to repeat its earlier triumph, amassing a score of 191 for the loss of three wickets. It was then that the right-arm medium paced seamer Anya Shrubsole MBE [born 1991] nicked the wicket of Punam Ganesh Raut [born 1989] lbw for 86, sparking an Indian collapse of seven wickets for the addition of a trifling 28 runs. England's remarkable comeback saw India off for 219 with eight balls left unused. Shrubsole finished her bowling spell with six wickets for 46 runs, the best bowling figures in a World Cup final.

And yet even in the midst of the stunning 19 over spell by Shrubsole, in which she collected five wickets for 11 runs, India were still within reach of winning its first major title, and pulling off the highest successful run chase in World Cup history. England's fears were intensified when Jenny Gunn dropped a sitter at mid-off from Poonam Yadav [born 1991], but Shrubsole was to re-ignite the enthusiasm both on the pitch and amongst the 26,500 sell-out crowd, the second largest in Women's World Cup history when she clean bowled Rajeshwari Gayakwad [born 1991] with her next ball.

More than 50 million people worldwide watched the group stages, and in an post-match interview for BBC Sport the ecstatic Knight proclaimed, *'Women's cricket has gone through the roof since 2009'*, the last time England won the coveted trophy. *'This is a watershed moment, to be playing at Lord's in front of a sell-out crowd in a World Cup final. You just don't think those things are going to happen. It's unbelievable. What a tournament it has been, the support, the cricket and everything about it.'*

In her speech at the prize presentation after the match, the inspirational England captain said, *'I can't stop smiling. I am so proud of this group of girls. We made it hard for ourselves but I couldn't care less. We won tight games and that was something we wanted to work on. Anya Shrubsole ... what a hero ! India batted brilliantly and put good partnerships together. But we knew if we hung in and kept the rate at five or six then we would always be in the game. And we held our nerve.'*

Holding the trophy aloft, the champagne flowed freely, before the skipper passed it down the line to her team-mates, and there were floods of tears all round. Danielle Hazell [born 1988] was half laughing and half crying, while Barnsley's Katherine Brunt [born 1985] was yelling *'We love you, Heather !'*

The England match winner Anya Shrubsole, moved by the moment, said, *'I am lost for words. One of the great things about this team is we never give up. It is a fitting final of what was a brilliant World Cup. There was a huge amount of pressure. We never let the run rate get away and we knew if we got a couple then we would be in the game. It is a dream. I never thought it would come true. To be back here as a World Cup winner is amazing.'*

Former right-arm fast-medium bowler, Mark Andrew Robinson OBE [born 1966], the current coach of the England women's cricket team, proudly commented, *'It has captured the imagination of everybody as the tournament has gone on. Hopefully, the women's game will go from strength to strength. It is getting the recognition, getting its proper place. People take it seriously and give it respect'*. Robinson was also awarded an OBE in the 2018 Queen's New Year Honours list.

BBC television broadcast ten games live throught the series, with the remaining 21 matches streamed live via the ICC website. Although all the matches took place in England, officially the tournament was hosted by England and Wales since the England and Wales Cricket Board [EWCB] is responsible for the organisation of cricket in both countries.

What a day to savour for the women cricketers of England ... and, for a while at least, not a *'pebble'* to be seen anywhere !

Eleventh Women's World Cup Final

England v India

Venue: Lord's, London, England – 23 July, 2017
Umpires: Gregory Brathwaite [West Indies]: Shaun George [South Africa]

England won the toss and elected to bat
England Women won by 9 runs
Player of the match: Anya Shrubsole [England]

England Women's Innings [50 overs maximum]:

Lauren Winfield		b Gayakward	24
Tamsin Beaumont [Wicket]	c Goswami	b Poonam	23
Sarah Taylor	c Devi	b Goswami	45
Heather Knight [Capt.]	lbw	b Poonam	1
Natalie Sciver	lbw	b Goswami	51
Fran Wilson	lbw	b Goswami	0
Katherine Brunt	run out		34
Jenny Gunn	not out		25
Laura Marsh	not out		14
Alex Hartley	did not bat		
Anya Shrubsole	did not bat		
Extras	[3lb, 1nb, 7w]		11
TOTAL	50 overs – Run Rate 4.56		**228**

Fall of wickets:
1-47 L.Winfield, 11.1 ov, 2-60 T.Beaumont, 14.3 ov, 3-63 H.Knight, 16.1 ov, 4-146 S.Taylor, 32.4 ov, 5-146 F.Wilson, 32.5 ov,6-164 N.Sciver, 37.1 ov, 7-196 K.Brunt, 45.6 ov.

India Bowling:	O	M	R	W	Econ.
Jhulan Goswami	10	3	23	3	2.30
Shikha Pandey	7	0	53	0	7.57
Rajeshwari Gayakwad	10	1	49	1	4.90

Deepti Sharma	9	0	39	0	4.33
Yadav Poonam	10	0	36	2	3.60
Harmanpreet Kaur	4	0	25	0	6.25

India Women Innings [50 overs maximum]:

Poonam Raut	lbw	b Shrubsole	86
Smritj Mandhana	b Shrubsole		0
Mithali Raj [Captain]	run out		17
Harmanpreet Kaur	c Beaumont	b Hartley	51
Veda Krishnamurthy	c Sciver	b Shrubsole	35
Sishma Verma [Wicketkeeper]	b Hartley	0	
Deepti Sharma	c Sciver	b Shrubsole	14
Jhulan Goswami	b Shrubsole		0
Shikha Pandey	runout		4
Poonam Yadav	not out		1
Rajeshwari Gayakwad		b Shrubsole	0
Extras	[3lb, 7w, 1 nb]		11
TOTAL	48.4 overs – Run Rate 4.52		**219**

Fall of wickets:
1-5 S.Mandhana, 1.4 ov, 2-43 M.Raj, 12.1 ov, 3-138 H.Kaur, 33.3 ov, 4-191 P.Raut, 42.5 ov, 5-196 S.Verma 43.3 ov, 6-200 V.Krishamurthy, 44.4 ov, 7-201 J.Goswami, 44.6 ov, 8-218 S.Pandey, 47.3 ov, 9-218 D.Sharma, 48.1 ov,10-219 R.Gayakwad, 48.4 ov.

England Bowling:	**O**	**M**	**R**	**W**	**Econ.**
K.H.Brunt	6	0	22	0	3.67
A.Shrubsole	9.4	0	46	6	4.76
N.Sciver	5	1	26	0	5.20
J.Gunn	7	2	17	0	2.43
L.A.Marsh	10	1	40	0	4.00
A.Hartley	10	0	58	2	5.80
H.Knight	1	0	7	0	7.00

Group Stage Standings:

Team	**Pld**	**W**	**L**	**T**	**NR**	**A**	**Pts**	**RR**
England	7	6	1	0	0	0	12	1.295
Australia	7	6	1	0	0	0	12	1.004
India	7	5	2	0	0	0	10	0.669
South Africa	7	3	3	0	1	0	7	1,183
New Zealand	7	3	3	0	1	0	7	0.309
West Indies	7	2	5	0	0	0	4	-1.522
Sri Lanka	7	1	6	0	0	0	2	-1.099
Pakiastan	7	0	7	0	0	0	0	-1.930

Pld=Played; **W** =Wins; **L**=Losses; **T**=Tied; **NR**=No result; **Pts**=Points; **RR** = Run rate was to be used as a tie-breaker in the event of teams finishing on an equal number of points.

Thirteen nations have qualified for the Women's Cricket World Cup at least once. The 2021 Women's World Cup is scheduled to be held in New Zealand.

Summary of the tournament history of the Women's World Cup

No.	Year	Winner	Runner up	Host	Venue	No. of teams
1	1973	England	Australia	England	Edbaston	7
2	1978	Australia	England	India	Hyderabad	4
3	1982	Australia	England	New Zealand	Christchurch	5
4	1988	Australia	England	Australia	Melbourne	5
5	1993	England	New Zealand	England	Lords, London	8
6	1997	Australia	New Zealand	India	Kolkata	11
7	2000	New Zealand	Australia	New Zealand	Lincoln	8
8	2005	Australia	India	South Africa	Centurion	8
9	2009	England	New Zealand	Australia	Sydney	8
10	2013	Australia	West Indies	India	Mumbai	8
11	2017	England	India	England	Lords, London	8

Team	Appearances	Wins	Runner up	Best finish
Australia	11	6 55%	2 18%	1
Denmark	2	0 0 %	0 0 %	7
England	11	4 36%	3 27%	1
India	9	0 0 %	2 22%	2
Ireland	5	0 0 %	0 0 %	4
Netherlands	4	0 0 %	0 0 %	5
New Zealand	11	1 9%	3 27%	1
Pakistan	4	0 0 %	0 0 %	5
South Africa	6	0 0 %	0 0 %	Lost in semi-final
Sri Lanka	6	0 0 %	0 0 %	5
West Indies	6	0 0 %	1 17%	2
Obsolete teams				
International XI	2	0 0 %	0 0 %	4
Jamaica	1	0 0 %	0 0 %	6
Trinidad & Tobago	1	0 0 %	0 0 %	5
Young England	1	0 0 %	0 0 %	7

Chapter 12

The Women's Ashes

And so the invitation eventually arrived, and England's women cricketers accepted the challenge and prepared to set sail for Australia from Tilbury in October 1934 in the SS Orion, for the first ever Women's Test series to be played between England and Australia.

It was generally accepted the England side was under represented, with players having to independently stump up the cash needed for the six-month trip. As a result some of the best players inevitably missed out, along with a number of married women, as it was considered inappropriate for them to spend time away from their husbands and the home. Those that could muster the finances were reduced from an original list of 35 fervent volunteers. All of which made their own fun on board ship throughout the voyage by playing deck cricket and posing for photographs, having agree not to smoke, drink or gamble *or 'be accompanied by a man'.*

The women's game was still at a stage when it struggled to be taken seriously, and as was to be expected the ground breaking tour failed to meet with widespread approval. The *Times* being particularly disrespectful, claiming, *'It does not seem nice to think that they are future mothers charged with the responsibility of setting an example of gentleness, refinement and restraint to the coming generation'.*

Consequently, the tour would inevirably prove to be a test for all three of the participating nations. In the words of Betty Archdale, the England women's team captain when she stepped off the boat in Australia, *'We're not here for any Ashes, but merely to play cricket'.* Women played only *'for love of the game'* and did not wish to be associated with the male concept of Test matches and *'Ashes'.*

'Down Under' cricket was still in its infancy, for although State cricket had been established for several years, the game had only just begun to be organised nationally. Similarly, and in common with Australia, New Zealand had itself only been playing the game for just under 50 years.

An under strength England still proved the strongest, but Australia played its cricket rough, and runs were hard earned, for there were no such thing as boundaries, and you had to run all your runs.

The English cricketer and author, Nancy Joy, would later report in her book, *'Maiden Over. A short history of women's cricket and a diary of the 1948-49 test tour to Australia', 'England brought victory but no blaze of glory, for nerves and spin combined to make the cricket on both sides less good than it might have been'.*

England Women's Cricket Team 1934-1935

Australia Women v England Women, at Brisbane.

1st Test - 28-31 December, 1934 – 3 day match

Australia won the toss and elected to bat first
Australia Women 47 & 138 - England Women 154 & 34 for 1[12.5 overs]

England Women won by 9 wickets
England lead the 3 match series 1-0

Umpires: Francis Bartlett [Australia]: John Scott [Austalia]

Note: H.D. Pritchard kept wicket for England Women in both innings due to H.M. Hills suffering a broken nose while batting in the first Australia Women innings

Australia Women First Innings

H.D. Pritchard	hit wicket	b Maclagan	4
R. Monaghan		c & b Maclagan	4
E.M. McLarty		c & b Maclagan	0
E.M. Shevill		b Maclagan	0
K.M. Smith	c Spear	b Maclagan	25
H.M. Hills [Wicket]	retired hurt		2
M.E.M. Peden [Captain]		b Taylor	1

L.W. Kettels	c Partridge	b Maclagan	9
A. Palmer	c Partridge	b Maclagan	1
P. Antonio	c Partridge	b Taylor	0
F.L. Blade	not out		0
Extras	[1 b]		1
TOTAL	49.3 overs – Run Rate 0.94		**47**

England Bowling First Innings	**O**	**M**	**R**	**W**	**Econ.**
M.E. Maclagan	17	11	10	7	0.58
M.I. Taylor	14.3	8	9	2	0.62
M.F. Spear	8	7	2	0	0.25
M.E. Hide	4	0	6	0	1.50
D.M. Turner	4	1	7	0	1.75
J.E. Partridge	2	0	12	0	6.00

England Women First Innings

M.E. Maclagan		b Palmer	72
E.A. Snowball [Wicket]	c Shevill	b Antonio	15
M.E. Hide	c Kettels	b Palmer	9
E.M.Child	c McLarty	b Palmer	5
J.E. Partridge		b Palmer	0
H.E. Archdale [Captain]	not out		32
D.M. Turner	c McLarty	b Palmer	2
J. Liebert		b McLarty	1
M.I. Taylor	c McLarty	b Smith	0
M.F. Spear		b Palmer	9
C. Valentine		b Palmer	0
Extras	[9 b]		9
TOTAL	73.2 overs – Run Rate 2.10		**154**

Australia Bowling First Innings	**O**	**M**	**R**	**W**	**Econ.**
F.L. Blade	0	2	24	0	2.40
K.M. Smith	13	2	32	1	2.46
E.M. McLarty	10	4	12	1	1.20
P. Antonio	15	1	41	1	2.73
A. Palmer	13.2	4	18	7	1.35
L.W. Kettels	8	2	8	0	1.00
E.M. Shevill	4	1	10	0	2.50

Australia Women Second Innings

H.D. Pritchard	c Snowball	b Spear	20
R. Monaghan	run out		4
E.M. Shevill	not out		63
K.M. Smith		b Valentine	12
E.M. McLarty	c Snowball	b Spear	8
L.W. Kettels		b Spear	0
M.E.M. Peden [Captain]	c Partridge	b Spear	11
P. Antonio		b Spear	5
F.L. Blade	c Child	b Hide	4
A. Palmer		b Partridge	4
H.M. Hills [Wicket]	absenthurt		

Extras	[5 b, 1 lb, 1 w]	7
TOTAL	125.3 overs – Run Rate 1.09	**138**

England Bowling Second Innings	O	M	R	W	Econ.
M.E. Maclagan	28	12	31	0	1.10
M.I. Taylor	19	6	30	0	1.57
M.F. Spear	34	24	15	5	0.44
M.E. Hide	21	7	26	1	1.23
D.M. Turner	13	7	14	0	1.07
J.E. Partridge	5.3	2	6	1	1.09
C. Valentine	5	1	9	1	1.80

England Women Second Innings			
M.E. Maclagan		b Antonio	9
E.A. Snowball [Wicketkeeper]	not out		18
M.E. Hide	not out		6
E.M.Child	did not bat		
J.E. Partridge	did not bat		
H.E. Archdale [Captain	did not bat		
D.M. Turner	did not bat		
J. Liebert	did not bat		
M.I. Taylor	did not bat		
M.F. Spear	did not bat		
C. Valentine	did not bat		
Extras	[1 b]		1
TOTAL	12.5 overs – Run Rate 2.64		**34**

Australia Bowling Second Innings	O	M	R	W	Econ.
E.M. McLarty	2	0	4	0	2.00
A. Palmer	6	1	9	0	1.50
P. Antonio	4.5	4	20	1	4.13

England also triumphed in the second Test match held in Sydney, especially England's Myrtle Maclagan, who having already taken the first wicket in a Test match, added yet another record when she became the first woman to record a Test century with a score of 119 before falling lbw to Peggy Antonio, in an opening 149 run partnership with Betty Snowball. Australia's batting included a 47-minute duck for Essie Shevill [1908-1989], and with Joy Evelyn Partridge [1899-1947] claiming six second innings wickets, England were left facing the trifling target of needing 10 runs, which they achieved for the loss of two wickets.

Australia Women v England Women, at Sydney Cricket Ground

2nd Test – 4-8 January, 1935 – 4 day match

Australia won the toss and elected to bat first
Australia Women 162 & 148 - England Women 301 for 5 declared & 10 for 2 [6 overs]

England Women won by 8 wickets
England lead the 3 match series 2-0

Umpires: Puffett[Australia]: Unknown [Austalia]

Note: No play took place on the Saturday, 5 January - 2nd day, on the Sunday, 6 January was taken as a rest day

Australia Women First Innings

R. Monaghan		b Maclagan	9
H.D. Pritchard		b Maclagan	0
E.M. Shevill	c Snowball	b Hide	0
K.M. Smith	lbw	b Spear	47
J.P. Brewer	c Hide	b Spear	34
B.C.C. Peden	lbw	b Turner	12
E.M. McLarty	run out		7
M.E.M. Peden [Captain]	run out		6
I.H. Shevill [Wicketkeeper]		b Maclagan	2
P. Antonio	not out		18
A. Palmer	lbw	b Maclagan	14
Extras	[9 b, lb 3, nb 1]		13
TOTAL	121.3 overs – Run Rate 1.33		**162**

England Bowling First Innings	O	M	R	W	Econ.
M.E. Maclagan	33.2	22	33	4	0.99
M.I. Taylor	11	5	29	0	2.63
M.F. Spear	20	11	19	2	0.95
M.E. Hide	30	21	18	1	0.60
M.E. Richards	9	5	13	0	1.44
D.M. Turner	11	6	12	1	1.09
J.E. Partridge	7	0	25	0	3.57

England Women First Innings

M.E. Maclagan	lbw	b Antonio	119
E.A. Snowball [Wicket]	lbw	b Smith	71
M.E. Hide		b Smith	34
H.E. Archdale [Captain]		b Smith	3
E.M.Child	not out		30
D.M. Turner		b Antonio	9

J.E. Partridge	not out	26
M.E. Richrards	did not bat	
J. Liebert	did not bat	
M.I. Taylor	did not bat	
M.F. Spear	did not bat	
Extras	[4 b, 5 lb]	9
TOTAL	87 overs – Run Rate 3.45	**301 for 5 decl.**

Australia Bowling First Innings	**O**	**M**	**R**	**W**	**Econ.**
E.M. McLarty	16	0	77	0	4.81
K.M. Smith	20	3	42	3	2.10
P. Antonio	17	4	53	2	3.11
B.C.C. Peden	8	1	23	0	2.87
A. Palmer	14	1	57	0	4.07
J.P. Brewer	2	0	3	0	1.50
E.M. Shevill	10	0	37	0	3.70

Australia Women Second Innings

R. Monaghan	st Snowball	b Partridge	12
H.D. Pritchard		b Maclagan	0
E.M. Shevill	run out		36
K.M. Smith	lbw	b Partridge	27
J.P. Brewer	st Snowball	b Spear	9
B.C.C. Peden	c Hide	b Partridge	4
I.H. Shevill	hit wicket	b Partridge	1 0
E.M. McLarty	st Snowball	b Partridge	8
P. Antonio		b Maclagan	8
M.E.M. Peden [Captain]	not out		4
A. Palmer	st Snowball	b Partridge	23
Extras	[5 b, 2 lb]		7
TOTAL	80.4 overs – Run Rate 1.83		**148**

England Bowling Second Innings	**O**	**M**	**R**	**W**	**Econ.**
M.E. Maclagan	29	15	35	2	1.20
M.F. Spear	10	6	7	1	0.70
M.E. Hide	5	5	0	0	0.00
M.E. Richards	1	0	3	0	3.00
J.E. Partridge	35.4	6	96	6	2.69

England Women Second Innings

M.E. Richards	c IH Shevill	b E.M Shevill	3
J. Liebert	lbw	b Smith	0
E.A. Snowball [Wicket]	not out		4
M.E. Hide	not out		1
M.E. Maclagan	did not bat		
H.E. Archdale [Captain]	did not bat		
E.M.Child	did not bat		
D.M. Turner	did not bat		

J.E. Partridge	did not bat	
M.I. Taylor	did not bat	
M.F. Spear	did not bat	
Extras	[1 b, 1 lb]	2
TOTAL	6 overs – Run Rate 1.66	**10**

Australia Bowling Second Innings	**O**	**M**	**R**	**W**	**Econ.**
K.M. Smith	3	0	5	1	1.66
P. Antonio	2	1	1	0	0.50
E.M. Shevill	1	0	2	1	2.00

With Australia's cricket improving quickly, the third Test in Melbourne ended in a draw, with the in-form Maclagan making 50 runs and claiming 7 match wickets.

Australia Women v England Women, at Melbourne Cricket Ground

3rd Test – 18-20 January, 1935 – 3 day match

England Women won the toss and elected to bat first
England Women 162 & 153 for 7 declared - Australia Women 150 & 104 for 8 [57 overs]

Match drawn England won the 3 match series 2-0
Umpires: Herbert Nichols [Australia]: William Wettenhall [Austalia]

England Women First Innings			
M.E. Maclagan		b Hudson	50
E.A. Snowball [Wicketkeeper]		b Smith	1
M.E. Hide		b Antonio	7
E.M.Child	c Hudson	b Antonio	3
J.E. Partridge		b Antonio	0
H.E. Archdale [Captain]	b B.C.C. Peden	32	
D.M. Turner		b Antonio	5
M.E. Richards	c Palmer	b Antonio	31
J. Liebert	lbw	b Antonio	13
M.I. Taylor	run out		9
M.F. Spear	not out		7
Extras	[2 b, 2 lb]		4
TOTAL	71.5 overs – Run Rate 2.25		**162**

Australia Bowling First Innings	**O**	**M**	**R**	**W**	**Econ.**
K.M. Smith	19	3	59	1	3.10
L.W. Kettels	8	3	15	0	1.87
A. Hudson	11	6	7	1	0.63
P. Antonio	21.5	7	49	6	2.24

A. Palmer	6	3	19	0	3.16
B.C.C. Peden	6	1	9	1	1.50

Australia Women First Innings

A.Hudson	run out		16
M.E.M. Peden [Captain]	c Snowball	b Hide	10
E.M. Shevill	c Maclagan	b Spear	11
K.M. Smith	run out		1
H.D. Pritchard	c Liebert	b Hide	5
P. Antonio		b Maclagan 16	
B.C.C. Peden	c Richards	b Turner	10
L.W. Kettels	c Hide	b Maclagan	9
J.P. Brewer		b Spear	26
A. Palmer		b Maclagan 39	
I.H. Shevill [Wicket]	not out		3
Extras	[2 b, 2 lb 3]		4
TOTAL	129.1 overs – Run Rate 1.16		**150**

England Bowling First Innings	O	M	R	W	Econ.
M.E. Maclagan	34.1	20	32	3	0.93
M.E. Hide	20	12	24	2	1.20
M.I. Taylor	12	4	21	0	1.75
M.F. Spear	31	20	21	3	0.67
J.E. Partridge	26	9	40	0	1.53
D.M. Turner	6	2	8	0	1.33

England Women Second Innings

E.M.Child	run out		4
H.E. Archdale [Captain]	lbw	b Smith	10
E.A. Snowball [Wicket]	not out		83
M.E. Maclagan	lbw	b Antonio	3
M.E. Hide		b Palmer 26	
J.E. Partridge	c Smith	b Palmer	1
M.E. Richards	c Kettels	b Antonio 18	
M.I. Taylor		b Palmer	5
D.M. Turner	not out		1
J. Liebert	did not bat		
M.F. Spear	did not bat		
Extras	[1 b, 1 lb]		2
TOTAL	57 overs – Run Rate 2.68		**153 for 7 decl.**

Australia Bowling Second Innings	O	M	R	W	Econ.
K.M. Smith	11	2	37	1	3.36
L.W. Kettels	6	3	11	0	1.83
A. Hudson	12	5	13	0	1.08
P. Antonio	15	1	55	2	3.66
A. Palmer	7	0	17	3	2.42
B.C.C. Peden	6	2	18	0	3.00

Australia Women Second Innings			
A.Hudson		c & b Maclagan	8
H.D. Pritchard	c Child	b Maclagan	5
K.M. Smith	c Partridge	b Maclagan	9
P. Antonio	lbw	b Spear	14
A. Palmer		b Taylor	11
E.M. Shevill		b Taylor	0
B.C.C. Peden	not out		24
J.P. Brewer		b Maclagan	31
L.W. Kettels	c Archdale	b Partridge	1
M.E.M. Peden [Captain]	not out		0
I.H. Shevill [Wicket]	did not bat		
Extras	[1 b]		1
TOTAL	57 overs – Run Rate 1.82		**104 for 8**

England Bowling Second Innings	**O**	**M**	**R**	**W**	**Econ.**
M.E. Maclagan	24	13	28	4	1.16
M.E. Hide	8	2	14	0	1.75
M.I. Taylor	9	5	13	2	1.44
M.F. Spear	5	3	7	1	1.40
J.E. Partridge	8	1	36	1	4.50
D.M. Turner	3	2	5	0	1.66

It was only retrospectively that the brave English women who made that historic voyage would be hailed as pioneers. It took a batswoman such as Molly Hide to help change the cynical opinion expressed by the *Times* newspaper, together with that of a few other critical parties. In the words of *Wisden*, *'her batting had a strength as well as a style that astonished sceptical male spectators, many of whom in her era thought women's cricket was like a dog on its hind legs'.*

And Doris Mildred Turner [1908-1986], not only made history as one of the English players, and although her personal performances were somewhat disappointing, she later progressed under her married name of Doris Coysh to become the first female cricket umpire in 1959, eventually standing in two Tests. The second Test match between England and

Australia held in 1963, and the third Test in 1966 between England and New Zealand.

With a touring side already selected, the plan was that there should have been a return visit made to Australia in 1939-1940, but World War II got in the way, and it wasn't until nearly a decade later that the next tour came along.

The Women's Ashes became formally identified in July 1998 when, on what seemingly was a particularly inauspicious day, a ceremony was held before the start of the first women's Test match at Lord's. Augmented by a few moderate outbreaks of sunlight, a disinterested grounds-man was busy rolling the pitch, and a team of players were ostensibly working out in the nets. A group of around thirty in number gathered together in the Harris Garden, with them they had a miniature bat, autographed by the English and Australian cricket squads, a copy of the WCA Constitution and Rules Book, some matches and a wok. The bat was burned in the wok and the remaining ashes carefully gathered up and sealed inside a replica of a hollowed-out wooden cricket ball. There was no fanfare, very little glamour, and after the inauspicious ceremony came to an end everyone went their separate ways.

This simple ceremony would ultimately become momentous in the history of women's cricket. Even after 64 years, it appears few, if any, of the England or Australian players who were part of the 1998 series knew the reason how, or why, it came about. In the words of eighteen year old Charlotte Edwards [born 1979], *'I didn't realise then what I was part of'.*

Nobody did !

Born in Barnstaple, Devon, the former right-handed batsman and right-arm medium pace bowler, Melanie 'Mel' Jones [born 1972] who played five Test matches for Australia between 1998 and 2003, summarised by saying, *'As players you just get told what you're doing and where you're going. You don't get told why.'*

And the former England captain, all-rounder Clare Joanne Connor, OBE [born 1976], later to become head of women's cricket at the ECB, and the creator of the multi-format, points-based women's Ashes, has but a few memories, *'Of course, it was a very momentous occasion. But I don't remember being given an explanation about it.'*

The British multi-national telecommunications company Vodaphone, eventually agreed to become the official sponsor the women's initial series, the same company that had given its support to the men's Ashes series in the previous year. It is reported that just prior to the Tests, a group of sport journalists were sent a bunch of red roses with a card reading, *'Eleven English roses playing cricket - watch this space.'*

1998 was a significant year for women's cricket, when Mrs. Norma Izard OBE [born 1934], the last President of the Women's Cricket Association [1994-1998], decided it was the right time the women's game had some *'ashes'* of its own, to commemorate the dissolution of the WCA. Especially since at an Extraordinary General Meeting of the WCA, which had been formed in 1926, its members voted to merge with the newly formed England

and Wales Cricket Board [ECB], and the 1998 Women's *'Ashes'* series would be the last one played under the auspices of the WCA.

'I was fed up,' said Norma, who presented the Women's *'Ashes'* Trophy, *'The Australians kept on saying, 'Why don't we have a trophy ?' But they never did anything about it. So I thought, 'Well, I'll do it then!' Why shouldn't we do the same as the men ? They've got Ashes, so we'll have some Ashes ! I talked about it with the WCA Committee, and they agreed it would be a good idea to create some 'ashes' by burning a bat'.*

Never known to dither or be indecisive, Norma approached a friend, Brian Hodges, a wood-carver at Twigfolly Trophies of Littlehampton, Sussex, the husband of the midwife who had years earlier, delivered her youngest son. *'Ever thought of making a trophy ? '*, she enquired. *'Something in the shape of a cricket ball.'*

'I'll give it a try', he replied. And dutifully designed and crafted the trophy of the hollowed-out wooden cricket ball, together with a suitable replica, constructed from a 300 year old English yew tree which had been blown down in the 1987 gales.

Born in Beckenham in 1933, at the age of 11 Norma Izard went to Beckenham Grammar School, where she was thrilled to discover cricket was played. She soon made the school team as wicketkeeper, and in 1948 attended one of the first schoolgirls' coaching sessions in Blackheath, Kent. At the age of 17 Norma was selected for the Kent Junior XI, and before long was playing for the senior Kent side. She married in 1955, and subsequently decided to give up cricket in order to start a family. It was only several years later, when her sons had grown up, that she re-emerged and once again became involved, initially as the manager of the first ever junior England side, and later as a national selector. Eventually a vacancy arose for the position as manager of the full England women's side. *'You were supposed to send your CV and all this sort of thing. I wrote a letter saying: 'I understand there may be a vacancy for manager. I wish to apply for it. I'm not putting any more on this letter because you know what I've done and what I can do !'* As a result the Executive Committee of the WCA made the appointment solely on that basis. To this day Norma Izard remains the longest-serving manager of any England cricket team, male or female, having served a nine-year stretch in charge of the England women's team from 1984 to 1994, overseeing a dozen international tours during her spell in charge, culminating with a World Cup win for England at Lord's in 1993.

Appointed when funds were tight, Norma combined the duties of manager, coach, and physiotherapist. When on tour Izard made sure players were *'correctly dressed'*, and conformed with the standards approved by the WCA. She also agreed and took care of every minute detail relating to accommodation, travel arrangements and official functions between games. She was a no-nonsense manager who imposed and rigorously enforced a 10 p.m. curfew on the players. Once, during a tour of Australia, she banned the consumption of alcohol after a player turned up drunk to a State game following rather excessive celebrations on the previous evening.

The job as the England women's cricket team manager was far from financially rewarding, and Izard never received a penny for her years of service. She saw it as a way of helping advance the cause of women's cricket.

Her ultimate triumph as team manager came at the very end of her nine-year reign, England's World Cup win at home at Lord's in 1993. Norma remains modest about her contribution to the overwhelming success, *'I was thrilled for them, but it wasn't a personal achievement for me. It was their win, not mine'*.

Her proudest moment was undoubtedly being invited to become one of the first ever female members of the MCC in 1999. As the first female member to walk through the door into the pavilion, she recalled, *'I just happened to be standing by the door when the doorman said, 'Come on in.' So in I walked ! It was a very special day'*.

Norma Izard was awarded an OBE for her services to women's cricket, all for love of the game, with no financial reward whatsoever. She dedicated a great deal of her life to women's cricket since first playing the sport in 1948 while at school in Beckenham. She continued to serve as Chairman of the Women's Cricket Association following its merger with the England and Wales ECB in 1999.

It is fair to say that the mounting success of women's cricket has been built on the strength and efforts of women like Norma Izard, who as amateurs, in a far from glamorous arena, pushed to remove the *'pebble from the shoe'* of women cricketers, with no thought for anything other than the game they loved so much.

The 1998 series turned out to be something of a blockbuster. England had crushed the Aussies in the 1993 World Cup, but five years later the *'Southern Stars'* had put together one of the finest women's sides ever to grace a cricket pitch in the history of the female game. Captained by Belinda Clark, a giant of Australian cricket both on and off the field, they were strong, aggressive, and fit. Fresh from a triumphant victory in the 1997 World Cup in India the previous winter, and energised from becoming the first women's cricket team to record a ODI double-century. Charlotte Marie Edwards CBE [born 1979] the youngest player ever to play for England when she made her debut against New Zealand in 1996, described them as having the best bowling attack she had ever faced. A fearsome strike force which included the great Cathryn Lorraine Fitzpatrick [born 1968], who was recognised as the world's fastest pace bowler the women's game had ever seen, frequently delivering the ball at terrified batsman at speeds reaching 125 km/h, just short of 80 miles per hour.

The Australians arrived in England for their two-month tour *'really revved up for the series and anxious to make a statement.'* Which they certainly did ! Socialising between the two teams was to say the least minimal. With the young Charlotte Edwards recalling she was *'quite frightened of most of the Australian players'.*

By the time the ceremony of the burning of the bat was held at Lord's, the Aussies had pulverised England in the first four of five ODIs. The Women's Ashes trophy, the perpetual trophy for the women's international cricket series between England and Australia, now remains in care at the Lord's Cricket Ground, with a replica held by the winning Country. The name is derived from the historic male precedent, and until 2013 was decided exclusively on the outcome of Test matches. After the newly created Women's Ashes trophy had been introduced, and since the Australian women's tour of England in 2013, the competition was decided by a points system, which takes into account the results of Test matches together with One Day Internationals and Twenty20 International matches. Currently, four points are awarded for a Test match win, with two points awarded to each side in the event of a draw, and two points for a victory in each of the limited-over games. Over the years the length of a series has varied, ranging from one to five Test matches. Since 2001 it has been played biennially, and usually includes only one or two Tests.

Since 1934, when Betty Archdale led her England team on that historic journey to Australia to play the first ever women's cricket international matches and the 20 July, 1998, England and Australia have met in 34 Test matches, more than any other pair of nations. They have ferociously competed against each other over decades, and in Sydney in 1992, played the only five-day women's Test match in history. Yet for all those years, there was never a trophy to compete for. In part this can be explained by the early principles of the English Women's Cricket Association, which proclaimed in its original Constitution of 1930 that *'no member of any affiliated club shall take part in any cricket challenge cup or prize competition'*. A rule abolished in 1966.

Results Summary	Played	Australian Wins	England Wins	Drawn
All Tests	49	12	9	28
Tests in Australia	24	6	5	13
Tests in England	25	6	4	5
All Series	22	8	6	8
Series in Australia	11	5	3	3
Series in England	11	3	3	5

Series decided on Test results

Series	Season	Host Nation	First Match	Tests Played	Aust. Wins	Eng. Wins	Tests Drawn	Series Result	Holder
1	1934-35	Aust.	Dec.1934	3	0	2	1	Eng.	Eng.
2	1937	Eng.	June 1937	3	1	1	1	Drawn	Eng.
3	1948-49	Aust.	Jan.1949	3	1	0	2	Aust.	Aust.
4	1951	Eng.	June 1951	3	1	1	1	Drawn	Aust.
5	1957-58	Aust.	Feb. 1958	3 [4]	0	0	0	Drawn	Aust.
6	1963	Eng.	June 1963	3	0	1	2	Eng.	Eng.
7	1968-69	Aust.	Dec.1968	3	0	0	3	Drawn	Eng.
8	1976	Eng.	June 1976	3	0	0	3	Drawn	Eng.
9	1984-85	Aust.	Dec.1984	5	2	1	2	Aust.	Aust.
10	1987	Eng.	Aug. 1987	3	1	0	2	Aust.	Aust.
11	1991-92	Aust.	Feb.1992	1	1	0	0	Aust.	Aust.

Ashes Trophy Inaugurated

Series	Season	Host Nation	First Match	Tests Played	Aust. Wins	Eng. Wins	Tests Drawn	Series Result	Holder
12	1998	Eng.	Aug.1998	3	0	0	3	Drawn	Aust.
13	2001	Eng.	June.2001	2	2	0	0	Aust.	Aust.
14	2002-03	Aust.	Feb.2003	2	1	0	1	Aust.	Aust.
15	2005	Eng.	Aug.2005	2	0	1	1	Eng.	Eng.
16	2008	Aust.	Feb.2008	1	0	1	0	Eng.	Eng.
17	2009	Eng.	July 2009	1	0	0	1	Eng.	Eng.
18	2011	Aust.	Jan.2011	1	1	0	0	Aust	Aust.

Series decided on Points System

Series	Season	Host Nation	First Match	Tests Played	Result	ODI's Wins	Twenty 20's	Points	Series Result	Holder
19	2013	Eng.	Aug. 2013	1	Draw	Eng. 2-1	Eng. 3-0	Aust. 4 Eng.12	Eng.	Eng.
20	2014	Aust.	Jan. 2014.	1	Eng.	Aust. 2-1	Aust. 2-1	Aust. 8 Eng.10	Eng.	Eng.
21	2015	Eng.	Jul. 2015	1	Aust.	Aust. 2-1	Eng. 2-1	Aust.10 Eng. 6	Aust.	Aust.
22	2017	Aust.	Oct. 2017	1	Draw	Aust. 2-1	Eng. 2-1	Aust.8 Eng.8	Draw	Aust.

Chapter 13

Women's World Twenty20

The ICC Women's World Twenty20 is a stand-alone tournament, similar in format to that of the men's event. Although the earlier Women's World T20 events were staged in parallel with the men's events, they are now run separately. The *'double-headers'* may well have raised the profile of the women's game, but they often resulted in the women's semi-finals and finals played to half-empty stadiums, with the crowd gradually arriving later for the men's matches. The Chairman of the ICC Governance Committee and Chairman of Cricket Australia, David Peever, said, *'Women's cricket is undoubtedly gaining in popularity. We felt that by separating the two events we could accelerate that growth.'* Adding, *'Having the ICC Women's World Twenty20 as a stand-alone event means we can hold it in stadiums that we can fill, put it on TV at prime-time, and ensure it has the space to be promoted away from the shadow of the men's game'*. Peever is less-widely known as head of the mining giant Rio Tinto.

ICC Womens' World Twenty20 Results:

Year	Hosts	Winners	Year	Hosts	Winners
2009	England	England	2010	West Indies	Australia
2012	Sri Lanka	Australia	2014	Bangladesh	Australia
2016	India	West Indies	2018	England	

First ICC Women's World Twenty20 - 2009

The 2009 tournament consisted of eight teams divided into two groups of four, followed by the semi-finals and final. In all, the tournament ran for a period of 10 days, with all the group stage matches played at the County Ground, Taunton in Devon

Group Stage Standings:

Group A

Team	Pld	W	L	T	NR	A	Pts	RR
New Zealand	3	3	0	0	0	0	6	1.676
Australia	3	2	1	0	0	0	4	0.242
West Indies	3	1	2	0	0	0	2	-1.137
South Africa	3	0	3	0	0	0	0	-0.717

Group B

Team	**Pld**	**W**	**L**	**T**	**NR**	**A**	**Pts**	**RR**
England	3	3	0	0	0	0	6	2.738
India	3	2	1	0	0	0	4	-0.025
Sri Lanka	3	1	2	0	0	0	2	-1.207
Pakistan	3	0	3	0	0	0	0	-1.481

Semi-Final – New Zealand v India - 18 June, 2009
Venue: Trent Bridge, Nottingham
Umpires: Asad Rauf [Pakistan] & Mark Benson [Australia]
New Zealand won by 52 runs.
New Zealand won the toss and elected to bat
New Zealand 145 for 5 wickets [20 overs] - India 93 for 9 wickets [20 overs]

Semi-Final – Australia v England - 19 June, 2009
Venue: Kennington Oval, London
Umpires: Billy Doctrove [West Indies] & Tony Hill [New Zealand]
England won the toss and elected to field
England won by 8 wickets.
Australia 163 for 5 wickets [20 overs] – England 165 for 2 wickets [19.3 overs]

England and New Zealand contested the final at Lord's which, after all the expectancy generated by the first women's World Twenty20 final, turned out to be a bit of an anti-climax. In the end the better team prevailed, and the match was won and lost in the first ten overs when the New Zealand women failed to deal with Katherine Helen Brunt's [born 1985] vicious in-swingers. In a career-best performance, Brunt collected 3 wickets for the loss of half-a-dozen runs, to set up a target of 86 for the hosts to chase, which England knocked off in 17 overs.

First ICC Women's World Twenty20 Final

New Zealand v England

Venue: Lord's, London, England – 21 June, 2009 – Attendance: 12,717
Umpires: Aleem Dar [Pakistan]: Rudi Koertzen [South Africa].

England Women won by 6 wickets
England won the toss and elected to field.
Player of the match: Katherine Brunt [England]

New Zealand Women's Innings [20 overs maximum]:

Suzannah Wilson Bates	st S.J. Taylor	b Marsh	1
Lucy Doolan	c S.J. Taylor	b Brunt	14
Aimee Watkins [Capt.]		b Brunt	2
Amy Satterthwiate	c S.C. Taylor	b Shaw	19
Rachel Priest [Wicketkeeper]		c & b Brunt	0
Nicola Browne		b Shaw	1
Sara McGlashan	c Greenway	b Gunn	9
Sarah Tsukigawa	c S.J. Taylor	b Gunn	5
Sophi Devine	run out		10
Katherine Pulford	c S.C. Taylor	b Edwards	14
Sian Ansley Ruck	not out		0
Extras	[1b, 4lb, 1nb, 4w]		10
TOTAL	20 overs – Run Rate 4.25		**85**

Fall of wickets:
1-2 S.W Bates, 0.5 ov, 2-10 A.L. Watkins, 3.1 ov, 3-23 L.R. Doolan, 7.2 ov, 4-23 R.H. Priest, 7.5 ov, 5-31 N.J. Browne,10.3 ov, 6-48 S.J. McGlashan, 14.3 ov, 7-58 S.J. Tsukigawa, 16.5 ov, 8-62 A.E. Satterthwaite. 17.4 ov, 9-84 K.L. Pulford, 19.5 ov, 10-85 S.F.M. Devine, 19.6 ov.

England Bowling:	**O**	**M**	**R**	**W**	**Econ.**	
Laura Alexandra	Marsh	4	0	16	1	4.00
Katherine Helen	Brunt	4	2	6	3	1.50
Nicola Jayne	Shaw	4	0	17	2	4.25
Holly Louise	Colvin	4	0	16	0	4.00
Jennifer Louise	Gunn	3	0	19	2	6.33

Charlotte Marie Edwards	1	0	6	1	6.00

England Women's Innings [20 overs maximum]:

Sarah Taylor [Wicket]	c Priest	b Pulford	23
Charlotte Edwards [Capt.]		b Ruck	9
Samantha Taylor	not out		39
Beth Morgan	c McGlashan	b Browne	6
Lydia Greenway		b Devine	3
Jennifer Gunn	not out		2
Caroline Atkins	did not bat		
Nicola Shaw	did not bat		
Katherine Brunt	did not bat		
Holly Colvin	did not bat		
Laura Marsh	did not bat		
Extras	[1lb, 3w]		4
TOTAL	17 overs – Run Rate 5.05		**86 for 4 wickets**

Fall of wickets:
1-19 C.M. Edwards, 3.5 ov, 2-39 S.J. Taylor, 8.6 ov, 3-70 B.L. Morgan, 14.3 ov, 4-74 L.S. Greenway, 15.4 ov.

New Zealand Bowling:	**O**	**M**	**R**	**W**	**Econ.**
Sophie Frances Monique Devine	3	0	12	1	4.00
Sian Elizabeth Ansley Ruck	4	0	17	1	4.25
Katherine Louise Pulford	4	0	20	1	5.00
Suzannah Wilson Bates	2	0	8	0	4.00
Nicola Jane Browne	3	0	18	1	6.00
Lucy Rose Doolan	1	0	10	0	10.00

Second ICC Women's World Twenty20 Final - 2010

The 2010 ICC Women's World Twenty20 was held in the West Indies from the 5-16 May 2010. With the group stage matches played at the Warner Park Sporting Complex, an athletic facility in Basseterre, St. Kitts, St. Kitts and Nevis. Named after Sir Thomas Warner [1580-1649], the Caribbean explorer who established the first English colony on St. Kitts in 1624, the eastern segment of the complex contains the cricket pitch, pavilion, media centre and seating for 4,000 which is capable of being increased to 10,000 for major events. The format of the tournament was similar to that of the inaugural event consisting of eight teams divided into two groups of four, followed by the semi-finals and final.

Group A

Team	Pld	W	L	T	NR	A	Pts	RR
Australia	3	3	0	0	0	0	6	0.550
West Indies	3	2	1	0	0	0	4	0.167
England	3	1	2	0	0	0	2	0.900
South Africa	3	0	3	0	0	0	0	-1.617

Group B

Team	Pld	W	L	T	NR	A	Pts	RR
New Zealand	3	3	0	0	0	0	6	2.514
India	3	2	1	0	0	0	4	1.452
Sri Lanka	3	1	2	0	0	0	2	-1.950
Pakistan	3	0	3	0	0	0	0	-1.733

Semi-Final – India v Australia - 13 May, 2010
Venue: Beausejour, Gros Islet, St Lucia
Umpires: Marias Esasmus [South Africa] & Tony Hill [New Zealand]
Australia won by 7 wickets.
India won the toss and elected to bat
India 119 for 5 wickets [20 overs] – Australia 123 for 3 wickets [20 overs]

Semi-Final – New Zealand v West Indies - 14 May, 2010
Venue: Beausejour, Gros Islet, St Lucia
Umpires: Asoka de Silva [Sri Lanka] & Rod Tucker [Australia]
West Indies won the toss and elected to field
New Zealand won by 56 runs
New Zealand 180 for 5 wickets [20 overs] – West Indies 124 for 8 wickets [20 overs]

The New Zealand women started very effectively in the final in Bridgetown, Barbados, after the Australian skipper Alexandra Joy Blackwell [born 1983] won the toss and elected to bat. The *'White Ferns'* opening fast bowler Nicola Jane Browne [born 1983] collected 2 wickets at a cost of 11 runs from her bowling quota of four overs. With Leah Joy Poulton [born 1984] and Jessica Evelyn Cameron [born 1989] responding for Australia with a partnership of 30 runs off 45 balls. They were however unable to noticeably increase the run rate and Poulton went after an unsuccessful attempt to loft a ball over cover, and two balls later, Cameron was clean bowled first ball by Kate Ellen Broadmore [born 1991], leaving Australia sitting on 5 for 51 in the thirteenth over. The overall total was helped by an unbeaten knock of 19 from Sarah Jane Elliott [born 1982] off 20 balls, and Lisa Carprini Sthalekar [born 1979] who contributed a further 18 runs off 13 deliveries. The *'Southern Stars'* innings was ended by a spectacular one-handed catch at cover by the New Zealand captain Aimee Louise Watkins [born 1982], preventing a drive from going for four, off the bowling of Rene Farrell [born 1987].

New Zealand deserved to come in to bat in confident mood after restricting Australia to 106 for 8, but was unable to satisfactorily deal with the suffocating Aussie pressure. In the fourth over, skipper Watkins was caught out by the leaping opposing skipper Blackwell at midwicket, off the bowling of Clea Rosemary Smith [born 1979]. And in the following over Blackwell ran out Sara McGlashan [born 1982] for 1, after a mix-up with Suzannah Wilson Bates [born 1987], leaving New Zealand struggling on 2 for 19, which would slump even further to 4 for 29 by the seventh over.

The New Zealand batting was further contained by a phase of spin attack delivered by Shelley Nitschke [born 1976] and Lisa Sthalekar. Rachel Holly Priest [born 1985] was given out stumped by Healy, after the television umpire Asad Rauf was forced to retract his initial decision after confessing to having pressed the wrong button. New Zealand was on 5 for 36 after 11 overs, leaving it 71 runs short of its target with 54 deliveries to come.

Nicola Jane Browne [born 1983] came to the crease and put on 41 runs from as many balls in a partnership with Devine, who carried her bat with a score 38 not out from 35 balls. However, the pair could not score quickly enough, and Browne went caught behind for 20. Sophie Frances Monique Devine [born 1989] came to the rescue hitting a four and a six from the final two balls of the 19th over, leaving the *'White Ferns'* with a realistic chance of victory, with 14 runs required from the final over. A single from the first ball put Devine on strike, who hit four consecutive twos. With five runs required to win off the last ball of the match, Devine struck a powerful straight drive, but Ellyse Alexandra Perry [born 1990], who had played football for Australia, stuck out her right foot and deflected the ball to Sthalekar at mid-on and only one run was scored.

The Australian women were absolutely ecstatic, they had held their nerve and managed to stage a dramatic comeback to seal a win by three runs in a low-scoring final, and it was easy to see how much the win meant to them. Fast bowler Perry finished with a highly impressive 3 for 18 and was named player of the match. However, it was a sad end to the event for New Zealand, and emotions were very low, for despite the loss of wickets, the *'White Ferns'* should have without doubt launched their charge sooner. There were a lot of dot balls in New Zealand's innings, as its batswomen struggled against a thoroughly professional Australian side in the field. Having lost the 50-over World Cup and World Twenty20 finals in 2009, New Zealand were disappointed to suffer a third consecutive loss in a global final.

Second Women's World Twenty20 Final

Australia v New Zealand – 16 May, 2010

Venue: Kensington Oval, Bridgetown, Barbados - Attendance: 8,332
Umpires: Asoka de Silva [Sri Lanka]: Marais Erasmus [South Africa]

Australia Women won by 3 runs
Australia won the toss and elected to bat
Player of the match: Ellyse Perry [Australia]

Australian Women's Innings [20 overs maximum]:

Elyse Villani	c McGlashan	b Browne	6
Shelly Nitschke	lbw	b Ruck	3
Leah Poulton	c Watkins	b Devine	20
Alexandra Blackwell [Capt.]	c Devine	b Browne	0
Jessica Cameron		b Broadmore	14
Sarah Elliott	not out		19
Alyssa Healey [Wicket]	run out		10
Lisa Sthalekar		b Devine	18
Rene Farrell	c Watkins	b Doolan	3
Ellyse Perry	did not bat		
Clea Smith	did not bat		
Extras	[1lb, 1nb, 11w]		13
TOTAL	20 overs – Run Rate 5.30		**106 for 8 wickets**

Fall of wickets:
1-10 S.Nitschke, 2.2 ov, 2-14 E.J. Villani, 3.1 ov, 3-20 A.J. Blackwell, 5.2 ov, 4-50 L.J. Poulton,11.5 ov, 5-51 J.E. Cameron, 12.1 ov, 6-72 A.J. Healy, 15.1 ov, 7-99 L.C. Sthalekar, 18.5 ov, 8-106R.M. Farrell. 19.6 ov.

New Zealand Bowling:	**O**	**M**	**R**	**W**	**Econ.**
Sara Elizabeth Ansley Ruck	3	0	18	1	6.00
Nicola Jane Browne	4	1	11	2	2.75
Aimee Louise Watkins	4	0	17	0	4.25
Sophie Frances Devine	3	0	21	2	7.00
Kate Ellen Broadmore	2	0	15	1	7.50
Lucy Rose Doolan	4	0	23	1	5.75

New Zealand Women's Innings [20 overs maximum]:

Suzanah Wilson Bates	c Elliott	b Perry	18
Aimee Watkins [Capt.]	c Blackwell	b Smith	2
Sara McGlashan	run out		1
Sophie Devine	not out		38
Amy Ella Satterthwaite		b Perry	4
Rachel Priest [Wicket]	c Blackwell	b Nitschke	5
Nicola Browne	c Healy	b Perry	20
Elizabeth Perry	not out		4
Lucy Doolan	did not bat		
Sara Ansley Ruck	did not bat		
Kate Broadmore	did not bat		

Extras	[3lb, 8w]	11
TOTAL	20 overs – Run Rate 5.15	**103 for 6 wickets**

Fall of wickets:
1-16 A.L. Watkins, 3.1 ov, 2-19 S.J. McGlashan, 4.3 ov, 3-24 S.W. Bates, 5.5 ov, 4-29 A.E. Satterthwaite,7.3 ov, 5-36 R.H. Proest, 10.6 ov, 6-77 N.J. Browne, 17.5 ov.

Australia Bowling:	**O**	**M**	**R**	**W**	**Econ.**
Rene Michele Farrell	4	0	31	0	7.75
Clea Rosemary Smith	4	0	22	1	5.50
Shelly Nitschke 4	0	10	1	2.50	
Ellyse Alexandra Perry	4	0	18	3	4.50
Lisa Carprini Sthalekar	4	0	19	0	4.75

Third ICC Women's World Twenty20 – 2012

The bi-annual ICC Women's World Twenty20 was held in the Sri Lanka from the 23 September to the 7 October 2012, and was run simultaneously alongside the men's ICC World Twenty20 tournament.

The women's group stage matches were played at the Galle International Stadium, fringed on two sides by the Indian Ocean it is considered one of the most picturesque cricket grounds in the world. The semi-finals and finals were played at the Ranasinghe Premadasa Cricket Stadium, in Maligawatta, Colombo, the largest stadium in Sri Lanka with a capacity for 35,000 spectators.

All the eight participating teams played a series of warm-up matches prior to the start of the tournament. The format being similar to that of the previous two events, with the teams divided into two groups of four. With the two best placed teams from each group progressing to the two-round knock-out stage, followed by the semi-finals and final. The teams which were eliminated played each other to establish qualification for the 2014 tournament.

Group A

Team	Pld	W	L	T	NR	A	Pts	RR
England	3	3	0	0	0	0	6	1.341
Australia	3	2	1	0	0	0	4	0.628
Pakistan	3	1	2	0	0	0	2	-1.367
India	3	0	3	0	0	0	0	0.607

Group B

Team	Pld	W	L	T	NR	A	Pts	RR
West Indies	3	2	1	0	0	0	4	1.602
New Zealand	3	2	1	0	0	0	4	0.638
Sri Lanka	3	1	2	0	0	0	2	-0.692
South Africa	3	1	2	0	0	0	2	-1.194

Semi-Finals – 4 October, 2012
New Zealand v England
Venue: Ranasinghe Premadasa Cricket Stadium, Colombo, Sri Lanka
Umpires: Marias Esasmus [South Africa] & Bruce Oxenford [Australia]
England won the toss and elected to field.
New Zealand 93 for 8 wickets [20 overs] – England 94 for 3 wickets [17.2 overs]
England won by 7 wickets.

Semi-Finals – 5 October, 2012
Australia v West Indies
Venue: Ranasinghe Premadasa Cricket Stadium, Colombo, Sri Lanka
Umpires: Billy Bowden [New Zealand] & Tony Hill [New Zealand]
Australia won the toss and elected to bat
Australia 115 for 7 wickets [20 overs] – West Indies 87 [19.2 overs]
Australia won by 28 runs.

Australia ran out winners and retained the Women's World T20 trophy with a 4 run win over England at the Premadasa Stadium, Colombo, Sri Lanka.

While England's record over the previous 18 months had been excellent, they looked nervous in the final against its time-honoured adversary. Australia set a challenging total and remained on top throughout the match. Jessica Evelyn Cameron [born 1989] quickly got into her stride, and her innings of 45 from 34 deliveries, including 5 fours and one six, was

Australia's highest of the tournament. She brought up the 100 for Australia with a well executed reverse sweep, clouting the ball for six off the right-arm medium pace of Anya Shrubsole, adding another couple of fours in what resulted as being an expensive over for England costing 17.

Australia held their nerve and continued to bowl with discipline as the England run chase became increasingly desperate. Needing to hit the final ball for six to secure an England win, Danielle Hazel [born 1988] mistimed her shot towards midwicket, and the overjoyed Australian women clinched the title and the trophy.

The defending champions were impressive throughout, exacting only England's second defeat from their previous twenty-five T20 internationals. After winning the toss they may well have reflected the decision to put Australia in to bat first to have backfired. By giving Australia the first use of a fine batting surface, it allowed them to build a commanding total. Following which England succumbed to the pressure of chasing down runs against a well-organised attack and some tight fielding. Indeed, in England's sixty-three match T20 history, it had only successfully chased down 142 to win on three occasions.

In truth, England did well to come so close, since it had been behind the run rate throughout its entire innings, and but for a enthralling display of agricultural batting in the dying overs from the right-hander Jenny Louise Gunn, the margin would have certainly been much greater. Thumping a four and a six off Julie Lauren Hunter [born 1984] Jenny succeeded in reducing the runs required from 35 from three overs, to 16 from the final over. But England had always left too much to do, even though the four run Aussie victory was the narrowest margin recorded against England in Women's Twenty20 internationals.

At the presentation ceremony the England captain, Charlotte Marie Edwards said, *'I am very proud of them, in the last 18 months we have worked towards this. It didn't go our way, but congratulations to Australia. I wouldn't change the decision to bowl first. Our bowling is good, the wicket is still good. It still came down to six off the last ball. It wasn't to be a fairy tale, but hope we have done the country proud'.*

'I'm so proud of this team,' responded Jodie Maree Fields, the Australian Women's captain. *'I love this jersey, I love playing with the girls. Such a good feeling. Whenever you put this jersey on, you have to fight hard. England played a really good match, but we had the belief in our team. Just an all-round performance. Just to be standing here is awesome. All the hard work has been worth it'.*

But while Australia enjoyed its moment of celebration, spare a thought for how frustrated and disappointed the girls of England must have felt. This was only the second game they had lost all year. It just happened to be the World Cup final !

2012 Women's World Twenty20 Final

Australia v England - Attendance: 9,321

Venue: Ranasinghe Premadasa Stadium, Colombo - 7 October, 2012
Umpires: Billy Bowden [New Zealand]: Marais Erasmus [South Africa]

Australia Women won by 4 runs
England won the toss and elected to field
Player of the match: Jess Cameron [Australia]

Australian Women's Innings [20 overs maximum]:

Meghann Lanning		c & b Colvin	25
Alyssa Healey [Wicket]		b Hazell	26
Jessica Cameron	c Gunn	b Colvin	45
Lisa Sthalekar	not out		23
Alexandra Blackwell	run out		13
Jodie Fields [Capt. & Wicket]	did not bat		
Rachael Haynes	did not bat		
Erin Osborne	did not bat		
Julie Hunter	did not bat		
Ellyse Perry	did not bat		
Jessica Jonasson	did not bat		
Extras	[1lb, 1nb, 8w]		10
TOTAL	20 overs – Run Rate 7.10		**142 for 4 wickets**

Fall of wickets:
1-51 MM Lanning, 6.5 ov, 2-68 AJ Healy, 10.1 ov, 3-119 JE Cameron, 16.1 ov, 4-142 AJ Blackwell, 19.6ov.

England Bowling:	O	M	R	W	Econ.
Katherine Helen Brunt	2	0	20	0	10.00
Danielle Hazell	4	0	23	1	5.75
Danielle Nicole Wyatt	3	0	20	0	6.66
Anya Shrubsole	3	0	31	0	10.33
Holly Louise Colvin	4	0	21	2	5.25
Laura Alexandra Marsh	4	0	26	0	6.50

England Women's Innings [20 overs maximum]:

Charlotte Edwards [Capt.]	c Perry	b Sthalekar	28
Laura Marsh		c & b Hunter	8
Sarah Taylor [Wicket]	c Fields	b Perry	19
Lydia Greenway	c Perry	b Jonassen	4
Arran Thompson		b Sthalekar	13
Danielle Wyatt	c Blackwell	b Jonassen	9
Jennifer Gunn	c Jonassen	b Hunter	19
Katherine Brunt		b Jonassen	3
Danielle Hazell	not out		16
Holly Colvin	run out		8
Anya Shrubsole	not out		0
Extras	[2b, 2lb, 1nb, 6w]		11
TOTAL	20 overs – Run Rate 6.90		**138 for 9 wickets**

Fall of wickets:
1-20 LA Marsh, 4.3 ov, 2-44 CM Edwards, 7.2ov, 3-61 SJ Taylor, 9.6 ov, 4-63 LS Greenway,10.5ov, 5-86 A Thompson, 13.5 ov, 6-90 DN Wyatt, 14.5 ov, 7-101 KH Brunt, 16.1 ov, 8-120 JL Gunn, 17.6 ov, 9-137 HL Colvin, 19.5 ov.

Australia Bowling:	O	M	R	W	Econ.
Ellyse Alexandra Perry	4	0	24	1	6.00
Lisa Carprini Sthalekar	4	0	16	2	4.00
Julie Lauren Hunter	4	0	36	2	9.00

Erin Alyse Osborne	4	0	33	0	8.25
Jessica Louise Jonasson	4	0	25	3	6.25

Fourth ICC Women's World Twenty20 – 2014

The fourth ICC Women's World Twenty20 tournament was played in the cities of Sylhet and Dhaka in Bangladesh from the 23 March to 6 April 2014.

For the first time the tournament included ten teams, rather than eight as in previous tournaments, with Bangladesh and Ireland making their first appearance in the event. The top six teams from the 2012 ICC World Twenty20 tournament, which included Australia, England, India, New Zealand, South Africa, and the West Indies, plus the host nation Bangladesh, qualified automatically for a place in the tournament, with three additional teams, Ireland, Pakistan and Sri Lanka, qualifying through the 2013 ICC Women's World Twenty20 Qualifier.

Each team played every other team in its appropriate group stage matches, all of which were played at the Sylhet Divisional Stadium. Previously known as the Sylhet Divisional Stadium, it was created in 2007 and extensively developed six years later to accommodate a capacity crowd of 18,500 spectators when Bangladesh were scheduled to host the men's and women's 2014 ICC World Twenty20 matches, which were to run concurrently.

The top two teams from each group would qualify automatically to compete in the 2016 ICC Women's World Twenty20 tournament, with the third and fourth placed teams from each group competing in a knockout competition in order to establish the remaining qualifying teams for the 2016 event.

In total the 2014 ICC Women's World Twenty20 included a total of 25 matches. All the ten competing teams featured in a series of ten warm-up matches in March prior to the start of the tournament proper. They were all played at the Bangladesh Krira Shikkha Protisthan cricket grounds [BKSP Grounds], a complex of four cricket grounds owned by the Bangladesh Cricket Board, in Savar, approximately 15 miles [24 kilometres] north west of Dhaka City,

The group stage matches were held at the Sylhet Divisional Stadium, with the semi-finals and final held at the Sher-e-Bangla National Cricket Stadium, Mirpur, Dhaka. Constucted in the late1980s, primarlily to accommodate football, the Sher-e-Benga ground lies ten kilometres outside the Mirpur city centre and has a capacity of 25,000.

Group A

Team	Pld	W	L	T	NR	A	Pts	RR
Australia	4	3	1	0	0	0	6	2,205
South Africa	4	3	1	0	0	0	6	1.606
New Zealand	4	3	1	0	0	0	6	1,275
Pakistan	4	1	3	0	0	0	2	-2.288
Ireland	4	0	4	0	0	0	0	-2.750

Group B

Team	Pld	W	L	T	NR	A	Pts	RR
England	4	3	1	0	0	0	6	1.363
West Indies	4	3	1	0	0	0	6	0.773
India	4	2	2	0	0	0	4	0.781
Sri Lanka	4	1	3	0	0	0	2	-0.437
Bangladesh	4	1	3	0	0	0	2	-2.388

Semi-Finals – 3 April, 2014
Australia v West Indies
Venue: Shere Bangla National Stadium, Mirpur, Dhaka, Bangladesh
Umpires: Aleem Dar [Pakistan] & Marais Erasmus [South Africa]
Australia won the toss and elected to field.
Australia won by 8 runs.
Australia 140 for 5 wickets [20 overs] – West Indies 132 for 4 wickets [20 overs]

The current holders of the Women's World Twenty20 trophy Australia, booked a place in their third successive final with an eight-run victory over West Indies in the semi-final at Mirpur. The *'Southern Stars'* opening bat Elyse Villani was top-scorer with 35, in a competitive total of 140 for the loss of 5 wickets from their 20 over spell at the crease. The *'Windies'* put on a good performance and showed their ability to manoeuvre the ball. And thanks to a contribution of 40 runs from Deandra Jalita Shakira Dottin, and Stacy-Ann King's 36 not out, were briefly threatening, but hopes collapsed when Dottin [born 1991] holed out to a pressure catch by Erin Alsye Osborne [born 1989] from a low full toss off the right-arm medium bowling of Sarah Jane Coyte [born 1991]. This left the *'Windies'* needing 20 runs from the last 10 balls, which although well within reach proved beyond them as the right-arm seamer Rene Michele Farrell [born 1987] bowled a tight final over.

Semi-Finals – 4 April, 2014

England v South Africa

Venue: Shere Bangla National Stadium, Mirpur, Dhaka, Bangladesh

Umpires: Steve Davis [Australia] & Bruce Oxenford [Australia]

England won the toss and elected to field.

England won by 9 wickets.

South Africa 101 all out [19.5 overs] – England 102 for 1 wicket [16.5 overs]

England, who had won the inaugural Women's World Twenty20 tournament in 2009, thrashed South Africa by nine wickets in the second of the 2014 semi-finals to secure a place in its second successive Women's World Twenty20 final.

After winning the coin toss England chose to put South Africa in to bat. Anya Shrubsole captured two early wickets in an innings in which included five run-outs. With the lack-lustre South Africa side seen off for the meagre total of 101. The only couple to make double figures for the *'Proteas'* were Chloe LesleighTryon [born1994] who knocked up 40 runs, and the South African skipper Mignon du Preez [born 1989] with a score of 23.

England easily passed its target inside 17 overs, with wicketkeeper Sarah Jane Taylor [born 1989] knocking up an unbeaten 44. Not only did the win give the women's captain, Charlotte Edwards, the satisfaction of avenging the defeat in Sri Lanka in 2012, but also completed a twelve month period in which England regained the Ashes at home, and successfully defended them down under. *'This gives us confidence going into the next game,'* she told Test Match Special. *'The batters are batting well and the bowlers have been exceptional all tournament. It was more of the same today'.*

In the final of the 2014 Women's World Twenty20 series held at the Shere Bangla National Stadium in Mirpur, Dhaka on the 6 April, the Australian women's team skipper, Meghann Lanning [born 1992], won the toss and chose to field. As the game progressed it soon became clear the England side was totally outperformed. The *'Southern Stars'* effortlessly triumphed by a comfortable wicket margin, to collect a third successive Women's World Twenty20 title with 29 balls left in reserve.

On a blameless pitch England failed to find form with the bat, collapsing from 55 for 1 to post a modest 105 for the loss of 8 wickets in its 20 over spell at the crease, with Heather Knight knocking up the team's highest score of 29 from two dozen deliveries. The England captain, Charlotte Edwards, batting alongside her opening partner Sarah Taylor, failed to score freely during a lifeless stand of 23, which endured for almost six overs. Both fell to the impressive right-arm medium pace of Sarah Jane Coyte, Edwards caught at mid-on for 13 by a diving Jess Cameron [born 1989], and Taylor fell for 18 after attempting a cheeky reverse-sweep, she was struck low on the back pad and given out lbw by umpire Aleem Dar. England laboured to reach three figures with four more wickets falling in the last five overs.

'We weren't good enough. 105 was never going to be good enough in a World Cup final', confessed the England captain Charlotte Edwards. *'We were completely outplayed'*.

Once Australia had raced to 43 for the loss of one wicket by the end of the first six-over power-play, the end result was never left in doubt. Left-hander Jess Jonassen [born 1992] set the pace of the Australian reply by pocketing two fours and a six off the second over, off the right-arm off-breaks bowled by Danielle Hazell [born 1988]. Meg Lanning added 44 runs from 30 deliveries, which included 4 fours and 2 sixes, in a 60 run third-wicket stand alongside Ellyse Perry [born 1990] who finished on 31 not out, resulting in a swift and comprehensive victory for Australia with 29 balls to spare. By way of contrast, not a single England player managed to hit a six during the entire competition.

The result was a thoroughly dispiriting end to the winter for the England women's team, which had been found badly wanting, and as a result would undoubtedly be subject far greater scrutiny.

2014 Women's World Twenty20 Final

England v Australia – 6 April, 2014

Venue: Shere Bangla National Stadium, Mirpur, Dhaka, Bangladesh
Umpires: Aleem Dar [Pakistan]: Marais Erasmus [South Africa]

Australia won the toss and elected to field.
Australia Women won by 6 wickets.
Player of the match: Sarah Coyte [Australia].

England Women's Innings [20 overs maximum]:

Sarah Taylor [Wicket]	lbw	b Coyte	18
Charlotte Edwards [Capt.]	c Cameron	b Coyte	13
Heather Knight	c Perry	b Osborne	29
Lydia Greenway	c Healy	b Perry	2
Natalie Sciver		b Farrell	9
Amy Jones	lbw	b Perry	12
Tamsin Beaumont		b Coyte	6
Jennifer Gunn	not out		7
Danielle Hazell	c Osborne	b Farrell	4
Anya Shrubsole	not out		1
Rebecca Grundy	did not bat		
Extras	[1nb, 3w]		4
TOTAL	20 overs – Run Rate 5.25		**105 for 8 wickets**

Fall of wickets:
1-23 CM Edwards, 5.4 ov, 2-55 SJ Taylor, 9.5 ov, 3-58 LS Greenway, 10.5 ov, 4-67 HC Knight, 12.5 ov, 5-85 NR Scriver, 15.5ov, 6-93 TT Beaumont, 16.3 ov, 7-95 AE Jones, 17.2 ov, 8-101 D. Hazell, 19.3 ov.

Australia Bowling:	**O**	**M**	**R**	**W**	**Econ.**
Rene Michell Farrell	4	0	27	2	6.75
Jessica Louise Jonassen	4	0	16	0	4.00
Ellyse Alexandra Perry	4	0	13	2	3.25
Sarah Jane Coyte	4	0	16	3	4.00
Erin Aylse Osborne	3	0	24	1	8.00
Julie Lauren Hunter	1	0	9	0	9.00

Australia Women's Innings [20 overs maximum]:

EJ Villiani	c Edwards	b Gunn	12
Jessica Jonassen	c Jones	b Shrubsole	15
MM Lanning [Captain]	c Knight	b Sciver	44
Ellyse Perry	not out		31
Alexandra Blackwell	lbw	b Sciver	0
Jessica Cameron	not out		0
Alyssa Healy [Wicket]	did not bat		
Erin Osborne	did not bat		
Sarah Coyte	did not bat		
Rene Farrell	did not bat		
Julie Hunter	did not bat		

Extras	[1lb, 1nb, 2w]	4
TOTAL	15.1 overs – Run Rate 6.98	**106 for 4 wickets**

Fall of wickets:
1-17 JL Jonassen, 2.4 ov, 2-44 EJ Villani, 6.2 ov, 3-104 JE MM Lanning, 14.4 ov, 4-105 AJ Blackwell, 14.6ov.

England Bowling:	**O**	**M**	**R**	**W**	**Econ.**
Anya Shrubsole	4	0	29	1	7.25
Danielle Hazell	3.1	0	29	0	9.15
Rebecca Louise Grundy	4	0	22	0	5.50
Jennifer Louise Gunn	2	0	13	1	6.50
Natalie Ruth Sciver	2	0	12	2	6.00

Fifth ICC Women's World Twenty20 – 2016

The fifth ICC Women's World Twenty20 tournament was hosted for the first time by India from the 15 March to the 3 April, 2016. The event was again run simultaneously with the men's World Twenty20 tournament, with the finals of both the women's and the men's events played on the same day at the famous Eden Gardens, Kolkata.

The top eight teams from the 2014 tournament qualified to compete in the 2016 tournament, with the remaining two spots decided at the 2015 World Twenty20 Qualifier, and awarded to Bangladesh and Ireland. The final list of the ten competing teams included Australia, England, the West Indies, South Africa, the host nation India, New Zealand, Pakistan, Sri Lanka, Ireland and Bangladesh.

A series of nine warm-up matches were played in Bangalore, which featured nine of the ten participating teams. A number of matches were held at the M. Chinnaswamy Stadium, in the heart of the city of Bengaluru, Karnataka. Bordered by the picturesque Cubbon Park, the stadium has a seating capacity of approaching 40,000, and is owned by the Government of Karnataka, with the ground and facilities leased for a term of 99 years by the Karnataka State Cricket Association [KSCA]. Formerly known as the Karnataka State Cricket Association stadium, the ground was re-named as a tribute to Mr. M. Chinnaswamy, who served the KSCA for forty years and was President of the Board of Control for Cricket in India [BCCI].

The remaining warm-up games were played in Chennai at the M. A. Chidambaram Stadium or Chepauk Stadium. Established in 1916, the stadium is the oldest of the continuously used cricket stadiums in India. Formerly known as the Madras Cricket Club Ground the stadium has a capacity of 50,000, it was re-named after M A Chidambaram, another former President of the BCCI.

As on previous occasions the ICC divided the 10 teams into two groups of five for the Group Stages of the competition, in which each team played every other team in its respective group, with the top two teams from each group qualifying to progress to the knockout phase of the tournament.

Group A

Team	Pld	W	L	T	NR	A	Pts	RR
New Zealand	4	4	0	0	0	0	8	2.430
Australia	4	3	1	0	0	0	6	0.613
Sri Lanka	4	2	2	0	0	0	4	-0.240
South Africa	4	1	3	0	0	0	2	0.173
Ireland	4	0	4	0	0	0	0	-2.817

Group B

Team	Pld	W	L	T	NR	A	Pts	RR
England	4	4	9	0	0	0	8	1.417
West Indies	4	3	1	0	0	0	6	0.688
Pakistan	4	2	2	0	0	0	4	-0.673
India	4	1	3	0	0	0	2	0.790
Bangladesh	4	0	4	0	0	0	0	-2.306

Semi-Finals – 30 March, 2016
England v Australia
Venue: Feroz Shah Kotla Ground, New Delhi

Umpires: Chris Gaffaney [New Zealand] & Sundaram Ravi [India]
England won the toss and elected to field.
Australia won by 5 runs
Australia 132 for 6 wickets [20 overs] – England 127 for 7 wickets [20 overs]
Player of the match: Meg Lanning [Australia].

Almost all international victories are sweet, no matter what the sport, but there are some that are sweeter than others. And it was the *'Southern Stars'* cock-a-hoop women's skipper Meg Lanning who earned the bragging rights over arch rivals England in the first of the 2016 semi-finals World Twenty20. England stumbled to another defeat, affording Australia the mouth-watering prospect of a fourth successive Women's World T20 title. Lanning's 55 off 50 deliveries on a slow Feroz Shah Kotla pitch was the cornerstone of Australia's total of 132 for 6 in its 20 over spell, leaving England needing to accomplish the highest run chase in the tournament in order to earn another crack at its second title. Lanning and Ellyse Perry did what they do best, harvesting runs in the middle overs through smart strike rotation, seldom looking for big hits against the defensive field set by the England captain Charlotte Edwards. England reprieved Lanning twice during her innings, once on 20 and again on 45, with the wicketkeeper Sarah Taylor [born 1989] the culprit on both occasions. Lanning went on to make a half-century, and help Australia post a very competitive score, ably supported by her deputy Alex Blackwell [born 1983] who contributed 11 in a 37-run stand for the fourth wicket.

England came out on the attack at the start of its run chase, and profited from a slice of good luck as a diving Beth Mooney [born 1994] put down a tough chance at mid-off in the fourth over from Tamsin Beaumont [born 1991]. Charlotte Edwards started slowly, before chipping a catch to cover in the tenth over, against the run of play and ending a 67 run opening partnership with fellow opener Beaumont. After much hard work, Beaumont nudged one to cover where Lanning pulled off a stunning catch diving forward.

Reduced to 91 for 3, England required 42 off the last five overs. Despite being flawed by a combination of tension and careless shots, they still managed to come within touching distance of the target set by the Aussies. In spite of the sterling effort by Katherine Brunt, who muscled a six and a four to leave England needing 17 runs off 10 balls, it was not enough and yet again the Australian killer instinct won through and England fell agonisingly short by a mere five runs.

Semi-Finals – 31 March, 2016

West Indies v New Zealand

Venue: Wankhede Stadium, Mumbai

Umpires: Richard Illingworth [England] & Nigel Llong [England]

New Zealand won the toss and elected to field.

West Indies won by 6 runs.

West Indies 143 for 6 wickets [20 overs] – New Zealand 137 for 8 wickets [20 overs].

Player of the match: Britney Cooper [West Indies].

Since the dawn of the game, those faced with the task of wielding the bat have needed to be imaginative and find a way to keep the scoreboard ticking along. Such assertiveness came to the fore at the Wankhede Stadium in Mumbai, in the second of the 2016 World Twenty20 semi-final matches between the West Indies and New Zealand. A high-scoring clash which the West Indies Women won by half-a-dozen runs, setting up a final date with the women of Australia in Kolkata.

New Zealand won the coin toss and put the *'Windies'* in to bat. Brim full of swagger and substance, they challenged the might of New Zealand's spin trio of Morna Nielsen, Leigh Kasperek and Erin Bermingham to post an imposing 143 for the loss of 6 wickets.

It was Britney Cooper who turned out to be the West Indies principal destroyer, delivering a forceful 61 runs off 48 deliveries, although it was far from a one-woman show, since both the skipper Stafanie Taylor and Deandra Dottin both played important roles.

New Zealand, who had stamped their authority over the rest of the field in the group stages, needed to produce the best batting display of the tournament in order to successfully chase down the total they had been set. With Rachel Priest falling early, Sophie Devine came out all guns blazing, hitting four boundaries off her first six deliveries to bring the chase back on track. But some half-hearted running coupled with a rocket of a throw by Deandra Dottin from point found Devine inches short of the crease. When Bates was poached off a leading edge at mid-off four balls later, New Zealand slipped to 49 for 3 to throw the chase off track again.

It was Sara McGlashan [born 1982] who took the onus upon herself to keep the scoreboard ticking along, without taking any unnecessary risks she combined with Amy Satterthwaite [born 1986] to eat into the target. Helped by a West Indies side that seemed to have momentarily switched off, both McGlashan and Satterthwaite overcame several slices of luck, as they might well have been run-out on a few occasions during the course of their fourth-wicket stand of 59. With 56 runs required off the last 36 balls, the game was delicately poised, but with Taylor's crucial double-strike in the 17th over, in which she claimed the scalp of Sattherthwaite, and that of McGlashan to a catch by Shemaine Campbelle at sweeper cover. Their eventual dismissal in the space of four deliveries frustrated the plans laid by the. *'White Ferns',* with their challenge evaporating as they finished the innings on 137 for 8. After notching up 20 to finish well with the bat, Deandra Dottin was summoned to bowl the final over in which she had to defend 19 the runs required to close out the game, which she did in style, and the elated West Indies were through to the final after three failed attempts.

In the final match of the 2016 Women's World Twenty20 series on the 3 April, and seeking a fourth successive World T20 title win, Australia won the toss and chose to open the batting against the West Indies at the iconic Eden Gardens. The stadium takes its name from the Eden Gardens, one of the oldest parks in Kolkata, which was named after the Eden sisters of Lord Auckland, the Governor-General of India at the time. Although it was initially named *the 'Auckland Circus Gardens'*, its name was later changed to Eden Gardens, said to be inspired by the biblical Garden of Eden.

The Australian women posted a target of 148 runs for the loss of 5 wickets in its 20 over spell at the crease, with Elyse Villani seizing upon some wayward full tosses on her way to the first half century in a World Twenty20 final. Boasting a total of nine boundaries in her fine 52 off 37 deliveries, she was finally caught by the *'Windies'* captain, Stafanie Taylor [born 1991], off a thick leading edge off the medium paced bowling of Deandra Dottin.

The West Indies, which had lost all eight of its previous T20 internationals against Australia, made an uneasy start in its first final. No doubt to the delight of the Australian skipper Meg Lanning, who hit three successive fours from a total of eight, to post an identical score to that of Villani, before falling lbw to Anisa Mohammed [born 1988] with 14 deliveries left in the innings. The all-rounder Ellyse Perry ultimately rounding off the *'Southern Stars'* innings with a fine half-hour cameo performance.

Having fought back briefly by conceding only a single from their final over in the field, the West Indies made a slow start in reply, taking the first two opening overs to put a parsimonious score of three runs on the board. But 18-year-old *'Windies'* opener Hayley Kristen Matthews [born 1998] hit a dazzling 66 off 45 balls with three sixes, in an opening stand of 120 with her skipper, Stafanie Taylor. Matthews eventually fell foul of a long-hop which she pulled straight to Alexandra Blackwell [born 1983] at mid-wicket off the spinner Kristen Beams [born 1984]. Matthews and Taylor recorded their century partnership in fourteen overs, before Taylor eventually fell on 59, leaving the *'Windies'* just five more runs to score from eight deliveries. Three runs were needed from the final over and after a routine run-out opportunity turned into an overthrow, the jubilant celebrations were launched, as the West Indies claimed its first Women's World Twenty20 victory with a pulsating eight-wicket win over Australia.

The euphoric West Indies captain Stafanie Taylor said, *'I've been waiting for this a long time and it has come at the right time. We didn't get the start we wanted but the batting has done it for us'.*

While the thwarted Australian skipper Meg Lanning conceded, *'Full credit to the West Indies, they came out with the bat, and we did not quite get the result we wanted. We felt we were a little short, 160 would have been nice, but if we bowled well we would have defended. It was a really exciting, tough road into the World Cup and I am proud of the effort that everyone has put in'.*

2016 Women's World Twenty20 Final – 3 April, 2016

Australia v West Indies

Venue: Eden Gardens, Kolkata
Umpires: Aleem Dar [Pakistan]: Richard Illingworth [England]

West Indies Women won by 8 wickets.
Australia won the toss and elected to bat
Player of the match: Hayley Matthews [West Indies]

Australia Women's Innings [20 overs maximum]:

Alyssa Healy [Wicket]		c & b Matthews	4
Elyse Villani	c Taylor	b Dottin	52
Meghann Lanning [Capt.]	lbw	b Mohammed	52
Ellyse Perry	lbw	b Dottin	28
Alexandra Blackwell	not out		3
Erin Osborne	run out		0
Jessica Jonassen	not out		0
Bethany Mooney	did not bat		
Megan Schutt	did not bat		
Rene Farrell	did not bat		
Kristen Beams	did not bat		
Extras	[4b, 2lb, 3w]		9
TOTAL	15.1 overs – Run Rate 7.40		**148 for 5 wickets**

Fall of wickets:
1-15 AJ Healy, 1.6 ov, 2-92 EJ Villani, 11.6 ov, 3-134 JE MM Lanning, 17.4 ov, 4-147 EA Perry, 19.4ov, 5-147 EA Osborne, 19.5 ov.

West Indies Bowling:	**O**	**M**	**R**	**W**	**Econ.**
Shamilia Shontell Connell	2	0	15	0	7.50
Hayley Kristen Matthews	2	0	13	1	6.50
Stafanie Roxann Taylor	3	0	26	0	8.66
Deandra Jalisa Shakira Dottin	4	0	33	2	8.25
Afy Samatha Sharlyn Fletcher	1	0	9	0	9.00
Anisa Mohammed	4	0	19	1	4.75
Shaquana Latish Quintyne	4	0	27	0	6.75

West Indies Women's Innings [20 overs maximum]:

Hayley Matthews	c Blackwell	b Beams	66
Stafanie Taylor [Capt.]	c Jonassen	b Farrell	59
Deandra Dottin	not out		18
Britney Cooper	not out		3
Stacy-Ann King	did not bat		
Merissa Aguilleira [Wicket]	did not bat		
Shemaine Campbelle	did not bat		
Shaquana Quintyne	did not bat		
Anisa Mohammed	did not bat		
Afy Fletcher	did not bat		
Shamilia Connell	did not bat		
Extras	[2lb, 1w]		3
TOTAL	19.3 overs – Run Rate 7.64		**149 for 2 wickets**

Fall of wickets:
1-120 HK Matthews, 15.4 ov, 2-144 SR Taylor, 18.4 ov.

Australia Bowling:	**O**	**M**	**R**	**W**	**Econ.**
Jessica Louise Jonassen	4	0	26	0	6.50
Ellyse Alexandra Perry	3.3	0	27	0	7.71
Megan Schutt	3	0	26	0	8.66
Rene Michele Farrell	4	0	35	1	8.75
Kristen Maree Beams	4	0	27	1	6.75
Erin Aylse Osborne	1	0	6	0	6.00
Shaquana Latish Quintyne	4	0	27	0	6.75

Sixth ICC Women's World Twenty20 – 2018

The sixth ICC Women's World Twenty20 is scheduled to be hosted by the West Indies during November 2018.The tournament was awarded to the West Indies Cricket Board [WICB] at the Annual Conference of the International Cricket Council in 2013. It will be the second time the tournament has been hosted by the West Indies, the first being in 2010. The ICC confirmed this would also be the first T20 tournament using the Umpire Decision Review System [UDRS], in which each team will be permitted one review in each.

Roy Case

The Umpire Decision Review System or [DRS] is a technological system used to assist match officials with decision-making. On-field umpires may choose to consult with the third umpire, this is known as an Umpire Review. Players are also permitted to request the third umpire to consider a decision which has been made by the on-field umpires, which is known as a Player Review. The main elements used are television replays, using technology that tracks the path of the ball, and predicts what it is likely to have done, and microphones to detect minute sounds made as the ball hitting bat or pad. Infra-red imaging is also used to identify changes in temperature as the ball hits the bat or pad.

While on-field Test match umpires have been able to refer some decisions to a third umpire since 1992, the formal DRS system in which Player Reviews was first used was in a Test match in 2008. The system was first used in a ODI match in 2011, and in a Twenty20 International in October 2017.

Eight teams qualified automatically from the 2016 tournament, including Australia, England, India, New Zealand, Pakistan, South Africa, Sri Lanka and the host nation West Indies. They will be joined by the teams from Ireland and Bangladesh teams from the qualifying tournament for the competition which was held in July 2018 in the Netherlands. Following the group-stage matches, Bangladesh and Papua New Guinea along with Ireland and Scotland progressed to the semi finals. Ireland beat Papua New Guinea by 27 runs, and in doing so qualified for the 2018 ICC Women's World Twenty20, in the second of the semi finals, Bangladesh also qualified after defeating Scotland by 49 runs. Bangladesh won the overall qualifying tournament, defeating Ireland by 25 runs in the final.

The ICC has announced that three venues will be used to host the games. The Providence Stadium, or Guyana National Stadium, which has a capacity of 15,000, and was built specifically to host Super Eight matches in the 2007 Cricket World Cup. The Daren Sammy Cricket Ground, previously known as the Beausejour Cricket Ground, which is located near Gros Islet, Saint Lucia. The stadium staged its first international Test match in 2003 against Sri Lanka, and can also accommodate around 15,000 spectators. And finally, the Sir Vivian Richards Stadium in North Sound, Antigua, situated a short drive from the capital city St. John's. It was completed in 2002 at a cost of approximately 60 million US dollars, funded primarily by a Chinese Government grant. Named after the former West Indies cricket captain Viv Richards, the stadium caters for around 10,000 spectators, although its capacity can be doubled by the addition of temporary seating as it was for the 2007 World Cup. The stadium staged its first Test match against Australia, with the match ending in a draw.

Chapter 14

England Women's Test Cricket Captains

Helen Elizabeth 'Betty' Archdale [née Russel] - 1934–1937

Born: Paddington, London, England - 21 August 1907

Died: Killara, New South Wales, Australia - 11 January 2000

Right-hand bat:

Batting: Runs scored: 133 Centuries 0 Highest score: 32 not out

Teams represented: England Women, East of England Women, Kent

Test debut: 28 December 1934 v Australia

Last Test: 13 July 1937 v Australia

Test matches: 5

Mary Edith 'Molly' Hide - 1934-1954

Born: Shanghai, China – 24 October 1913

Died: Guildford, Surrey, England - 10 September 1995

Right hand bat: Right-arm medium bowler:

Batting: Runs scored: 872 Centuries 2 Highest score: 124 n/o o

Bowling: Balls bowled: 2,064 Wickets: 36 Best bowling: 5/20

Teams represented: England Women

Test debut: 28 December 1934 v Australia

Last Test: 27 July 1954 v New Zealand

Test matches: 15

Myrtle Ethel Maclagan MBE - 1934-1951

Born: Ambala [now Haryana], United Provinces, India

2 April 1911

Died: Farnham, Surrey, England - 11 March 1993

Right-arm bat: Right-arm off-break bowler:

Batting: Runs scored: 1,007 Centuries 2 Highest score: 119

Bowling; Balls bowled: 3,432 Wickets: 60 Best bowling: 7/10

Teams represented: England Women, South Women, Surrey

Test debut: 28 December 1934 v Australia

Last Test: 31 July 1951 v Australia

Test matches: 14

Mary Beatrice Duggan -1949-196

Born: Worcester, Worcestershire, England – 7 November 1925

Died: Colwall, Herefordshire, England - 10 March 1973

Right hand bat: Slow left-arm orthodox & left-arm medium fast:

Batting: Runs scored: 652 Centuries 2 Highest score: 108

Bowling: Balls bowled: 3,734 Wickets: 77 Best bowling: 7/6

Teams represented: England Women,South Women, Middlesex, Yorkshire

Test debut: 15 January 1949 v Australia

Last Test: 20 July 1963 v Australia

Test matches: 17

Mary Cecilia Robinson - 1949-1963

Born: Canterbury, Kent, England –22 May1924

Roy Case

Right hand bat:

Batting: Runs scored: 829 Centuries 2 Highest score: 105

Teams represented: England Women, East Women, Kent

Test debut: 15 January 1949 v Australia

Last Test: 29 June 1963 v Australia

Test matches: 14

Helen Margaret Sharpe [Also known as Helen Griffiths] - 1957-1961

Born: England – 23 February 1937

Died: England – 7 December 1996

Right hand bat:

Batting: Runs scored: 296 Centuries 1 Highest score: 126

Bowling: Balls bowled: 54 Wickets: 0

Wicketkeeper: Caught: 1 Stumped: 1

Teams represented: England Women, Middlesex

Test debut: 27 December 1957 v New Zealand

Last Test: 13 January 1961 v South Africa

Test matches: 5

Baroness Rachael Heyhoe-Flint OBE, DL [1939-2017] - 1960-1979

Born: Wolverhampton, Staffordshire, England – 11 June 1939

Died: England – 18 January 2017

Right hand bat: Right-arm leg-spin:

Batting: Runs scored: 1,594 Centuries: 3 Highest score: 179

ODI: Runs scored: 643 Centuries: 1 Highest score: 114

Bowling: Balls bowled: 402 Wickets: 3 Best bowling: 1/3

ODI: Balls bowled: 18 Wickets: 1 Best bowling: 1/13

Teams represented:

England Women, West Midlands Women

Test debut: 2 December July, 1960 v South Africa

Last Test: 1 July, 1979 v West Indies

ODI debut: 23 June 1973 v International XI

Last ODI: 7 February 1982 v Australia

Test matches: 22 ODI: 23

Janet 'Jan' Southgate [Also known as Janet Allen] - 1976-1985

Born: Eastcote, Middlesex, England – 24 September 1955

Right hand bat:

Batting: Runs scored: 490 Centuries: 0 Highest score: 74

ODI: Runs scored: 372 Centuries: 0 Highest score: 82

Bowling: Balls bowled: 238 Wickets: 2 Best bowling: 1/13

ODI: Balls bowled: 138 Wickets: 4 Best bowling: 2/28

Teams represented: England Women, Sussex

Test debut: 19 June, 1976 v Australia

Last Test: 25 January 1985 v Australia

ODI debut: 1 August 1976 v Australia

Last ODI: 3 February 1985 v Australia

Test matches: 13 ODI: 17

Susan Goatman - 1979

Born: Thanet, Kent, England – 5 February 1945

Right hand bat:

Batting: Runs scored: 158 Centuries: 0 Highest score: 71

ODI: Runs scored: 498 Centuries: 0 Highest score: 83

Teams represented: England Women, East Women, Kent

Test debut: 16 June 1979 v West Indies

Roy Case

Last Test: 1 July 1979 v West Indies

ODI debut: 23 June 1973 v Australia

Last ODI: 7 February 1982 v Australia

Test matches: 3 ODI: 21

Carole Ann Hodges [Also known as Carole Cornthwaite] - 1984–1992

Born: Blackpool, Lancashire, England – 1 September 1959

Right hand bat: Right-arm off-break bowler:

Batting: Runs scored: 1,164 Centuries: 2 Highest score: 158 n/o

ODI: Runs scored: 1,073 Centuries: 2 Highest score: 113

Bowling: Balls bowled: 2,556 Wickets: 23 Best bowling: 4/21

ODI: Balls bowled: 2,207 Wickets: 58 Best bowling: 4/3

Teams represented: England Women, Lancashire, Cheshire

Test debut: 6 July 1984 v New Zealand

Last Test: 19 February 1992 v Australia

ODI debut: 14 January 1973 v International XI

Last ODI: 1 August 1993 v New Zealand

Test matches: 18 ODI: 47

Karen Smithies OBE [Also known as Karen Hicken] - 1987-1999

Born: Ashby de la Zouch, Leicestershire, England

20 March 1969

Left hand bat: Right-arm medium bowler

Batting: Runs scored: 443 Centuries: 0 Highest score: 64

ODI: Runs scored: 921 Centuries: 1 Highest score: 110 not out

Bowling: Balls bowled: 2,196 Wickets: 16 Best bowling: 3/63

ODI: Balls bowled: 2,681 Wickets: 64 Best bowling: 3/6

Teams represented: England Women, East Midlands Women

Test debut: 21 August 1987 v Australia

Last Test: 15 July 1999 v India

ODI debut: 28 June 1986 v India

Last ODI: 15 February 2000 v New Zealand

Test matches: 15 ODI: 69

Helen Clare Plimmer - 1992-1996

Born: Solomon Islands – 3 June 1965

Right hand bat:

Batting: Runs scored: 243 Centuries: 0 Highest score: 46

ODI: Runs scored: 886 Centuries: 1 Highest score: 118

Teams represented: England Women, Yorkshire

Test debut: 11 January 1992 v New Zealand

Last Test: 4 July 1996 v New Zealand

ODI debut: 19 July 1989 v Netherlands

Last ODI: 26 December 1997 v New Zealand

Test matches: 9 ODI: 37

Clare Joanne Connor CBE - 1995–2005

Born: Brighton, Sussex, England – 1 September 1976

Right hand bat:

Batting: Runs scored: 502 Centuries: 0 Highest score: 61

ODI: Runs scored: 1.087 Centuries: 0 Highest score: 85 n/o

T20I: Runs scored: 15 Centuries: 0 Highest score: 9 not out

Bowling: Balls bowled: 2,061 Wickets: 24 Best bowling: 5/65

ODI: Balls bowled: 3,580 Wickets: 80 Best bowling: 5/49

T20I: Balls bowled: 36 Wickets: 0 Best bowling: -

Teams represented: England Women, Sussex

Roy Case

Test debut: 10 December 1995 v India

Last Test: 24 August 2005 v Australia

ODI debut: 19 July 1995 v Denmark

Last ODI: 1 September 2005 v Australia

T20I debut: 5 August 2004 v New Zealand

Last T20I: 2 September 2005 v Australia

Test matches: 16 ODI: 93 T20I: 2

Charlotte Marie Edwards CBE - 1996-2015

Born: Huntingdon, Cambridgeshire, England

17 December 1979

Right hand bat: Leg-break bowler

Batting: Runs scored: 1,676 Centuries: 4 Highest score: 117

ODI: Runs scored: 5,992 Centuries: 9 Highest score: 173 n/o

T20I: Runs scored: 2,605 Centuries: 0 Highest score: 92 n/o

Bowling: Balls bowled: 1,118 Wickets: 12 Best bowling: 2/28

ODI: Balls bowled: 1,627 Wickets: 54 Best bowling: 4/30

T20I: Balls bowled: 303 Wickets: 9 Best bowling: 3/21

Teams represented: England Women, East Anglia Women, Northern Districts Women, Kent

Test debut: 12 July 1996 v New Zealand

Last Test: 1 August 2015 v Australia

ODI debut: 19 August 1997 v South Africa

Last ODI: 14 February 2016 v South Africa

T20I debut: 5 August 2004 v New Zealand

Last T20I: 30 March 2016 v Australia

Test matches: 23 ODI: 191 T20I: 95

Heather Clare Knight OBE - 2011-2018

Born: Plymouth, Devon, England – 26 December 1990

Right hand bat: Right-arm off-break bowler

Batting: Runs scored: 358 Centuries: 1 Highest score: 157

ODI: Runs scored: 2,067 Centuries: 1 Highest score: 106

T20I: Runs scored: 426 Centuries: 0 Highest score: 51

Bowling: Balls bowled: 179 Wickets: 2 Best bowling: 1/7

ODI: Balls bowled: 1,331 Wickets: 43 Best bowling: 5/26

T20I: Balls bowled: 339 Wickets: 12 Best bowling: 3/10

Teams represented: England Women, England Academy Women, Diamonds, Rubies

Test debut: 22 January 2011 v New Zealand

Last Test: 9 November 2017 v Australia

ODI debut: 1 March 2010 v India

Last ODI: 29 October 2017 v Australia

T20I debut: 22 November 2010 v Sri Lanka

Last T20I: 25 March 2018 v India

Test matches: 6 ODI: 78 T20I: 41

Chapter 15

Extras

These days cricket is governed by the International Cricket Council [ICC], and is played mainly in Australasia, the Indian sub-continent, Southern Africa, the West Indies, and of course Great Britain and Ireland. The ICC has a diverse membership numbering in excess of a 100 countries. Twelve of which are full members and eligible to play Test cricket.

The rules of the game are known as the *'Laws of Cricket'*, and are regulated and maintained by the Marylebone Cricket Club [MCC] in London.

The modern game offers something to suit the taste of almost everyone, with several distinctive forms of the game, ranging from the popular Twenty20 version, through to International Test matches. Each in its turn is designed to meet the needs of the judicious cricket enthusiast. Whether the obdurate supporter, who seeks the satisfaction of an end result within a few hours of play, or the time-honoured purist, preferring a more arduous examination lasting several days.

Twenty20 is a much shorter form of the game, in which each of the two competing teams is allowed a single innings, limited to a maximum of

20 overs. A much quicker form of the game, it was initially introduced to be more compatable with the time-span generally associated with other popular team sports, arguably more appealing to spectators and television viewers. The duration of a conventional Twenty20 game is around three and a half hours, with each team innings lasting around 100 minutes. It was first introduced at the professional level by the England and Wales Cricket Board [ECB] in 2003, for inter-county competition in England and Wales and List A and first-class cricket.

The Twenty20 game has successfully spread throughout the cricket world, and is one of three current forms of cricket recognised by the International Cricket Council [ICC] as being at the highest international or domestic level.

The categorisation of cricket matches as List A was officially approved by the International Cricket Council in 2006, and these days most Test cricketing nations have introduced some form of domestic List A competition, together with some nations who have as yet not achieved official ODI status.

List A cricket is classified as form of of limited-over [one-day] cricket, which includes One Day International [ODI] matches and various other forms of domestic competitions. The number of overs in an innings for each of the competing teams ranging from between forty to sixty.

First-class cricket is designated as the highest official classification of important domestic or international cricket matches. A first-class match is deemed worthy of the title according to the merit of the competing teams, and is played over a period of three or more days between two teams of eleven players. Matches must allow for each of the teams to play two innings, although in practice a team might only play a single innings or part of an innings.

A peculiarity of a two-innings match is the *'follow-on'* law. Namely, if the team batting second is 200 runs, or more, behind the opposing team's first innings total, it may be required to bat again. That is to say, to immediately *'follow on'* from its first innings, rather than alternating as would normally be the case.

Undoubtedly the highest standard of cricket remains Test cricket, statistically a form of first-class cricket, played between teams representing full member countries of the ICC.

The origin of the term 'first-class cricket' is unknown, but it was used loosely before it acquired official status. The term was subsequently classified on a global basis by the Imperial Cricket Conference [ICC] in May 1947, when *'first-class cricket'* became a term generally used when referring to the highest form of domestic contest.

The official County Championship was first constituted in a meeting at Lord's in December 1889, and is an annual domestic first-class cricket competition consisting of eighteen competing clubs from historic cricketing counties, organised by the ECB. Participating teams accumulate league points throughout the season, with the overall winning team in Divisions 1 and 2 determined by the aggregate number of points accrued. Additional bonus points may also be collected through the batting and bowling performance in the first 110 overs of each team's opening innings, which are retained regardless of the eventual outcome of the match. From time to time, a team may also have match points deducted for specific reasons.

The inaugural Women's County Championship was introduced in 1997, replacing the Women's Area Championship. The first tournament was organised by the WCA [Women's Cricket Association], and has subsequently been organised and administered by the ECB since its merger with the WCA in 1998.

A 50 over competition, the Women's County Championship is the women's equivalent of the men's County Championship. The thirty-six competing teams are also drawn from the historic counties of England, and has also include representation by the Scottish women's national side since 2007, the Wales women's national team since 2008, and the Netherlands women who joined the Championship in 2009. The Ireland women's national team also played in the competition from 2009 to 2015, but withdrew from the Championship in early 2016, causing the designated fixtures for that particular season to be rescheduled.

Initially four divisions were sub-divided with four teams in each, and a *'festival finale'* was held at the County Ground, Taunton, but this system was abandoned to avoid the risk of rain affecting the matches. From 2009 the teams making up the Championship were also organised into four divisions, with the fourth division divided into two groups based upon geographical location. Eight years later, in 2017, division four was eliminated with all its teams promoted to division three which is now sub-divided geographically into groups of at least 4 teams.

The competition is the longest established women's cricket competition in England and Wales, operating alongside the Women's Twenty20 Cup [2009] and the Women's Cricket Super League, a franchise league with six teams playing Twenty20 cricket. Traditionally the players wear a uniform of all-white clothing, although in limited over matches it is customary for teams to wear distinctive club colours, in common with the men's game.

There is evidence to suggest twomen may well have initially played the game with a different coloured ball. Some years ago, Zoe English, a cricket historian and Cataloguing Assistant at the MCC, was listening to an interview on the MCC audio archive. In which Ken Medlock OBE, a former chairman of John Wisden & Co, and the cricket historian, writer and broadcaster, David Rayvern Allen [1938-2014], were discussing the manufacture of cricket balls. During the discussion it was suggested that in the early days of women's cricket a blue cricket ball had been used in the women's game, with the only known remaining example of such a ball exhibited in the MCC collections on loan from the Women's Cricket Association. According to a catalogue from a 1963 Exhibition of Women's Cricketana, it is claimed, *'The blue ball made specially by Alfred Reader at the request of Gamages Limited in 1897, to ensure that lady cricketers would not swoon at the sight of a red one, did not prove practical as it could not be seen again the background of grass and sky.'*

So there you have it, a limited supply of the blue ball was produced, the weight of which was 5 ounces. The same weight as that used by women cricketers since 1926, when a special standardised 5 ounce ball was adopted. It was manufactured for the WCA by Wisden, with a 4¾ ounce ball developed for use in schools.

The manufacture and weight of a cricket ball at first-class level is now regulated by cricketing law, with the construction detail, dimensions, quality and performance strictly controlled. Composed of a core of cork, they are layered with tightly wound string, and covered by a leather case stitched with string to form the ball's slightly raised prominent seam.

Cricket ball specifications:	Weight:	Circumference:
Men, and boys 13 and over:	5 1/2–5 3/4 ounces	8 13/16–9 inches
	156–163 grams	224–229 mm
Women, and girls 13 and over:	4 15/16–5 5/16 ounces	8 1/4-8 7/8 inches
	140–151 grams	210–225 mm
Children under 13:	4 11/16-5 1/16 ounces	8 – 8 7/8 inches
	133–144 grams	203–225 mm
Younger children:	A plastic ball such as the *'Kwik cricket'* ball is often used.	

In professional *'day'* cricket, when domestic games may stretch over several days, and in almost all amateur matches the traditional red cricket ball is used. While in most one day matches a white ball is used in order that it may remain visible under floodlights. Since 2010, a pink ball has occasionally been introduced, to contrast with the players clothing, and improve visibility during day/night matches.

Even though manufacturers claim white and red balls are made using the same methods and materials, other than the dye used in the treatment of the leather, it is claimed the white ball has a tendency to behave differently to the red ball. They are said to deteriorate more quickly and have a tendency to swing more during the first half of an innings.

Although it may appear to be stating the obvious the bat is a specific piece of equipment, first cited in 1624, which is used by the batsman to strike the ball. Usually constructed out of *'white willow'*, often referred to as *'cricket bat willow'*, it consists of a cylindrical cane handle, covered with a rubber grip, attached by a tapered splice to a flat-fronted wooden blade with a ridge on the back. The finished bat is then treated with a protective coat of raw linseed oil.

The Laws of Cricket state that the length of the bat may not exceed 38 inches [965 mm] and be no wider than 4.25 inches [108 mm], and typically weigh from 2 lb 7 oz [1.2 kg] to 3 lb [1.4 kg].

This rule was introduced following the *'Monster Bat Incident of 1771'*, when during a cricket match between Chertsey and Hambledon, a squabble arose as the Chertsey player, Thomas *'Daddy'* White [1740-1831], attempted to use a bat as wide as the wicket. Although the Hambledon players made an objection, although they did go on to win the match by a single run, a formal protest was written after the match which eventually brought about a change in the laws of the game. The maximum width of the bat was set at 4.25 inches in 1774, a ruling which remains intact to this day.

Since 1979, the Laws stipulate that bats may only be constructed from wood. They are made available in a range of sizes, including those designated to accommodate children. Bats may be increased in length and width, with the *'short handle'* [SH] the most commonly used adult size, although *'long handle'* and *'long blade'* options are also available. The edges of the blade closest to the handle are known as the *'shoulders'* of the bat, and the bottom of the blade is known as the *'toe'* of the bat.

Most modern bats are not ready for immediate use, and require' *knocking-in'* before striking a hard new cricket ball, in order to avoid causing damage and the risk of the bat breaking. This involves striking the blade of the bat with an old cricket ball or a special mallet.

The oldest bat still in existence is dated 1729 and is on display in the Sandham Room at The Oval in London, when they were not always the shape and style of the modern bat used today. Prior to the 18th century, they were often a similar shape to that of a hockey stick. Although the origin remains obscure, the shape may have been a legacy from the time when it is thought a shepherd's crooks may have been used as a form of bat, and a more suitable method of dealing with the early under-arm bowling style.

Historically cricket wickets had only two stumps and one bail, and resembled a small *'wicket'* gate. The third stump, the middle stump, was introduced in 1775, and today each wicket consists of a set of three stumps, consisting of three upright wooden poles hammered into the ground and topped with two wooden crosspieces known as the bails.

The size and shape of the wicket has changed several times during the past 300 years. Its dimension and placing, now determined in the Laws of the Game as consisting of three wooden stumps that are 28 inches [71 cm] tall. The stumps are positioned along the batting crease, with equal distances between each stump, so that they are 9 inches [23 cm] wide overall. The wickets are placed at either end of the pitch, sometimes also known as the *'wicket'*, although according to the Laws of the Game this term is technically incorrect.

Two wooden bails are placed in shallow grooves on top of the stumps, which must not project more than 0.5 inches [1.3 cm] above the stumps, and must be 4 $\frac{5}{16}$ inches [10.95 cm] long. If playing conditions are deemed to be unfit, the umpires are granted the discretion to dispense with the use of the bails. A modified specification may be used for the wickets and bails in junior cricket.

The size of the field on which the game is played varies from ground to ground, with the cricket pitch a central rectangular strip of the field between the wickets 10ft [3.05m] in width, and 22 yards [20.12m] in length, which in earlier times this precise distance was known as a *'chain'*. The surface is flat and usually covered with extremely short grass, ordinarily quickly worn away at the ends of the pitch. Accurate markings define the creases as specified by the Laws of Cricket, four feet [1.22m] in front of the stumps at each end of the pitch.

The rectangular central area of the cricket field used for pitches is known as the *'square'*, usually positioned as close to the north-south direction as practical, in order to avoid the low afternoon sun which may prove dangerous for a batsman facing west.

Although extremely rare, injuries do occasionally occur during a game of cricket. This has led to the gradual introduction of various items of protective equipment, which most professional players now choose to wear to guard against potential injury, generally caused by the hard ball.

Two cricket sight screens are deployed during play, positioned at each end of the pitch, behind the wickets a short distance beyond the boundary rope. They are usually coloured black or white, depending upon the type of match and the colour of the ball being used. The purpose is to offer the batsman a clear view of the bowler's delivery, and provide a visual contrast to the cricket ball, which helps the batsman see its movement through the air. The sight screen also helps avoid any distraction, including that of spectators, which may disturb the concentration of the batsman.

Limited over matches, such as One Day Internationals, or Twenty20 Internationals, are usually played with a white ball, and the sight screen is usually black, or dark in colour. In first-class matches and Test matches, in which the traditional red ball is used, the sight screen usually white.

A pitch with grass longer, or more moist than usual, is often described as a *'green pitch'*. This tends to favour the bowler as the ball can be made to behave unpredictably on longer or wet grass. A *'sticky wicket'* refers to a pitch that has become wet and is drying out, often quite quickly in a hot sun. This can cause the ball to behave erratically, particularly for slower, or spin, bowlers. These days, since modern pitches are well protected before and during games, a *'sticky'* pitch is rarely seen in first-class cricket. However, the phrase has become extended beyond cricket to mean any *'difficult situation'*.

As a match progresses, and the pitch begins to dry out, batting generally becomes easier. However, over the course of a four or five-day match, the pitch may begin to crack, crumble and become dusty. This kind of pitch is colloquially known as a *'dust bowl'*. Once again favouring the spin bowlers, who are able to get considerable traction off the surface and impart significant spin. Potential changes in the state of the pitch as the game progresses is one of the strategic considerations a captain of the team that wins the coin toss may take into account when deciding whether to bat of field first.

Over the years the women's game has enjoyed outstanding success, both on and off the field, and should be truly proud of its achievement along the way.

It is perhaps not generally known that it was the England Women who were the first to play a Twenty20 International match, when in August 2004 they took on New Zealand at the County Cricket Ground in Hove. New Zealand won the toss and decided to bat, scoring 131 runs, at a run rate of 6.55, for the loss of 8 wickets in their 20 overs. The England Women forfeited 7 of its wickets, on the way to a total score of 122 runs, at a run rate of 6.10 an over, conceding defeat by just 9 runs. This historic match was held six months before the first men's Twenty20 International was contested between Australia and New Zealand.

Moreover, in 1982, in their opening game of the third Women's World Cricket Cup, the England women were the first to tie a one-day international match. The event was particularly notable since two of the same series of matches resulted in ties, a first for women's international cricket. The first came in January, in the match between England and the host country New Zealand at Cornwall Park, Auckland. New Zealand, won the toss and elected to bat, scoring 147 runs for the loss of 9 wickets. England matched the score losing 8 of its wickets in the allotted 60 overs. The second was played the following month, between England and Australia at Christ's College Christchurch. Australia won the toss and chose to bowl first. England scored 167 for the loss of 8 wickets in its innings of

60 overs, which Australia matched for the loss of all its wickets. The two teams met again later in February in the World Cup final at Lancaster Park, Christchurch, where Australia emerged triumphant with a 3 wicket win. A further fifteen years would elapse before another tie in ODI cricket came about, in December 1997.

In addition, the women's game has produced some outstanding individual cricketers too, exemplified by the following noteworthy examples.

Born in Lancaster, England in 1963, Sarah Illingworth represented New Zealand as captain in all six of the women's Test matches in which she played, racking up six draws. She also led the New Zealand side in 29 Women's One-Day International matches. Illingworth holds the joint record as the first female wicket- keeper to claim 6 dismissals in a single innings in the Women's Cricket World Cup match held at Beckenham against Australia, capturing 4 catches and stumping 2 victims. She shares the record with the former Indian Test and One-Day International cricketer Venkatacher Kalpana, who took one catch and made 5 stumpings in the Women's Cricket World Cup match against Denmark held at Slough on the same day, the 29 July1993.

Belinda Clark played international cricket for Australia for 14 years, and represented her Country in an astounding 118 One-Day International matches. Born in Newcastle, New South Wales in 1970, she was the first person to score a double century in the Women's ODI against Denmark at The Middle Income Group Ground, Bandra, Mumbai in 1997, where she recorded a score of 229 not out.

Syeda Sajjida Shah, became the youngest player to appear in an international cricket match when she made her debut for Pakistan in a One-Day International against Ireland in July 2000, four months after celebrating her twelfth birthday. Born in Hyderabad, Sindh, in Pakistan in February, 1988, Syeda played in four ODI matches on that tour, making her first appearance in what was also Ireland's first women's Test match. But perhaps the finest moment of Syeda's cricketing career came in 2003, in the International Women's Cricket Council [IWCC] Trophy in the Netherlands. At the age of fifteen she played in all five of Pakistan's series of matches, and in the opening contest against Japan, at the Sportpark Drieburg, Amsterdam, destroyed its batting line-up, taking seven wickets for just four runs. This bowling performance remains the best in a single innings in the history of women's ODI cricket

More recently, in 2009, the right-handed England batswoman and *'occasional'* wicket-keeper Samantha Claire Taylor was named as one of Wisden's five cricketers of the year, and became the first woman to be honoured with the award in the 120 year history of the celebrated yearbook. The editor at the time wrote, *'There is no element of political correctness or publicity-seeking about her selection, she has been chosen on merit, for being pre-eminent in her form of the game.'* In May of the same year Samantha was also named as the England and Wales Cricket Board's Women's Player of the Year. The following year Taylor was appointed a Member of the Order of the British Empire [MBE] in the New Year Honours list. Upon her retirement The Guardian's cricket correspondent and former England Test and county cricketer Mike Selvey wrote, *'she was perhaps the finest batsman the women's game has seen.'*

Born in Amersham Buckinghamshire in September 1975, Taylor did not play cricket until the age of 13, when she was initially judged to be a wicket-keeper with limited batting ability. Despite which she developed into one of the leading batswomen in women's cricket. She made her international debut for England in the ODI against Australia in 1998, represented her Country on more than 150 occasions, and played a key role as the batting mainstay in England's two world cup titles.

In spite of the proverbial *'pebble lodged in their shoe'*, numerous influential women have *'climbed the mountain'* and helped spearhead the development of modern one-day cricket.

Baroness Rachael Heyhoe-Flint's contribution to women's cricket is incalculable, her boundless energy and dedication helped assure what would eventually become an amazing period of change at all levels of the women's game. In 2010 she became one of the first female board members at the ECB, and continued to play an integral role until the latter stage of her life, in particular with regard to England women's professional contracts. She was always there to support, inform, and offer good counsel. Rachael came from the age of the enthusiastic amateur, together with a closely knit group of women who were also passionate about the game.

Today's leading professional players live their lives in a harsh, judgemental world, a world in which they are frequently confronted with diverse challenges, where dealing with pressure is paramount. In the sporting world a commonly used term for handling pressure is being *'in the arena',* and in recent years the England women's team performance has probably been subjected to closer inspection than ever before.

The ECB has recently restructured its England Women's Development Pathway and has a wealth of talented players incorporated within its four coaching modules. Supported by an assortment of dedicated coaches and medical science staff, the ECB performance team's quest is to ensure the players become *'the best they can be'*. The updated structure is made up of four modules, designed to help and assist the development of players within the age range of 13 to 31.

England Women's Squad. Responsible for progressing the development of the members of the England women's squad who are on the verge of qualification for the next ICC Women's World Cup.

England Women's Senior Academy. . Drawn from a pool of players from various counties it is responsible for the development of the next generation of England players, assisting in improving the experience, performance and conditioning of promising talent, utilising the facilities of the National Cricket Performance Centre in Loughborough, Leicestershire,

England Women's Academy. Also based at the National Cricket Performance Centre, it is responsible for the development of promising young talent.

Regional Development Centres. This new tier incorporates six Regional Development Centres, directly aligned with the Kia Super League structure, providing an opportunity for young developing players to grow and evolve in training environments which are local to them. Clare Connor, the Director of England Women's Cricket, said, *'The pinnacle for any talented, aspiring young cricketer is to play and win matches for England, and through the*

England Women's Pathway we believe that we are developing a structure to support their journey. We want players to be constantly challenging and vying to make the next step towards wearing an England shirt'.

The ambition and dedication of Connor, together with Jo Kirk, the Kia Super League General Manager, along with a host of other colleagues at the ECB, they collectively delivered the inaugural KSL in the space of eight months. It features six teams formed with the best players from around the world. According to Jo Kirk, *'The KSL exceeded all of our expectations. During the group stage it drew an average of more than 1,000 spectators per game, a diverse mix, 42 per cent of which came with families'.*

'We had a blank canvas and we weren't threatening any existing structures,' said Connor. *'There's been lots of positive feedback that the KSL has shown how cricket can do things differently, that cricket can change. It can find ways to thrive, be relevant and reach a new audience. The women's game was crying out for a premier domestic competition. We created something that is modern, dynamic and aspirational and will hopefully continue to grow.'*

The challenge now faced must be to invest in the energy and resources to strategically improve participation and growth, especially in relation to the club game. Ten years ago there were 90 clubs in the country incorporating women and girls sections. Now there are more than 700.

Even so Government figures published in 2016 indicated a significant slump in the population of those aged 14 and over who engaged in some form of sporting activity at least once a week. The figures of just short of

16 million resulted in the Parliamentary Under Secretary of State for Sport, Tourism and Heritage announcing its intention to launch an extensive strategic review. More emphasis would be placed upon developing exercise and activity, at the expense of formal sport. At the same time it was planned to introduce a system designed to measure the ability of sport to facilitate social change. Such an initiative would require modification of the current Sport England policy of distributing more than half its money through sports governing bodies.

Subsequently, the Chief Executive of Sport England, Jennie Price, declared, *'This represents a stabilisation. If we want another big jump we need to move on. We need to do some different things'.* Sport England claims its multi-million pound *'This Girl Can'* advertising campaign helped drive almost 150,000 more women into playing sport. Yet figures indicate overall participation, especially amongst the lower socio-economic groups and the disabled, was in decline. The report suggests only 26% of people in the lowest socio-economic groups play sport at least once a week, while in the more affluent socio-economic groups 39% of people regularly take part in some form of weekly sporting activity.

On the whole, annual funding for Sport England was largely protected in a recent Government spending review, and although Sport England's Active People survey revealed an increase in the number of people running, and those participating in the sports of boxing, cricket, gymnastics, rugby union and tennis, some concern was expressed that the Government's long-term austerity measures, and subsequent cuts made to local authority budgets, may have had an adverse effect on the development of grassroots sport.

There can be little doubt women's sport has grown in stature over time. What is more, participation and a rapid improvement in expertise ensure it continues to enjoy increasing popularity. As a consequence media coverage is spreading, especially within the popular professional sports of tennis, football, cricket and rugby union. Yet most women's sport remains starved of adequate financial support, especially through medium of sponsorship deals. Give the girls a break and help them *'climb the mountain'* by removing the *'pebble from their shoes'*. Surely they've done enough to deserve that favour !

About the Author

Born in the village of Kirkby-in-Ashfield in Nottinghamshire at the start of the Second World War, Roy Case was educated at the Queen Elizabeth Grammar School in Mansfield. He retired from the position of Managing Director of a large interior contracting company at the age of 55, subsequently devoting his time to his true passion of sport.

After voluntarily serving England Golf for a number of years he was elected its President in 2008, and in the Millennium Year was presented with the Gerald Micklem Award for his outstanding service to amateur golf. Case also served for more than a decade on the Great Britain & Ireland Boys Selection Committee of the Royal & Ancient Golf Club of St. Andrews.

A keen follower of cricket, Case is a member of the Nottinghamshire County Cricket Club and the Association of Cricket Statisticians and Historians.

Other Publications include:

The McGregor Story: The First Thirty Years. Many of the world's leading professional golfers competed in the McGregor Trophy as youngsters, and fondly remember the important part the tournament played in their development.

The Victorian Pioneers: An appealing story of a dozen English cricketers which travelled to Canada and North America in 1859 to compete in the first inter-continental cricket tour.

Printed in Great Britain
by Amazon